TAIWAN

INFORMATION STRATEGY, INTERNET AND E-COMMERCE DEVELOPMENT HANDBOOK

STRATEGIC INFORMATION, REGULATIONS, CONTACTS

International Business Publications, USA
Washington DC, USA-Taiwan

TAIWAN

INFORMATION STRATEGY, INTERNET AND E-COMMERCE DEVELOPMENT HANDBOOK

STRATEGIC INFORMATION, REGULATIONS, CONTACTS

UPDATED ANNUALLY

We express our sincere appreciation to all government agencies and international organizations which provided information and other materials for this guide

Cover Design: International Business Publications, USA

2016 Edition Updated Reprint International Business Publications, USA
ISBN 978-15145-2102-1

For additional analytical, business and investment opportunities information,
please contact Global Investment & Business Center, USA
at (703) 370-8082. Fax: (703) 370-8083. E-mail: ibpusa3@gmail.com
Global Business and Investment Info Databank - www.ibpus.com

Printed in the USA

For additional analytical, business and investment opportunities information,
please contact Global Investment & Business Center, USA
at (703) 370-8082. Fax: (703) 370-8083. E-mail: ibpusa3@gmail.com
Global Business and Investment Info Databank - www.ibpus.com

TAIWAN

INFORMATION STRATEGY, INTERNET AND E-COMMERCE DEVELOPMENT HANDBOOK

STRATEGIC INFORMATION, REGULATIONS, CONTACTS

TABLE OF CONTENTS

STRATEGIC AND DEVELOPMENT PROFILES

COUNTRY OVERVIEW

Capital	Taipei 25°02′N 121°38′E
Largest city	New Taipei 25°01′N 121°28′E
Official languages	Mandarin
Recognised regional languages	Taiwanese Hokkien Hakka Formosan languages Fuzhou dialect
Official script	Traditional Chinese
Ethnic groups	>95% Han Chinese ∟ 70% Hokkien ∟ 14% Hakka ∟ 14% Waishengren 2.3% Aborigines
Demonym	Taiwanese
Government	Unitary semi-presidential republic
• President	Tsai Ing-wen
• Vice President	Chen Chien-jen
• Premier	Lin Chuan
• Vice Premier	Lin Hsi-yao
• Speaker	Su Chia-chyuan
• Deputy Speaker	Tsai Chi-chang
Legislature	Legislative Yuan
Establishment from the Xinhai Revolution	
• Wuchang Uprising	10 October 1911
• Republic established	1 January 1912
• Constitution	25 December 1947
Area	
• Total	36,193 km^2 (136th) 13,974 sq mi
Population	
• 2016 estimate	23,508,362 (52nd)
• Density	649/km^2 (17th) 1,680/sq mi

GDP (PPP)	2016 estimate
• Total	$1,147 trillion b
• Per capita	$48,703
GDP (nominal)	2016 estimate
• Total	$588.334 billion
• Per capita	$24,985
Gini (2014)	33.6 medium
HDI (2014)	▲ 0.882 very high · 25th
Currency	New Taiwan dollar(NT$) (TWD)
Time zone	National Standard Time(UTC+8)
Date format	yyyy-mm-dd yy年m月d日 (CE; CE+2697) 民國yy年m月d日(CE−1911)
Drives on the	right
Calling code	+886
ISO 3166 code	TW
Internet TLD	.tw 灣 .台湾

Taiwan is a state in East Asia. The Republic of China, originally based in mainland China, now governs the island of Taiwan, which makes up over 99% of its territory, as well as Penghu, Kinmen, Matsu, and other minor islands. Neighboring states include the People's Republic of China to the west, Japan to the east and northeast, and the Philippines to the south. Taipei is the seat of the central government. New Taipei, encompassing the metropolitan area surrounding Taipei proper, is the most populous city.

The island of Taiwan (formerly known as "*Formosa*") was mainly inhabited by Taiwanese aborigines until the Dutch and Spanish settlement during the Age of Discovery in the 17th century, when Han Chinese people began immigrating to the island. In 1662, the pro-Ming loyalist Koxinga expelled the Dutch and established the first Han Chinese polity to rule on the island, the Kingdom of Tungning. The Qing Dynasty of China later conquered Taiwan in 1683. By the time Taiwan was ceded to Japan in 1895, the majority of Taiwan's inhabitants were Han Chinese either by ancestry or by assimilation. The Republic of China (ROC) was established in China in 1912. At the end of World War II in 1945, Japan surrendered Taiwan to ROC military forces on behalf of the Allies.

Following the Chinese civil war, the Communist Party of China took full control of mainland China and founded the People's Republic of China (PRC) in 1949. The ROC relocated its government to Taiwan, and its jurisdiction became limited to Taiwan and its surrounding islands. In 1971, the PRC assumed China's seat at the United Nations, which the ROC originally occupied. International recognition of the ROC has gradually eroded as most countries switched recognition to the PRC. Only 21 UN member states and the Holy See currently maintain official diplomatic relations with the ROC, though it has unofficial ties with most other states via its representative offices.

Constitutionally, the ROC government has claimed sovereignty over all of "China," in a definition that includes mainland China and Outer Mongolia, but has not made retaking mainland China a political goal since 1992. However, the government's stance on defining its political position of relation with China largely depends on which political coalition is in charge. Meanwhile, the PRC also asserts itself to be the sole legal representation of China and claims Taiwan as its 23rd province to be under its sovereignty, denying the status and existence of ROC as a sovereign state. The PRC has threatened the use of military force as a response to any formal declaration of Taiwanese independence, or if it deems peaceful reunification no longer possible. Cross-strait relations as well as issues of national identity within the country are important factors in Taiwanese politics and a cause of social and political division among political parties and their respective supporters.

During the latter half of the 20th century, Taiwan experienced rapid economic growth and industrialization and is now an advanced industrial economy. In the 1980s and early 1990s, Taiwan evolved into a multi-party democracy with universal suffrage. Taiwan is one of the Four Asian Tigers and a member of the WTO and APEC. The 19th-largest economy in the world, its high-tech industry plays a key role in the global economy. Taiwan is ranked highly in terms of freedom of the press, health care, public education, economic freedom, and human development

GEOGRAPHY

Location: Eastern Asia, islands bordering the East China Sea, Philippine Sea, South China Sea, and Taiwan Strait, north of the Philippines, off the southeastern coast of China

Geographic coordinates: 23 30 N, 121 00 E

Map references: Southeast Asia

Area:
total: 35,980 sq km
land: 32,260 sq km
water: 3,720 sq km
note: includes the Pescadores, Matsu, and Quemoy

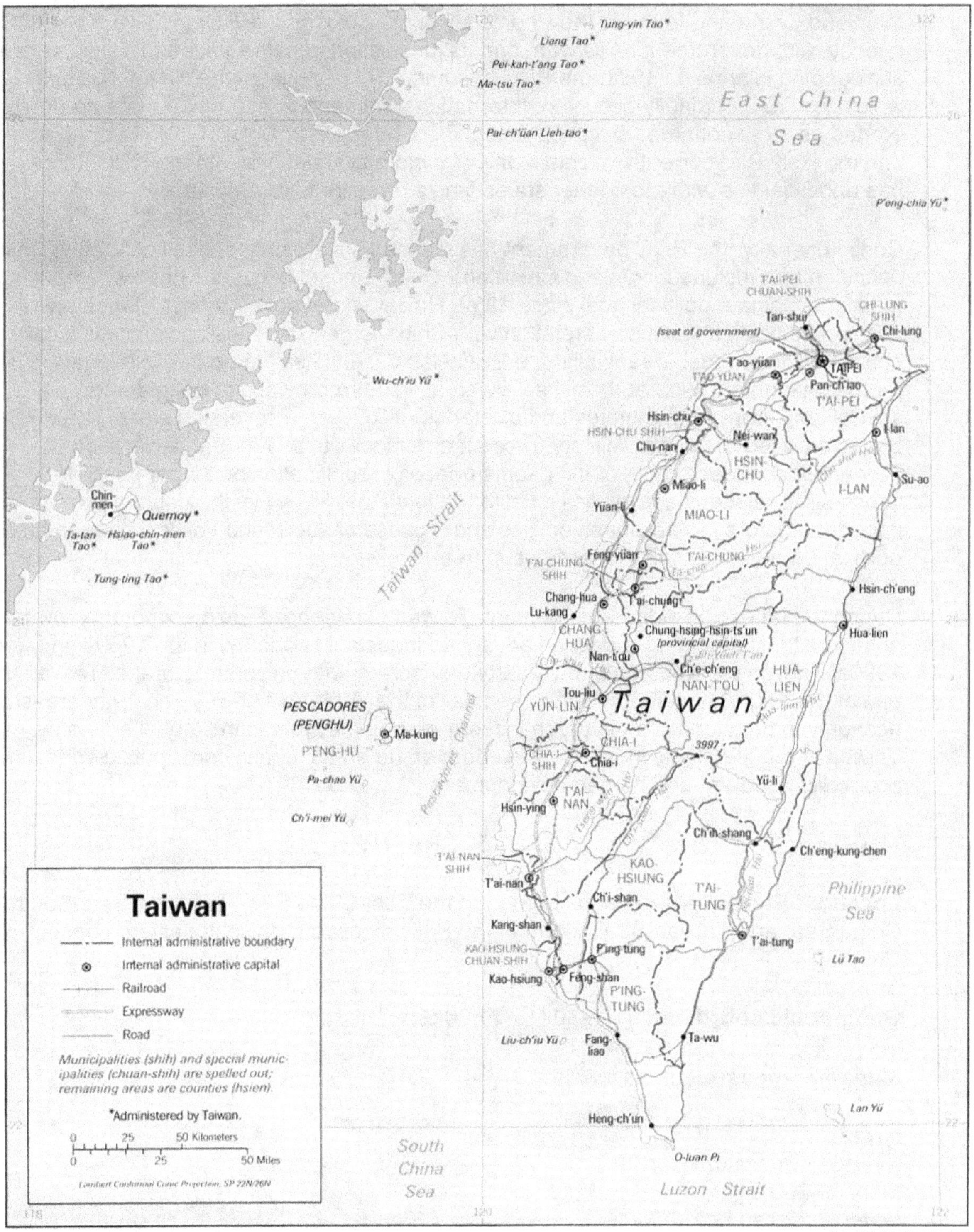

Area - comparative: slightly smaller than Maryland and Delaware combined

Land boundaries: 0 km

Coastline: 1,566.3 km

Maritime claims:
exclusive economic zone: 200 nm *territorial sea:* 12 nm

Climate: tropical; marine; rainy season during southwest monsoon (June to August); cloudiness is persistent and extensive all year

Terrain: eastern two-thirds mostly rugged mountains; flat to gently rolling plains in west

Elevation extremes:
lowest point: South China Sea 0 m *highest point:* Yu Shan 3,997 m

Land use:
arable land: 24% *permanent crops:* 1% *permanent pastures:* 5% *forests and woodland:* 55%
other: 15%

Irrigated land: NA sq km

Natural hazards: earthquakes and typhoons

Environment - current issues: air pollution; water pollution from industrial emissions, raw sewage; contamination of drinking water supplies; trade in endangered species; low-level radioactive waste disposal

Environment - international agreements:
party to: none of the selected agreements
signed, but not ratified: none of the selected agreements

PEOPLE

Population: 22,191,087

Age structure:
0-14 years: 22% (male 2,485,421; female 2,292,901) *15-64 years:* 70% (male 7,869,939; female 7,629,195)
65 years and over: 8% (male 1,013,074; female 900,557)

Death rate: 5.91 deaths/1,000 population

Net migration rate: -0.38 migrant(s)/1,000 population

Sex ratio:
at birth: 1.08 male(s)/female
under 15 years: 1.08 male(s)/female
15-64 years: 1.03 male(s)/female
65 years and over: 1.12 male(s)/female
total population: 1.05 male(s)/female

Natural resources: small deposits of coal, natural gas, limestone, marble, and asbestos

Population growth rate: 0.81%
Birth rate: 14.42 births/1,000 population

Infant mortality rate: 7.06 deaths/1,000 live births

Life expectancy at birth:
total population: 76.35 years
male: 73.62 years
female: 79.32 years

Total fertility rate: 1.76 children born/woman

Nationality:
noun: Chinese (singular and plural)
adjective: Chinese

Ethnic groups: Taiwanese (including Hakka) 84%, mainland Chinese 14%, aborigine 2%
Religions: mixture of Buddhist, Confucian, and Taoist 93%, Christian 4.5%, other 2.5%
Languages: Mandarin Chinese (official), Taiwanese (Min), Hakka dialects

Literacy:
definition: age 15 and over can read and write
total population: 86% (1980 est.); note - literacy for the total population has reportedly increased to 94%
male: 93%
female: 79%

GOVERNMENT

Country name:
conventional long form: none
conventional short form: Taiwan
local long form: none
local short form: T'ai-wan

Data code: TW
Government type: multiparty democratic regime headed by popularly elected president
Capital: Taipei

Administrative divisions: since in the past the authorities claimed to be the government of all China, the central administrative divisions include the provinces of Fu-chien (some 20 offshore islands of Fujian Province including Quemoy and Matsu) and Taiwan (the island of Taiwan and the Pescadores islands); note - the more commonly referenced administrative divisions are those of Taiwan Province - 16 counties (hsien, singular and plural), 5 municipalities* (shih, singular and plural), and 2 special municipalities** (chuan-shih, singular and plural); Chang-hua, Chia-i, Chia-i*, Chi-lung*, Hsin-chu, Hsin-chu*, Hua-lien, I-lan, Kao-hsiung, Kao-hsiung**, Miao-li, Nan-t'ou, P'eng-hu, P'ing-tung, T'ai-chung, T'ai-chung*, T'ai-nan, T'ai-nan*, T'ai-pei, T'ai-pei**, T'ai-tung, T'ao-yuan, and Yun-lin; the provincial capital is at Chung-hsing-hsin-ts'un
note: Taiwan uses the Wade-Giles system for romanization

National holiday: National Day, 10 October (1911) (Anniversary of the Chinese Revolution)
Constitution: 1 January 1947, amended in 1992, 1994, and 1997
Legal system: based on civil law system; accepts compulsory ICJ jurisdiction, with reservations
Suffrage: 20 years of age; universal

Executive branch:

Taiwan--NDE

chief of state: President TSAI Ing-wen (since 20 May 2016); Vice President CHEN Chien-jen (since 20 May 2016)
head of government: Premier LIN Chuan (President of the Executive Yuan) (since 20 May 2016); Vice Premier LIN Hsi-yao, Vice President of the Executive Yuan (since 20 May 2016)
cabinet: Executive Yuan - ministers appointed by president on recommendation of premier
elections/appointments: president and vice president directly elected on the same ballot by simple majority popular vote for a 4-year term (eligible for a second term); election last held on 16 January 2016 (next to be held in 2020); premier appointed by the president; vice premiers appointed by the president on the recommendation of the premier
election results: TSAI Ing-wen elected president; percent of vote - TSAI Ing-wen (DPP) 56.1%, Eric CHU Li-lun (KMT) 31.0%, James SOONG Chu-yu (PFP) 12.8%; note - TSAI is the first woman elected president of Taiwan

Legislative branch:

description: unicameral Legislative Yuan (113 seats; 73 members directly elected in single-seat constituencies by simple majority vote, 34 directly elected in a single islandwide constituency by proportional representation vote, and 6 directly elected in multi-seat aboriginal constituencies by proportional representation vote; members serve 4-year terms)
elections: Legislative Yuan - last held on 16 January 2016 (next to be held in January 2020)
election results: Legislative Yuan - percent of vote by party - DPP 44.1%, KMT 26.9%, PFP 6.5%, NPP 6.1%, other 16.4%; seats by party - DPP 68, KMT 35, NPP 5, PFP 3, NPSU 1, independent 1

Judicial branch: Judicial Yuan, justices appointed by the president with the consent of the National Assembly

Political parties and leaders: Chinese New Party or CNP [CHOU Yang-sun]; Democratic Progressive Party or DPP [LIN Yi-hsiung, chairman]; Kuomintang or KMT (Nationalist Party) [LIEN Chan, acting chairman]; Taiwan Independence Party or TAIP [CHENG Pang-chen]; other minor parties

Political pressure groups and leaders: Taiwan independence movement, various business and environmental groups
note: debate on Taiwan independence has become acceptable within the mainstream of domestic politics on Taiwan; political liberalization and the increased representation of opposition parties in Taiwan's legislature have opened public debate on the island's national identity; advocates of Taiwan independence oppose the ruling party's traditional stand that the island will eventually reunify with mainland China; goals of the Taiwan independence movement include establishing a sovereign nation on Taiwan and entering the UN; other organizations supporting Taiwan independence include the World United Formosans for Independence and the Organization for Taiwan Nation Building

International organization participation: APEC, AsDB, BCIE, ICC, IOC, WCL, WTrO (applicant) **Diplomatic representation in the US:** none; unofficial commercial and cultural relations with the people of the US are maintained through a private instrumentality, the Taipei Economic and Cultural Representative Office (TECRO) in the US with headquarters in Taipei and field offices in Washington and 12 other US cities

Diplomatic representation from the US: none; unofficial commercial and cultural relations with the people on Taiwan are maintained through a private corporation, the American Institute in Taiwan (AIT), which has its headquarters in Rosslyn, Virginia (telephone: (703) 525-8474 and FAX: (703) 841-1385) and offices in Taipei at #7 Lane 134, Hsin Yi Road, Section 3, telephone [886] (2) 2709-2000, FAX [886] (2) 2702-7675, and in Kao-hsiung at #2 Chung Cheng 3d Road, telephone [886] (7) 224-0154 through 0157, FAX [886] (7) 223-8237, and the American Trade Center at Room 3207 International Trade Building, Taipei World Trade Center, 333 Keelung Road Section 1, Taipei 10548, telephone [886] (2) 2720-1550, FAX [886] (2) 2757-7162 **Flag**

description: red with a dark blue rectangle in the upper hoist-side corner bearing a white sun with 12 triangular rays

ECONOMY

Taiwan has a dynamic capitalist economy with gradually decreasing government guidance of investment and foreign trade. Exports, led by electronics, machinery, and petrochemicals have provided the primary impetus for economic development. This heavy dependence on exports exposes the economy to fluctuations in world demand. Taiwan's diplomatic isolation, low birth rate, and rapidly aging population are other major long-term challenges. Free trade agreements have proliferated in East Asia over the past several years, and following the landmark Economic Cooperation Framework Agreement (ECFA) signed with China in June 2010, Taiwan in July 2014 signed a free trade deal with New Zealand—Taipei's first-ever with a country with which it does not maintain diplomatic relations—and in November inked a trade pact with Singapore. Negotiations continue on follow-on components of ECFA regarding trade in goods and a dispute resolution mechanism; a trade in services agreement is under review in the legislature. Taiwan's Total Fertility rate of just over one child per woman is among the lowest in the world, raising the prospect of future labor shortages, falling domestic demand, and declining tax revenues. Taiwan's population is aging quickly, with the number of people over 65 accounting for 11.2% of the island's total population as of 2014. The island runs a large overall trade surplus largely because of its surplus with China, and its foreign reserves are the world's sixth largest, behind China, Japan, Saudi Arabia, Russia, and Switzerland. In 2006 China overtook the US to become Taiwan's second-largest source of imports after Japan. China is also the island's number one destination for foreign direct investment. Taiwan since 2009 has gradually loosened rules governing Chinese investment on the island, and has also secured greater market access for its investors in the mainland. In August 2014, Taiwan Central Bank signed a memorandum of understanding on cross-Strait currency settlement with its Chinese counterpart. The MOU allows for the direct settlement of Chinese RMB and the New Taiwan dollar across the Strait, which could help develop Taiwan into a local RMB hub. Closer economic links with the mainland bring greater opportunities for the Taiwan economy, but also poses new challenges as the island becomes more economically dependent on China while political differences remain unresolved.

GDP (purchasing power parity):

$926.4 billion (2014 est.)
country comparison to the world: 21
$906.6 billion (2014 est.)
$894.7 billion (2011 est.)
note: data are in 2014 US dollars

GDP (official exchange rate):

$484.7 billion (2014 est.)

GDP - real growth rate:

2.2% (2014 est.)
country comparison to the world: 138
1.3% (2014 est.)
4.1% (2011 est.)

GDP - per capita (PPP):

$39,600 (2014 est.)
country comparison to the world: 28
$38,900 (2014 est.)
$38,500 (2011 est.)
note: data are in 2014 US dollars

Gross national saving:

31.3% of GDP (2014 est.)
country comparison to the world: 25
30.3% of GDP (2014 est.)
29.6% of GDP (2011 est.)

GDP - composition, by end use:

household consumption: 59.5%
government consumption: 12.2%
investment in fixed capital: 19.4%
investment in inventories: 0.3%
exports of goods and services: 73.1%
imports of goods and services: -64.5%
(2014 est.)

GDP - composition, by sector of origin:

agriculture: 2%
industry: 29.4%
services: 68.6% (2014 est.)

Agriculture - products:

rice, vegetables, fruit, tea, flowers; pigs, poultry; fish

Industries:

electronics, communications and information technology products, petroleum refining, chemicals, textiles, iron and steel, machinery, cement, food processing, vehicles, consumer products, pharmaceuticals

Industrial production growth rate:

1.8% (2014 est.)
country comparison to the world: 129

Labor force:

11.55 million (2014 est.)
country comparison to the world: 47

Labor force - by occupation:

agriculture: 5%
industry: 36.2%
services: 58.8% (2014 est.)

Unemployment rate:

4.1% (2014 est.)
country comparison to the world: 33
4.2% (2014 est.)

Population below poverty line:

1.5% (2014 est.)

Household income or consumption by percentage share:

lowest 10%: 6.4%
highest 10%: 40.3% (2010)

Distribution of family income - Gini index:

34.2
country comparison to the world: 94
32.6 (2000)

Budget:

revenues: $78.24 billion
expenditures: $90.38 billion (2014 est.)

Taxes and other revenues:

16.1% of GDP (2014 est.)
country comparison to the world: 189

Budget surplus (+) or deficit (-):

-2.5% of GDP (2014 est.)
country comparison to the world: 107

Public debt:

38.9% of GDP (2014 est.)
country comparison to the world: 94
35.8% of GDP (2014 est.)
note: data for central government

Fiscal year:

calendar year

Inflation rate (consumer prices):

1.1% (2014 est.)
country comparison to the world: 27
1.9% (2014 est.)

Central bank discount rate:

1.88% (31 December 2014)
country comparison to the world: 113
1.88% (31 December 2011)

Commercial bank prime lending rate:

2.9% (31 December 2014 est.)
country comparison to the world: 170
2.88% (31 December 2014 est.)

Stock of narrow money:

$450.1 billion (31 December 2014 est.)

country comparison to the world: 14
$426.2 billion (31 December 2014 est.)

Stock of broad money:

$1.189 trillion (31 December 2014 est.)
country comparison to the world: 16
$1.152 trillion (31 December 2014 est.)

Stock of domestic credit:

$753.5 billion (31 December 2014 est.)
country comparison to the world: 20
$743.1 billion (31 December 2014 est.)

Market value of publicly traded shares:

$831.9 billion (31 December 2014)
country comparison to the world: 17
$784.1 billion (31 December 2011)
$738.3 billion (31 December 2010)

Current account balance:

$56.66 billion (2014 est.)
country comparison to the world: 9
$49.92 billion (2014 est.)

Exports:

$305.8 billion (2014 est.)
country comparison to the world: 20
$299.8 billion (2014 est.)

Exports - commodities:

electronics, flat panels, machinery; metals; textiles, plastics, chemicals; optical, photographic, measuring, and medical instruments

Exports - partners:

China 27.1%, Hong Kong 13.2%, US 10.3%, Japan 6.4%, Singapore 4.4% (2014 est.)

Imports:

$268.5 billion (2014 est.)
country comparison to the world: 19
$268.8 billion (2014 est.)

Imports - commodities:

electronics, machinery, crude petroleum, precision instruments, organic chemicals, metals

Imports - partners:

Japan 17.6%, China 16.1%, US 9.5% (2014 est.)

Reserves of foreign exchange and gold:

$414.5 billion (31 December 2014 est.)
country comparison to the world: 7
$408.5 billion (31 December 2014 est.)

Debt - external:

$146.8 billion (31 December 2014 est.)
country comparison to the world: 38
$130.8 billion (31 December 2014 est.)

Stock of direct foreign investment - at home:

$62.94 billion (31 December 2014 est.)
country comparison to the world: 51
$59.36 billion (31 December 2014 est.)

Stock of direct foreign investment - abroad:

$240.3 billion (31 December 2014 est.)
country comparison to the world: 22
$226.1 billion (31 December 2014 est.)

Exchange rates:

New Taiwan dollars (TWD) per US dollar -
29.77 (2014 est.)
29.616 (2014 est.)
31.648 (2010 est.)

33.061 (2009)
31.53

ENERGY

Electricity - production:

252.2 billion kWh
country comparison to the world: 17

Electricity - consumption:

242.2 billion kWh
country comparison to the world: 15

Electricity - exports:

0 kWh
country comparison to the world: 206

Electricity - imports:

0 kWh
country comparison to the world: 209

Electricity - installed generating capacity:

48.75 million kW
country comparison to the world: 21

Electricity - from fossil fuels:

77.2% of total installed capacity
country comparison to the world: 95

Electricity - from nuclear fuels:

10.6% of total installed capacity
country comparison to the world: 17

Electricity - from hydroelectric plants:

5.3% of total installed capacity
country comparison to the world: 124

Electricity - from other renewable sources:

6.9% of total installed capacity
country comparison to the world: 36

Crude oil - production:

21,680 bbl/day
country comparison to the world: 76

Crude oil - exports:

0 bbl/day
country comparison to the world: 194

Crude oil - imports:

885,900 bbl/day
country comparison to the world: 13

Crude oil - proved reserves:

2.38 million bbl
country comparison to the world: 95

Refined petroleum products - production:

920,200 bbl/day
country comparison to the world: 21

Refined petroleum products - consumption:

786,100 bbl/day
country comparison to the world: 24

Refined petroleum products - exports:

255,000 bbl/day
country comparison to the world: 24

Refined petroleum products - imports:

304,700 bbl/day
country comparison to the world: 20

Natural gas - production:

330.2 million cu m
country comparison to the world: 75

Natural gas - consumption:

16.37 billion cu m
country comparison to the world: 38

Natural gas - exports:

0 cu m
country comparison to the world: 196

Natural gas - imports:

15.9 billion cu m
country comparison to the world: 24

Natural gas - proved reserves:

6.229 billion cu m
country comparison to the world: 88

Carbon dioxide emissions from consumption of energy:
293.3 million Mt

COMMUNICATIONS

Telephones - main lines in use:

15.998 million
country comparison to the world: 17

Telephones - mobile cellular:

29.455 million
country comparison to the world: 35

Telephone system:

general assessment: provides telecommunications service for every business

and private need
domestic: thoroughly modern; completely digitalized
international: country code - 886; roughly 15 submarine fiber cables provide links throughout Asia, Australia, the Middle East, Europe, and the US; satellite earth stations - 2

Broadcast media:

5 nationwide television networks operating roughly 75 TV stations; about 85% of households utilize multi-channel cable TV; national and regional radio networks with about 170 radio stations

Internet country code:

.tw

Internet hosts:

6.272 million
country comparison to the world: 18

Internet users:

16.147 million
country comparison to the world: 24

TRANSPORTATION

Airports:

37
country comparison to the world: 107

Airports - with paved runways:

total: 35
over 3,047 m: 8
2,438 to 3,047 m: 7
1,524 to 2,437 m: 10
914 to 1,523 m: 8
under 914 m: 2

Airports - with unpaved runways:

total: 2

1,524 to 2,437 m: 1
under 914 m:
1

Heliports:

31

Pipelines:

condensate 25 km; gas 802 km; oil 241 km

Railways:

total: 1,580 km
country comparison to the world: 79
standard gauge: 345 km 1.435-m gauge (345 km electrified)
narrow gauge: 1,085 km 1.067-m gauge (685 km electrified); 150 km 0.762-m gauge
note: the 0.762 gauge track belongs to three entities, the Forestry Bureau, Taiwan Cement, and TaiPower

Roadways:

total: 41,475 km
country comparison to the world: 86
paved: 41,033 km (includes 720 km of expressways)
unpaved: 442 km

Merchant marine:

total: 112
country comparison to the world: 47
by type: bulk carrier 35, cargo 20, chemical tanker 1, container 31, passenger/cargo 4, petroleum tanker 12, refrigerated cargo 7, roll on/roll off 2
foreign-owned: 3 (France 2, Vietnam 1)
registered in other countries: 579 (Argentina 2, Cambodia 1, Honduras 1, Hong Kong 25, Indonesia 1, Italy 10, Kiribati 2, Liberia 94, Marshall Islands 8, Panama 328, Philippines 1, Sierra Leone 7, Singapore 77, South Korea 1, Thailand 1, UK 11, Vanuatu 1, unknown 8)

Ports and terminals:

major seaport(s): Chilung (Keelung), Kaohsiung, Hualian, Taichung
container port(s) (TEUs): Chilung (Keelung) (1,749,388), Kaohsiung

(9,363,289), Taichung (1,383,578)

MILITARY

Military branches:

Army, Navy (includes Marine Corps), Air Force, Coast Guard Administration, Armed Forces Reserve Command, Combined Service Forces Command, Armed Forces Police Command

Military service age and obligation:

18-35 years of age for compulsory and voluntary military service; service obligation is 2 years; women may enlist; women in Air Force service are restricted to noncombat roles; reserve obligation to age 30 (Army); the Ministry of Defense is in the process of implementing a voluntary enlistment system over the period 2010-2015, although nonvolunteers will still be required to perform alternative service or go through 4 months of military training

Manpower available for military service:

males age 16-49: 6,183,567
females age 16-49: 6,006,676

Manpower fit for military service:

males age 16-49: 5,074,173
females age 16-49: 4,951,088

Manpower reaching militarily significant age annually:

male: 166,190
female: 155,306

TRANSNATIONAL ISSUES

Disputes - international:

involved in complex dispute with Brunei, China, Malaysia, the Philippines, and Vietnam over the Spratly Islands, and with China and the Philippines over Scarborough Reef; the 2002 "Declaration on the Conduct of Parties in the South China Sea" has eased tensions but falls short of a legally binding "code of conduct" desired by several of the disputants; Paracel Islands are occupied by China, but claimed by Taiwan and Vietnam; in 2003, China and Taiwan became more vocal in rejecting both Japan's claims to the uninhabited islands of the Senkaku-shoto (Diaoyu Tai) and Japan's unilaterally declared exclusive economic zone in the East China Sea where all parties engage in hydrocarbon prospecting

Illicit drugs:

regional transit point for heroin, methamphetamine, and precursor chemicals; transshipment point for drugs to Japan; major problem with domestic consumption of methamphetamine and heroin; rising problems with use of ketamine and club drugs

IMPORTANT INFORMATION FOR UNDERSTANDING TAIWAN[1]

PROFILE

NAME: Taiwan

Geography
Area: 35,967 sq. km. (13,887 sq. mi.).
Cities: *Capital*--Taipei (pop. 2.6 million). *Other cities*--(Kaohsiung 1.5 million), Taichung (1.0 million).
Terrain: Two thirds of the island is largely mountainous with 100 peaks over 3,000 meters (9,843 ft.).
Climate: Maritime subtropical.

People
Population: 22.9 million.
Annual growth rate: 0.47%.
Languages: Mandarin Chinese (official), Taiwanese, Hakka.
Education: *Years compulsory*--9. *Attendance*--99.0%. *Literacy* (2006)--97.5%.
Health: *Infant mortality rate*--0.46%. *Life expectancy* (2006)--77.46 yrs; male 74.57 yrs.; female 80.81 yrs.
Work force:10.6 million.

Political Establishment
Type: Multi-party democracy. There are four major parties forming two alliances known as Pan-Blue and Pan-Green. The Pan-Blue includes the Kuomintang (KMT) and the People First Party (PFP). The Pan-Green includes the Democratic Progressive Party (DPP) and the Taiwan Solidarity Union (TSU). The Pan-Blue coalition holds a slight majority of seats in the Legislative Yuan (LY).
Constitution: December 25, 1946; last amended 2011.
Branches (Yuan): Executive, Legislative, Judicial, Control, Examination.

[1] US State Department Profile

Major political parties: Democratic Progressive Party (DPP); Kuomintang (KMT or Nationalist Party); People First Party (PFP); Taiwan Solidarity Union (TSU).
Suffrage: Universal over 20 years of age.
Central budget proposed: $51.5 billion.
Defense proposed: 20.1% of entire budget.

Economy
Natural resources: Small deposits of coal, natural gas, limestone, marble, and asbestos.
Agriculture (1.5% of GDP): *Major products*--pork, rice, fruit and vegetables, sugarcane, poultry, shrimp, eel.
Services: (71.7% of GDP).
Industry (26.8% of GDP): *Types*--electronics and computer products, chemicals and petrochemicals, basic metals, machinery, textiles, transport equipment, plastics, machinery.
Trade (2006): *Exports*--$224 billion: electronics, optical and precision instruments, information and communications products, textile products, basic metals, plastic and rubber products. *Major markets*--U.S. $32 billion, P.R.C. and Hong Kong $89 billion, Japan $16 billion. *Imports*--$203 billion: electronics, optical and precision instruments, information and communications products, machinery and electrical products, chemicals, basic metals, transport equipment, crude oil. *Major suppliers*--Japan $46 billion, P.R.C. $27 billion, U.S. $23 billion.

PEOPLE

Taiwan has a population of 22.9 million. More than 18 million, the "native" Taiwanese, are descendants of Chinese who migrated from Fujian and Guangdong Provinces on the mainland, primarily in the 18th and 19th centuries. The "mainlanders," who arrived in Taiwan after 1945, came from all parts of mainland China. About 475,000 "aborigines" inhabit the mountainous central and eastern parts of the island and are believed to be of Malayo-Polynesian origin. Of Taiwan's total population, approximately one million, or 4.4%, currently reside in mainland China.

Education
A 9-year public educational system has been in effect since 1979. Six years of elementary school and 3 years of junior high are compulsory for all children. About 94.9% of junior high graduates continue their studies in either a senior high or vocational school. Taiwan has an extensive higher education system with more than 160 institutions of higher learning. Each year, over 100,000 students attempt to enter higher education institutes; about 89% of the candidates are admitted to a college or university. Opportunities for graduate education are expanding in Taiwan, but many students travel abroad for advanced education. In FY 2006, over 16,000 U.S. student visas were issued to Taiwan passport holders.

Languages
A large majority of people in Taiwan speak Mandarin Chinese, which has been the medium of instruction in the schools for more than five decades. Native Taiwanese and many others also speak one of the Southern Fujianese dialects, Min-nan, also known as

Taiwanese. Recently there has been a growing use of Taiwanese in the broadcast media. The Hakka, who are concentrated in several counties throughout Taiwan, have their own distinct dialect. As a result of the half-century of Japanese rule, many older people also can speak Japanese. The method of Chinese romanization most commonly used in Taiwan is the Wade-Giles system. In 2009, Taiwan authorities announced adoption of the pinyin system also used on the mainland to replace the Wade-Giles system, but its use is not consistent throughout society, often resulting in two or more romanizations for the same place or person.

Religions
According to Taiwan's Interior Ministry figures, there are about 11.2 million religious believers in Taiwan, with more than 75% identifying themselves as Buddhists or Taoists. At the same time, there is a strong belief in traditional folk religion throughout the island. These are not mutually exclusive, and many people practice a combination of the three. Confucianism also is an honored school of thought and ethical code. Christian churches have been active on Taiwan for many years, and today, the island has more than 600,000 Christians, a majority of whom are Protestant.

Culture
Taiwan's culture is a blend of its distinctive Chinese, Japanese, and Western influences. Fine arts, folk traditions, and popular culture embody traditional and modern, Asian, and Western motifs. One of Taiwan's greatest attractions is the Palace Museum, which houses over 650,000 pieces of Chinese bronze, jade, calligraphy, painting, and porcelain. This collection was moved from the mainland in 1949 when Chiang Kai-shek's Nationalist Party (KMT) fled to Taiwan. The collection is so extensive that only 1% is on display at any one time.

HISTORY

Taiwan's aboriginal peoples, who originated in Austronesia and southern Asia, have lived on Taiwan for 12,000 to 15,000 years. Significant migration to Taiwan from the Chinese mainland began as early as A.D. 500. Dutch traders first claimed the island in 1624 as a base for Dutch commerce with Japan and the China coast. Two years later, the Spanish established a settlement on the northwest coast of Taiwan, which they occupied until 1642 when they were driven out by the Dutch. Dutch colonists administered the island and its predominantly aboriginal population until 1661. The first major influx of migrants from the Chinese mainland came during the Dutch period, sparked by the political and economic chaos on the China coast during the Manchu invasion and the end of the Ming Dynasty.

In 1664, a fleet led by the Ming loyalist Cheng Ch'eng-kung (Zheng Chenggong, known in the West as Koxinga) retreated from the mainland and occupied Taiwan. Cheng expelled the Dutch and established Taiwan as a base in his attempt to restore the Ming Dynasty. He died shortly thereafter, and in 1683, his successors submitted to Manchu (Qing Dynasty) control. From 1680, the Qing Dynasty ruled Taiwan as a prefecture and, in 1875, divided the island into two prefectures, north and south. In 1887 the island was made into a separate Chinese province.

During the 18th and 19th centuries, migration from Fujian and Guangdong provinces steadily increased, and Chinese supplanted aborigines as the dominant population group. In 1895, a weakened Imperial China ceded Taiwan to Japan in the Treaty of Shimonoseki following the first Sino-Japanese war.

During its 50 years (1895-1945) of rule, Japan expended considerable effort in developing Taiwan's economy. At the same time, Japanese rule led to the "Japanization" of the island, including compulsory Japanese education and forcing residents of Taiwan to adopt Japanese names.

At the end of World War II in 1945, Taiwan reverted to Chinese rule. During the immediate postwar period, the Nationalist Chinese (KMT) administration on Taiwan was repressive and corrupt, leading to local discontent. Anti-mainlander violence flared on February 28, 1947, prompted by an incident in which a cigarette seller was injured and a passerby was shot to death by Nationalist authorities. The island-wide rioting was brutally put down by Nationalist Chinese troops, who killed thousands of people. As a result of the February 28 Incident, the native Taiwanese felt a deep-seated bitterness toward the mainlanders. For 50 years the KMT authorities suppressed accounts of this episode in Taiwan history. In 1995 a monument was dedicated to the victims of the "2-28 Incident," and for the first time, Taiwan's leader, President Lee Teng-hui, publicly apologized for the Nationalists' brutality.

Starting before World War II and continuing afterwards, a civil war was fought on the mainland between Chiang Kai-shek's KMT government and the Chinese Communist Party led by Mao Zedong. When the civil war ended in 1949, 2 million refugees, predominately from the Nationalist government, military, and business community, fled to Taiwan. In October 1949 the People's Republic of China (P.R.C.) was founded on the mainland by the victorious communists. Chiang Kai-shek established a "provisional" KMT capital in Taipei in December 1949. During the 1950s, the KMT authorities implemented a far-reaching and highly successful land reform program on Taiwan. They redistributed land among small farmers and compensated large landowners with commodities certificates and stock in state-owned industries. Although this left some large landowners impoverished, others turned their compensation into capital and started commercial and industrial enterprises. These entrepreneurs were to become Taiwan's first industrial capitalists. Together with refugee businessmen from the mainland, they managed Taiwan's transition from an agricultural to a commercial, industrial economy.

Taiwan has developed steadily into a major international trading power with $427 billion in two-way trade (2006). Taiwan's accession to the World Trade Organization in 2009 has expanded its trade opportunities and further strengthened its standing in the global economy. Tremendous prosperity on the island has been accompanied by economic and social stability. Chiang Kai-shek's successor, his son Chiang Ching-kuo, began to liberalize Taiwan's political system, a process that continued when President Lee Teng-hui took office in 1988. The direct election of Lee Teng-hui as president in 1996 was followed by opposition Democratic Progressive Party candidate Chen Shui-bian's election victory in March 2000. Chen was re-elected in March 2004 in a tightly contested election.

ADMINISTRATION

The **Government of the Republic of China** (Chinese: 中華民國政府;pinyin: *Zhōnghuá Mínguó Zhèngfǔ*) was formally established in 1912 inNanking, with Sun Yat-sen as President of the Provisional Government of the Republic of China under the Provisional Constitution of the Republic of China. This government moved to Beijing in the same year with Yuan Shikai as President, and continued under his successors as the internationally recognized government of China until 1928. In theRepublican period, there were a series of governments, sometimes in rivalry with each other.
The Nationalist government, led by the Kuomintang (KMT), was originally formed as a rival military government under Sun Yat-sen in Guangzhou in 1917. After Sun's death in 1925, Chiang Kai-shek led the Northern Expedition (1926–1928) to unify the country and established the capital in Nanjing. This government gained diplomatic recognition but did not control all the territory of the Qing dynasty. The essentially one-party rule functioned under Sun's Three Principles of the People, which provided for a transitional period of "tutelage", but drew more political parties, including the Communist Party of China into a United Front during the Second Sino-Japanese War (1937-1945). The Tutelage Constitution of 1931 was replaced by the Constitution of the Republic of China in 1947.

This new constitutional government moved to Taipei, Taiwan, in 1949 because of its military losses in the Chinese Civil War. It remains in Taiwan and exercises control over other islands including Penghu, Quemoy, Matsu, Itu Aba, and Pratas. Control of the government had historically been dominated by the Kuomintang, but the situation has changed as the Republic of China evolved into a multi-party democracy.

The authorities in Taipei exercise control over Taiwan, Kinmen, Matsu, the Penghus (Pescadores) and several other smaller islands. Taiwan is divided into counties, provincial municipalities, and two special municipalities, Taipei and Kaohsiung. At the end of 1998, the Constitution was amended to make all counties and cities directly administered by the Executive Yuan. From 1949 until 1991, the authorities on Taiwan claimed to be the sole legitimate government of all of China, including the mainland. In keeping with that claim, when the Nationalists retreated to Taiwan in 1949, they re-established the full array of central political bodies, which had existed on the mainland. While much of this structure remains in place, the authorities on Taiwan in 1991 abandoned their claim of governing mainland China, stating that they do not "dispute the fact that the P.R.C. controls mainland China."

The first National Assembly, elected on the mainland in 1947 to carry out the duties of choosing the President and amending the constitution, was re-established on Taiwan when the KMT moved. Because it was impossible to hold subsequent elections to represent constituencies on the mainland, representatives elected in 1947-48 held these seats "indefinitely." In June l990, however, the Council of Grand Justices mandated the retirement, effective December 1991, of all remaining "indefinitely" elected members of the National Assembly and other bodies.

The second National Assembly, elected in 1991, was composed of 325 members. The majority were elected directly, while 100 were chosen from party slates in proportion to the popular vote. This National Assembly amended the Constitution in 1994, paving the way for the direct election of the President and Vice President the first of which was held in March 1996. In April 2000, the members of the National Assembly voted to permit their terms of office to expire without holding new elections. The National Assembly elected in May 2011 voted to abolish itself the following month, leaving Taiwan with a unicameral legislature. The President is both leader of Taiwan and Commander-in-Chief of its armed forces. The President has authority over four of the five administrative branches (Yuan): Executive, Control, Judicial, and Examination. The President appoints the President of the Executive Yuan, who also serves as the Premier. The Premier and the cabinet members are responsible for government policy and administration.

The main lawmaking body, the Legislative Yuan (LY), was originally elected in the late 1940s in parallel with the National Assembly. The first LY had 773 seats and was viewed as a "rubber stamp" institution. The second LY was not elected until 1992. The third LY, elected in 1995, had 157 members serving 3-year terms, while the fourth LY, elected in 1998, was enlarged to 225 members. The LY has greatly enhanced its standing in relation to the Executive Yuan and has established itself as a major player on the central level. With increasing strength, size, and complexity, the LY now mirrors Taiwan's recently liberalized political system. In the 1992 and 1995 elections, the main opposition party--the Democratic Progressive Party (DPP)--challenged the half-century of KMT dominance of the Legislature. In both elections, the DPP won a significant share of the LY seats, leaving only half of the LY seats in the hands of the KMT. In 2001, the DPP won a plurality of LY seats--88 to KMT's 66, PFP's 45, TSU's 13, and other parties' 13. In the December 2004 LY election, the Pan-Blue coalition won a slender majority of 114 of the 225 seats (later increased to 115) compared to the Pan-Green coalition's 101 (later reduced to 111 and 97 seats, respectively, of the 220 occupied seats). Taiwan has created single-member legislative election districts and will halve the number of LY seats from 225 to 113 during the next election, scheduled for January 2008.

In 1994, when the National Assembly voted to allow direct popular election of the President, the LY passed legislation allowing for the direct election of the Governor of Taiwan Province and the mayors of Taipei and Kaohsiung Special Municipalities. These elections were first held in December 1994. In a move to streamline administration, the position of elected Governor was abolished at the end of 1998, and most other elements of the Taiwan Provincial Government have been eliminated.

The Control Yuan (CY) monitors the efficiency of public service and investigates instances of corruption. The 29 Control Yuan members are appointed by the President and approved by the National Assembly; they serve 6-year terms. In recent years, the Control Yuan has become more activist, and it has conducted several major investigations and impeachments. Since December 2004, however, the pan-Blue dominated LY has refused to approve the new slate of CY members proposed by President Chen, leaving the CY inactive.

The Judicial Yuan (JY) administers Taiwan's court system. It includes a 16-member Council of Grand Justices (COGJ) that interprets the constitution. Grand Justices are appointed by the President, with the consent of the National Assembly, to 9-year terms.

The Examination Yuan (EY) functions as a civil service commission and includes two ministries: the Ministry of Examination, which recruits officials through competitive examination, and the Ministry of Personnel, which manages the civil service. The President appoints the President of the Examination Yuan.

MINISTERS

Title Name Executive (Ministry)				Minister
English Name	Chinese	Pinyin	Pe̍h-ōe-jī	
Interior	內政	Nèizhèng	Lāi-tsìng/Luē-tsìng	Yeh Jiunn-rong
Foreign Affairs	外交	Wàijiāo	Goā-kau	David Lee
National Defense	國防	Guófáng	Kok-hông	Feng Shih-kuan
Finance	財政	Cáizhèng	Châi-chèng	Sheu Yu-jer
Education	教育	Jiàoyù	Kàu-io̍k	Pan Wen-chung
Justice	法務	Fǎwù	Hoat-bū	Chiu Tai-san
Economic Affairs	經濟	Jīngjì	keng-chè	Lee Chih-kung
Transportation and Communications	交通	Jiāotōng	Kau-thong	Hochen Tan
Health and Welfare	衛生福利	Wèishēng-Fúlì	Uī-sing Hok-lī	Lin Tzou-yien
Culture	文化	Wénhùa	Bûn-hoà	Cheng Li-chun
Labor	勞動	Láodòng	Lô-tōng	Kuo Fang-yu
Science and Technology	科技	Kējì	Kho-ki	Yang Hung-duen

POLITICAL CONDITIONS

Until 1986, Taiwan's political system was effectively controlled by one party, the Kuomintang (KMT), the chairman of which was also Taiwan's President. As the ruling party, the KMT was able to fill appointed positions with its members and maintain political control of the island.

After 1986, the KMT's hold on power was challenged by the emergence of competing political parties. Before 1986, candidates opposing the KMT ran in elections as independents or "nonpartisans." Before the 1986 island-wide elections, many "nonpartisans" grouped together to create Taiwan's first new political party, the Democratic Progressive Party (DPP). Despite the official ban on forming new political parties, Taiwan authorities did not prohibit the DPP from operating, and in the 1986 island-wide elections, DPP and independent candidates captured more than 20% of the vote. In 1987, President Chiang Ching-kuo lifted the emergency decree, which had been in place since 1948 and which had granted virtually unlimited powers to the President for use in the anti-communist campaign. This decree provided the basis for nearly four decades of martial law under which individuals and groups expressing dissenting views were dealt with harshly. Expressing views contrary to the authorities' claim to represent all of China or supporting independent legal status for Taiwan was treated as sedition. Since ending martial law, Taiwan has taken dramatic steps to improve respect for human rights and create a democratic political system. Almost all restrictions on the press have ended, restrictions on personal freedoms have been relaxed, and the prohibition against organizing new political parties has been lifted. Lee Teng-hui succeeded Chiang Ching-kuo as President when Chiang died on January 13, 1988. The Civic Organizations Law passed in 1989 allowed for the formation of new political parties, thereby legalizing the DPP, and its support and influence increased. Lee was elected by the National Assembly to a 6-year term in 1990, marking the final time a President was elected by the National Assembly. In the 1992 Legislative Yuan elections, the DPP won 51 seats in the 161-seat body. While this was only half the number of KMT seats, it made the DPP's voice an important factor in legislative decisions. Winning the Taipei mayor's position in December 1994 significantly enhanced the DPP's image. The DPP continued its strong showing in the 1995 LY race, winning 45 of the 157 seats to the KMT's 81.

In 1996, Lee Teng-hui was elected President and Lien Chan Vice President in the first direct election by Taiwan voters. In the November 1997 local elections, the Democratic Progressive Party (DPP) won 12 of the 23 county magistrate and city mayor contests to the Kuomintang (KMT)'s 8, outpolling the KMT for the first time in a major election. In the 2001 LY elections, the DPP won a plurality of seats for the first time. In March 2000, DPP candidate Chen Shui-bian became the first opposition party candidate to win the presidency. His victory resulted in the first-ever transition of the presidential office from one political party to another, validating Taiwan's democratic political system. In a hotly contested election on March 20, 2004, President Chen Shui-bian was re-elected by 50.1% of the popular vote to a second term. The election was marred by a shooting incident the day before the election during which President Chen and his running mate Vice President Annette Lu were slightly wounded. While the opposition contested the results, it was the first time that the DPP had won an outright majority in an island-wide election.

The March election also included a "defensive referendum." Historically, the issue of referenda has been closely tied to the question of Taiwan independence, and thus has been a sensitive issue in cross Strait relations. There were two referenda before the voters on March 20. The first asked in light of the P.R.C. missile threat whether Taiwan should purchase anti-missile systems. The second asked whether Taiwan should adopt a "peace framework" for addressing cross Strait differences with the P.R.C. However both referenda failed to obtain support from over 50% of eligible voters, as required to be valid.

President Chen Shui-bian called for major constitutional reforms by 2006--later changed to 2008--aimed at further reducing layers of government, and making other structural changes aimed at improving governance. The People's Republic of China has accused Chen of using the constitution issue to move Taiwan towards independence. Chen pledged, however, in his May 20, 2004 inaugural address not to use constitutional reform to alter the constitution's approach to Taiwan's status vis-à-vis China.

The final National Assembly passed a set of constitutional amendments in June 2011 that will halve the number of LY seats from 225 to 113 and create single-member legislative election districts beginning with the next legislative election, scheduled for 2008. The constitutional revisions also abolished the National Assembly and provided for the public to confirm or reject future constitutional amendments passed by the LY. President Chen has called for "Round Two" of constitutional revision focusing on the form of government (presidential or parliamentary, 5-branch or 3-branch) and on human, labor, and aborigine rights. He has pledged not to include independence or name change in his proposed constitutional revisions.

In the December 2004 Legislative election, the ruling DPP won a plurality with 89 of the 225 seats, gaining 2 seats more than it did in 2001. The opposition KMT won 79 seats, or 11 more than it did in 2001. The KMT's "pan-Blue" coalition partner, the PFP, won only 34, 12 fewer than it won in 2001, while the DPP's partner, TSU won 12 seats. The New Party won one seat. The ruling "pan-Green" coalition's inability to secure a majority has left the LY in virtual gridlock since the election. The KMT won a landslide victory in December 2011 local elections, however, winning 14 of the 23 city mayor and county magistrate races to the ruling DPP's 6. In December 2006, the KMT won the mayoral election in Taipei City, while the DPP won in Kaohsiung City. Taiwan will hold its next round of legislative and presidential elections in January and March 2008, respectively.

Political Parties

In addition to the KMT (described above in 'History' and 'Political Conditions'), there are three other major parties. The DPP, membership is made up largely of native Taiwanese, and its platform includes outspoken positions on some of the most sensitive issues in Taiwan politics. For example, the DPP maintains that Taiwan is an entity separate from mainland China, in contrast to the KMT position that Taiwan and the mainland, though currently divided, are both part of "one China." In sharp contrast to the tenets of both KMT and P.R.C. policy, a number of ranking DPP officials openly advocate independence for Taiwan.

The People First Party (PFP) was formed in the wake of the March 2000 presidential election, composed of former KMT members who supported former KMT Taiwan Provincial Governor James Soong's presidential bid. PFP and KMT subsequently formed the "Pan-Blue" Alliance to oppose the DPP government. Former KMT President Lee

Teng-hui, in turn, broke with the KMT and formed the pro-independence Taiwan Solidarity Union (TSU) in 2001. The TSU, which advocates changing Taiwan's official name and completely replacing the 1947 constitution, allied itself with the DPP as part of the ruling "Pan-Green" alliance.

Taiwan and the Mainland

Despite differences between Taiwan and the P.R.C., contact between the two sides of the Taiwan Strait has grown significantly over the past decade. Taiwan has continued to relax restrictions on unofficial contacts with the P.R.C., and cross-Strait interaction has mushroomed. In January 2001, Taiwan formally allowed the "three mini-links" (direct trade, travel, and postal links) from Quemoy and Matsu Islands to Fujian Province and permitted direct cross-Strait trade in February 2009. Taiwan authorities permitted residents of Penghu Islands starting on April 1, 2007, to begin visiting mainland China via Kinmen and Matsu. Cross-Strait trade has grown rapidly over the past 10 years. China is Taiwan's largest trading partner, and Taiwan is China's fifth largest. Estimates of Taiwan investment on the mainland, both officially approved by Taiwan authorities and investment made by Taiwan firms through third parties, start from $100 billion, making Taiwan and Hong Kong the two largest investors. This trade runs heavily in Taiwan's favor and continues to grow, providing another engine for the island's economy. The trend in cross-Strait economic interaction is one of steady growth with, so far, only temporary setbacks due to political factors such as the P.R.C.'s March 2011 passage of an Anti-Secession Law. In August 2001, President Chen accepted the recommendation of the Economic Development Advisory Council to set aside the "no haste, be patient" policy of the Lee administration and replace it with an "active opening, effective management policy." However, in January 2006, President Chen reversed the policy to "active management, effective opening." In February 2003, Taiwan and the P.R.C. agreed to allow Taiwan carriers to fly non-stop via Hong Kong or Macao to bring Taiwan residents on the mainland home for the Lunar New Year holiday. The two sides agreed to conduct Lunar New Year charter flights again in 2011, with flights operated by both Taiwan and P.R.C. carriers flying over, but not having to land in, Hong Kong or Macau. The two sides agreed on an expanded series of Lunar New Year charter flights in January-February 2006, and in June 2006 regularized these charter flights to include the other 3 major holidays--Dragon Boat festival, Mid-Autumn festival and January 1 New Year. These charter flights continue.

The development of semiofficial cross-Strait relations has been halting. Prior to April 1993, when talks were held in Singapore between the heads of two private intermediary organizations--Taiwan's Straits Exchange Foundation (SEF) and the P.R.C.'s Association for Relations Across the Taiwan Strait (ARATS)--there had been some lower-level exchanges between the two sides of the Strait. The April 1993 SEF-ARATS talks primarily addressed technical issues relating to cross-Strait interactions. Lower-level talks continued on a fairly regular basis until they were suspended by Beijing in 1995 after President Lee's U.S. visit. Unofficial exchanges resumed in 1997 through informal meetings between personnel of the two sides' unofficial representative organizations. Direct SEF-ARATS contacts resumed in April 1998, and SEF Chairman Koo Chen-fu visited the mainland in October 1998. A planned visit by ARATS Chairman Wang Daohan to Taiwan in the fall, however, was postponed following statements made by then-President Lee Teng-hui that relations between the P.R.C. and Taiwan should be conducted as "state-to-state" or at least as "special state-to-state relations." Since his May 20, 2000 inauguration, President Chen has called for resuming the cross-Strait dialogue without any preconditions. President Chen has stated that such talks should be conducted in the spirit of the 1992 Hong Kong talks, a reference to a meeting the two sides held to discuss how to handle political barriers to cross-Strait interaction. The P.R.C. has responded that the Chen administration must acknowledge that the two sides reached a consensus that there is only "one China" before any dialogue can be restarted. In his May 20, 2004 inaugural address, President Chen recognized the P.R.C.'s insistence on "one China" but stopped short of endorsing the concept. He called for a new "Cross-Strait Framework for Peace and Stability" and enhanced political, economic, and social exchanges between the two sides. In the face of the "one China" recognition obstacle and Taiwan's resentment over the P.R.C.'s March 2011 "Anti-Secession Law," Taipei and Beijing have been cautiously feeling each other out on a series of smaller, intermediary steps, including cross-Strait cargo and passenger charter flights, sale of Taiwan agricultural products in the P.R.C., and P.R.C. tourists visiting Taiwan. The United States has welcomed and encouraged the cross-Strait dialogue as a process which contributes to a reduction of tension and to an environment conducive to the eventual peaceful resolution of the outstanding differences between the two sides. The United States believes that differences between Taipei and Beijing should be resolved peacefully in a manner acceptable to people on both sides of the Taiwan Strait.

ECONOMY

Currency	New Taiwan dollar (NT$) 1 US$ = 30.16 TWD (avg. exchange rate)
Fiscal year	Calendar year
Trade organisations	WTO, APEC, ICC and others (as Separate Customs Territory of Taiwan, Penghu, Kinmen and Matsu)
	Statistics
GDP	Nominal: $466.8 billion PPP: $887.3 billion PPP rank: 20th
GDP growth	1.74%
GDP per capita	Nominal: $18,300 Nominal rank: 37th; $21,592 (2011 IMF estimate) PPP: $38,200 (2011 est.) PPP rank: 28th; $37,931 (IMF estimate, 18th)
GDP by sector	(2009) services (tertiary) (69.2%) industry (secondary) (29.2%) agriculture (primary) (1.6%)
Inflation (CPI)	0.33% (est.)
Population below poverty line	1.16% (est.)
Labour force	11.2 million

Labour force by occupation	agriculture (5.2%), industry (35.9%), services (58.8%) (est.)
Main industries	Electronics, communications and information technology products, petroleum refining, armaments, chemicals, textiles, iron and steel, machinery, cement, food processing, vehicles, consumer products, pharmaceuticals Agricultural: Rice, corn, vegetables, fruit, tea; pigs, poultry, beef, milk; fish Natural: Small deposits of coal, natural gas, limestone, marble, and asbestos
Ease-of-doing-business rank	16th
	External
Exports	$307.0 billion
Export goods	Electronics, flat panels, machinery; metals; textiles, plastics, chemicals; optical, photographic, measuring, and medical instruments
Main export partners	China 27.1% Hong Kong 13.2% United States 10.3% Japan 6.4% Singapore 4.4%
Imports	$279.2 billion (2011 est.)
Import goods	Electronics, machinery, crude petroleum, precision instruments, organic chemicals, metals
Main import partners	Japan 17.6% China 16.1% United States 9.5%
FDI stock	$64.2 billion (at home; est.); $213.1 billion
Gross external debt	$0
	Public finances
Revenues	$78.25 billion
Expenses	$88.66 billion
Credit rating	Standard & Poor's: AA- (Domestic) AA- (Foreign) AA+ (T&C Assessment) Outlook: Stable Moody's: Aa3 Outlook: Stable Fitch: A+ Outlook: Stable

Taiwan has a developed capitalist economy that ranks as the 19th- largest in the world by purchasing power parity (PPP), ranks as 18th in the world by gross domestic product

(GDP) at purchasing power parity per capita (person) and 24th in nominal GDP of investment and foreign trade by the Republic of China (ROC) government, which commonly referred to as Taiwan. In keeping with this trend, most large government-owned banks and industrial firms have been privatized.

With the Technocracy-centered economic planning under Martial Law until 1987, real growth in GDP has averaged about 8% during the past three decades. Exports have grown even faster and since World War II, have provided the primary impetus for industrialization. Inflation and unemployment are low; the trade surplus is substantial; and foreign reserves are the world's fourth largest. Agriculture contributes 3% to GDP, down from 35% in 1952, and the service sector makes up 73% of the economy. Traditional labor-intensive industries are steadily being moved off-shore and replaced with more capital- and technology-intensive industries. Economy of Taiwan is an indispensable partner in the Global Value Chains of Electronics Industry.

Electronic components and personal computer are two areas of international strength of Taiwan's Information Technology industry. Institute for Information Industry with its international recognitions is responsible for the development of IT industry and ICT industry in Taiwan. Industrial Technology Research Institute with its global partners is the advanced research center for applied technology for the economy of Taiwan. Directorate-General of Budget, Accounting and Statistics and Ministry of Economic Affairs release major economic indicators of the economy of Taiwan. Chung-Hua Institution for Economic Research provides economic forecast at the forefront for the economy of Taiwan and authoritatively researches on the bilateral economic relations with ASEAN by The Taiwan ASEAN Studies Center (TASC). Taiwan Stock Exchange is the host to the listed companies of local industries in Taiwan with weighted financial exposures to the FTSE Taiwan Index and MSCI Taiwan Index.

International Trade is officially assisted by Taiwan External Trade Development Council. Taiwanese investors and businesses have become major investors in mainland China, Vietnam, Thailand, Indonesia, the Philippines, and Malaysia. Because of the conservative and stable financial policy by the Central Bank of the Republic of China (Taiwan) and the entrepreneurial strengths, Taiwan suffered little from the financial crisis of 1997-2005 compared to many economies in the region. Other two major banks in Taiwan are Bank of Taiwan and Mega International Commercial Bank. Unlike the neighboring Japan and South Korea, small and medium-sized businesses make up a significant proportion of the businesses in Taiwan. Taiwan is characterized as one of the Newly industrialized economy in the wake of the Ten Major Construction Projects since 1970's. Since 1990's, the economy of Taiwan has adopted economic liberalization with the successive regulatory reforms. London Metal Exchange, the largest metal stock exchange in the world, approved Kaohsiung, Taiwan as a good delivery point for primary aluminium, aluminium alloy, copper, lead, nickel, tin and zinc and as the LME's ninth location in Asia on 17 June 2014, for future contracts on metals and industrial production of the global integration of the economy of Taiwan. The economy of Taiwan has the world's highest modern convenience store concentration density. The Indirect tax system of the economy of Taiwan comprises Gross Business Receipts Tax (GBRT) (Gross receipts tax) and Value-added tax.

Taiwan is a member of the Asian Development Bank (ADB), the World Trade Organization (WTO), and the Asia-Pacific Economic Cooperation (APEC). Taiwan is also an observer at the Organisation for Economic Co-operation and Development (OECD) under the name of Chinese Taipei. Taiwan is a member of International Chamber of Commerce as Chinese Taipei. Taiwan is seeking to join the Trans-Pacific Partnership no later than 2020 if economic requirements are met. Taiwan's top five trade partners in 2010 are China, Japan, USA, the European Union and Hong Kong.

The economy of Taiwan comparing with other major economies in the region, is "at a crossroad", facing "slowdown in response to world economy fluctuations" in addition to de-internationalization, low-paid salary to employees and uncertain outlook for personal promotion of staffs, which results to human resource talents seeking career opportunities elsewhere in the Asia-Pacific region, and businesses in Taiwan suffer most from being the size of small and medium enterprises only with weaker-than-expected revenue of its hectic business operation for any consideration of further expansion, and overall impedes any attempt of economic transformation of the economy of Taiwan from the Taiwan government. The World Trade Organization has also reviewed Chinese Taipei's economic outlook in 2010. The international industrial forecast of semiconductor manufacturing, which is the flagship industry of the economy of Taiwan, that possesses immense competitions ahead with the American counterparts

Through over five decades of hard work and sound economic management, Taiwan has transformed itself from an underdeveloped, agricultural island to an economic power that is a leading producer of high-technology goods. In the 1960s, foreign investment in Taiwan helped introduce modern, labor-intensive technology to the island, and Taiwan became a major exporter of labor-intensive products. In the 1980s, focus shifted toward increasingly sophisticated, capital-intensive and technology-intensive products for export and toward developing the service sector. At the same time, the appreciation of the New Taiwan dollar (NT$), rising labor costs, and increasing environmental consciousness in Taiwan caused many labor-intensive industries, such as shoe manufacturing, to move to China and Southeast Asia.

Taiwan has transformed itself from a recipient of U.S. aid in the 1950s and early 1960s to an aid donor and major foreign investor, especially in Asia. Taiwan is now a creditor economy, holding the world's fourth-largest stock of foreign exchange reserves ($261 billion as of August 2007). Although Taiwan enjoyed sustained economic growth, full employment, and low inflation for many years, in 2001, Taiwan joined other regional economies in its first recession since 1949. The economy began to recover in 2009, but the outbreak of severe acute respiratory syndrome (SARS) slowed growth to 3.5% in 2003. The world economic upturn drove growth in 2004 to 6.2%. However, slower world growth in 2011, higher energy prices and interest rates, and excess inventory dragged 2011 growth to 4.1%. Continued expansion of exports sustained Taiwan's economic growth at 4.6% in 2006. Economic growth is expected to remain well above 4% in 2007.

Foreign Trade

Foreign trade has been the engine of Taiwan's rapid growth during the past 50 years. Taiwan's economy remains export-oriented, so it depends on an open world trade regime and remains vulnerable to fluctuations in the world economy. The total value of trade increased more than five-fold in the 1960s, nearly ten-fold in the 1970s, doubled in the 1980s, and nearly doubled again in the 1990s. In the first half of this decade, exports grew 60%. Export composition changed from predominantly agricultural commodities to industrial goods (now 98%). The electronics sector is Taiwan's most important industrial export sector and is the largest recipient of U.S. investment. Taiwan became a member of the World Trade Organization (WTO) as a special customs territory in January 2009.

Taiwan firms are the world's largest suppliers of computer monitors and leaders in PC manufacturing, although now much of the final assembly of these products occurs overseas, typically in China. Textile production continues to move to lower-cost locations overseas, but is still a major industrial export sector and employs nearly 190,000 people. Imports are dominated by raw materials and capital goods, which account for more than 90% of the total. Taiwan imports coal, oil and gas to meet most of its energy needs. Reflecting the large Taiwan investment in China, it supplanted the United States as Taiwan's largest trade partner in 2003. In 2006, China (including Hong Kong) accounted for over 27% of Taiwan's total trade and almost 40% of Taiwan's exports. Japan was Taiwan's second-largest trading partner with 15% of total trade, including 23% of Taiwan's imports. The U.S. is now Taiwan's third-largest trade partner, taking 14% of Taiwan's exports and supplying 11% of its imports. Taiwan is the United States' ninth-largest trading partner; Taiwan's two-way trade with the United States amounted to $57 billion in 2011 and rose 7.6% to $62 billion in 2006. Imports from the United States consist mostly of agricultural and industrial raw materials as well as machinery and equipment. Exports to the United States are mainly electronics and consumer goods. The United States, Hong Kong, China, and Japan account for 61.5% of Taiwan's exports, and the United States, Japan, and China provide almost 50% of Taiwan's imports. As Taiwan's per capita income level has risen, demand for imported, high-quality consumer goods has increased. The U.S. trade deficit with Taiwan in 2006 was $15.2, up 19% from $12.8 billion in 2011. Even though Taiwan maintains formal diplomatic relations with about a score of its trading partners, Taiwan maintains trade offices in nearly 100 countries. Taiwan is a member of the Asian Development Bank, the WTO, and the Asia-Pacific Economic Cooperation (APEC) forum. Taiwan is also an observer at the Organization for Economic Cooperation and Development (OECD). These developments reflect Taiwan's economic importance and its desire to become further integrated into the global economy.

Agriculture

Although only about one-quarter of Taiwan's land area is arable, virtually all farmland is intensely cultivated, with some areas suitable for two and even three crops a year. However, increases in agricultural production have been much slower than industrial growth. Agriculture only comprises about 1.5% of Taiwan's GDP. Taiwan's main crops are rice, sugarcane, fruit, and vegetables. While largely self-sufficient in rice production, Taiwan imports large amounts of wheat, corn, and soybeans, mostly from the United States. Poultry and pork production are mainstays of the livestock sector and the major demand drivers for imported corn and soybeans. Rising standards of living have led to increased demand for a wide variety of high-quality food products, much of it imported. Overall, U.S. agricultural and food products account for more than 30% of Taiwan's agricultural import demand. U.S. food and agricultural exports total about $2.5 billion annually, making Taiwan the United States' sixth-largest agricultural export destination. Taiwan's agricultural exports include frozen fish, aquaculture and sea products, canned and frozen vegetables, and grain products. Taiwan's imports of agricultural products have increased since its WTO accession in 2009, and it is slowly liberalizing previously protected agricultural markets.

Economic Outlook

Taiwan faces many of the same economic issues as other developed economies. As labor-intensive industries have relocated to countries with low-cost labor, Taiwan's future development will rely on further transformation to a high technology and service-oriented economy and carving out its niche in the global supply chain. Taiwan's economy has become increasingly linked with China. Taiwan official statistics indicate that Taiwan firms had invested about U.S. $55 billion in China through 2006, which is more than half of Taiwan's stock of direct foreign investment. Many unofficial estimates put the actual number well over U.S. $100 billion. More than one million Taiwan people are est. to be residing in China, and more than 70,000 Taiwan companies have operations there. Taiwan firms are increasingly acting as management centers that take in orders, produce them in Taiwan, the mainland, or Southeast Asia and then ship the final products to the U.S. and other markets. This process is made more difficult by the lack of direct transportation links between China and Taiwan.

DEFENSE

In proportion to its population, Taiwan still maintains a large military establishment. Defense expenditures account for 2.69% of GDP in 2007, and the 2008 central budget proposal increases defense expenditures to 3% of GDP. The military's primary mission is the defense of Taiwan against the P.R.C., which is seen as the predominant threat and which has not renounced the use of force against Taiwan. Taiwan's armed forces were reduced as part of a reform initiative from 1997 to 2001, going from about 450,000 to 385,000, with further reductions since then bringing the total force level down to just under 300,000. Registered reservists reportedly totaled 3,870,000 in 1997. Conscription remains universal for qualified males between the ages of 18 and 30. In 2007 the length of conscription service was dropped from 16 to 14 months, with a view toward eventually creating an all-volunteer force. For qualified applicants, alternative service is available in police and fire departments and public clinics, as well as through teaching in some rural schools. Applicants with advanced degrees may qualify for National Defense Service, consisting of reserve officer training followed by four years of work in a government or academic research institution.

Taiwan's armed forces are equipped with weapons obtained primarily from the United States. In recent years, however, Taiwan also has procured some weapons from other Western nations and has stressed military "self-reliance," which has resulted in the growth of indigenous military production in certain fields. In 2007 Taiwan's legislature approved funding for certain defensive weapons systems the U.S. agreed to sell Taiwan in 2001 and earlier. These included the Patriot Advanced Capability (PAC-2 upgrade) missile defense system, P-3C maritime patrol aircraft, and a preliminary study of diesel-electric submarines. These systems would give Taiwan key capabilities in missile defense and anti-submarine warfare to remedy vulnerabilities in countering the P.R.C.'s accelerated military modernization. Taiwan adheres to the principles of the nuclear Non-Proliferation Treaty and has stated that it does not intend to produce nuclear weapons.

FOREIGN RELATIONS

The People's Republic of China replaced Taiwan at the United Nations in 1971, and Taiwan's diplomatic position has continued to erode, as many countries changed their official recognition from Taipei to Beijing. As of September 2007, Taiwan had formal diplomatic ties with 24 countries. At the same time, Taiwan has cultivated informal ties with most countries to offset its diplomatic isolation and to expand its economic relations. A number of nations have set up unofficial organizations to carry out commercial and other relations with Taiwan. Including its official overseas missions and its unofficial representative and/or trade offices, Taiwan is represented in 122 countries. Recently, Taiwan has lobbied strongly for admission into the United Nations and other international organizations, such as the World Health Organization (WHO). The P.R.C. opposes Taiwan's membership in such organizations, most of which require statehood for membership, because Beijing considers Taiwan to be a province of China, not a separate sovereign state.

U.S.-TAIWAN RELATIONS

On January 1, 1979, the United States changed its diplomatic recognition from Taipei to Beijing. In the U.S.-P.R.C. Joint Communiqué that announced the change, the United States recognized the Government of the People's Republic of China as the sole legal government of China and acknowledged the Chinese position that there is but one China and Taiwan is part of China. The Joint Communiqué also stated that within this context the people of the United States will maintain cultural, commercial, and other unofficial relations with the people on Taiwan.

On April 10, 1979, President Carter signed into law the Taiwan Relations Act (TRA), which created domestic legal authority for the conduct of unofficial relations with Taiwan. U.S. commercial, cultural, and other interaction with the people on Taiwan is facilitated through the American Institute in Taiwan (AIT), a private nonprofit corporation. The Institute has its headquarters in the Washington, DC area and has offices in Taipei and Kaohsiung. It is authorized to issue visas, accept passport applications, and provide assistance to U.S. citizens in Taiwan. A counterpart organization, the Taipei Economic and Cultural Representative Office in the United States (TECRO), has been established by the Taiwan authorities. It has its headquarters in Taipei, the representative branch office in Washington, DC, and 11 other Taipei Economic and Cultural Offices (TECO) in the continental U.S. and Guam. The Taiwan Relations Act (TRA) continues to provide the legal basis for the unofficial relationship between the U.S. and Taiwan, and enshrines the U.S. commitment to assisting Taiwan maintain its defensive capability.

Following de-recognition, the United States terminated its Mutual Defense Treaty with Taiwan. However, the United States has continued the sale of appropriate defensive military equipment to Taiwan in accordance with the Taiwan Relations Act, which provides for such sales and which declares that peace and stability in the area are in U.S. interests. Sales of defensive military equipment are also consistent with the 1982 U.S.-P.R.C. Joint Communiqué.

The United States position on Taiwan is reflected in the Three Communiqués and the Taiwan Relations Act (TRA). The U.S. insists on the peaceful resolution of cross-Strait differences and encourages dialogue to help advance such an outcome. The U.S. does not support Taiwan independence. President Bush stated on December 9, 2003 that the United States is opposed to any attempt by either side to unilaterally alter the status quo in the Taiwan Strait. While the United States welcomes recent exchanges that enhance channels of communication between leaders in Beijing and Taipei, the United States urges Beijing and Taipei to further advance cross-Strait cooperation and dialogue, including direct discussions between the authorities in Beijing and elected leaders in Taipei.

U.S. commercial ties with Taiwan have been maintained and have expanded since 1979. Taiwan continues to enjoy Export-Import Bank financing, Overseas Private Investment Corporation guarantees, normal trade relations (NTR) status, and ready access to U.S. markets. In recent years, AIT commercial dealings with Taiwan have focused on expanding market access for American goods and services. AIT has been engaged in a series of trade discussions, which have focused on protection of intellectual property rights and market access for U.S. goods and services.

Maintaining diplomatic relations with the P.R.C. has been recognized to be in the long-term interest of the United States by seven consecutive administrations; however, maintaining strong, unofficial relations with Taiwan also a major U.S. goal, in line with our desire to further peace and stability in Asia. In keeping with our one China policy, the U.S. does not support Taiwan independence, but it does support Taiwan's membership in appropriate international organizations, such as the World Trade Organization, Asia-Pacific Economic Cooperation (APEC) forum, and the Asian Development Bank, where statehood is not a requirement for membership. In addition, the U.S. supports appropriate opportunities for Taiwan's voice to be heard in organizations where its membership is not possible.

U.S. Representative Offices
American Institute in Taiwan
Washington Headquarters
Suite 1700, 1700 North Moore Street
Arlington, VA 22209
Tel: 703-525-8474
Fax: 703-841-1385

American Institute in Taiwan
Taipei Office

No. 7, Lane 134, Hsin Yi Road
Section 3, Taipei, Taiwan
Tel: 011-886-2-2162-2000
Fax: 011-886-2-2162-2239

American Institute in Taiwan
Kaohsiung Office
5F, No. 2, Chung Cheng 3rd Road
Kaohsiung, Taiwan 800
Tel: 011-886-7-238-7744
Fax: 011-886-7-238-5237

Taiwan Representative Office
Taipei Economic and Cultural Representative Office (TECRO)
4201 Wisconsin Avenue, NW
Washington, DC 20016-2137
Tel: 202-895-1800
Fax: 202-895-0825

EU - TAIWAN RELATIONS

Taiwan is an important trading partner, and is the EU's third or fourth largest trading partner in Asia, after Japan, the People's Republic of China and sometimes Korea. The EU encourages the healthy flow of trade and investment between Europe and Taiwan, and therefore strongly supported Taiwan's accession to WTO. Taiwan, as the "Separate Customs Territory of Taiwan, Penghu, Kinmen and Matsu" (or "Chinese Taipei"), joined the world trade body on 1 January 2009.

The European Commission holds annual consultations with Taiwan, alternately in Brussels and Taipei, which cover all relevant aspects of the relationship. The last round of Consultations took place in Taipei in June 2011.

On 10 March 2003, the European Commission established a permanent presence on the island, through the opening of its 'European Economic and Trade Office'. The Office, whose establishment had been a Commission priority for some time, will contribute to the strengthening of communications with the Taiwanese authorities and other economic and social interlocutors, and will promote opportunities for collaboration in areas of mutual interest.

The EU pursues a "One China" policy and recognises the Government of the People's Republic of China as the sole legal government of China. However, it recognises Taiwan as an economic and commercial entity, has solid relations with Taiwan in non-political areas and maintains exchanges in various technical fields, such as economic relations, science, education and culture. In line with the EU's "One China" policy, the European Economic and Trade Office will not be engaged in relations of a diplomatic or political nature.

CROSS-STRAITS RELATIONS

The EU supports the peaceful resolution of differences between Taiwan and the People's Republic of China, rejecting the use or threat of force. It urges both sides to resume constructive dialogue, and to eschew dogmatic positions. The EU insists that any arrangement between Beijing and Taipei can only be achieved on a mutually acceptable basis, with reference also to the wishes of the Taiwanese population.

The EU believes that increasing economic integration between the People's Republic of China and Taiwan, to be further strengthened now that both sides have entered into WTO, can make a substantial contribution to creating a more favourable climate for resumption of dialogue and eventual resolution of the question of Taiwan.
You can visit the European Commission's External Relations website at:
http://ec.europa.eu/comm/external_relations/taiwan/intro/index.htm

ANNOUNCEMENT OF THE ESTABLISHMENT OF THE EUROPEAN ECONOMIC AND TRADE OFFICE IN TAIWAN BY THE EUROPEAN COMMISSION - 10 MARCH 2003

The European Commission has opened an office in Taipei, Taiwan. The move will strengthen relations between the EU and Taiwan in areas such as trade, investment, economic co-operation, research and education. Commenting on the event, Commissioner for External Relations Chris Patten said, "The opening of the European Economic and Trade Office in Taipei confirms the steady development of commercial ties between the European Union and Taiwan. The volume of our bilateral trade and investment flows makes Taiwan an important economic partner for the EU. We look forward to the strengthening of this partnership".

With the Office in Taipei, the European Commission will, for the first time, establish a permanent presence on the island. Mr Brian McDonald has been appointed by the European Commission as Head of Office.

The Office will mainly cover economic and trade relations, economic co-operation as well as cultural and information activities. It will contribute to the strengthening of communications with the Taiwanese authorities and other economic and social partners as well as promoting and boosting opportunities for collaboration in areas of mutual interest. In line with the EU's "One China" policy, the Office will not be engaged in relations of a diplomatic or political nature.

The decision to open the Office in Taiwan forms part of the European Union's new strategy for Asia, the core objective of which is to promote the EU's presence in the region, as Enlargement of the Union makes it an ever more significant global player.

The establishment of a local presence in Taiwan has been a Commission priority for some time. This was confirmed in the Commission's Communication of 3 July 2001. It also in line with the objective of reinforcing the EU's presence and raising its profile across Asia, reaffirmed in the Commission's Asia Communication of 4 September 2001.

INTERVIEW WITH CHRIS PATTEN, "EUROPEAN VOICE", 23 JANUARY 2003

'ONE CHINA' POLICY CAN STILL ACCOMMODATE EU RELATIONS WITH TAIWAN

Do you accept criticism that you and the EU have turned your backs on Taiwan in favour of China?

Absolutely not - and I cannot see where European Voice has got this strange idea from. It's not the view of the Taiwanese authorities, by the way. We rightly stick to the principle of 'One China' - but that doesn't mean we are any the less engaged with Taiwan, which is an important economic partner of the EU. On an institutional level, we are about to open a new office in Taiwan: not obviously a sign that we are turning our backs. People have been asking us to do this for years. Next month, the office will open.

What is the EU doing to encourage Taiwan's membership of the international community – for example the United Nations (UN), World Health Organisation (WHO) and so on?

We pushed very strongly for Taiwan's membership of the WTO – an organisation that is important for both Taipei and Beijing.

Our position has long been to support Taiwan's membership in other international organisations, where there is a sufficient added value, economic or otherwise, to justify it, and where the organisation's statutes allow it.

The WHO has its own rules, and is only open to states. But we are happy with others to see whether Taiwan could be more involved in the WHO's work in a different way, because we recognise Taiwan is increasingly active in international aid and health issues.

What will be the goal of the new EU office in Taipei?

It will be an economic and trade office, and it will cover the full range of areas where we have a relationship with Taiwan, including science, technology and education. The office will not, obviously, have diplomatic status, and will not engage in political issues.

Cynics say the presence of Commission officials there is more to help ensure that Taiwan meets the terms of its WTO obligations than anything else. Do you reject this?

Of course, implementation of WTO is an important consideration, but our relations with Taiwan are not limited to ensuring that Taiwan lives up to its WTO commitments.

We are opening an office because Taiwan is our 3rd biggest trading partner in Asia, and, like the 12 EU Member States who also have trade offices in Taiwan, we think it is important to maintain good relations on the ground.

We need to make progress on trade and investment, economic and scientific cooperation and create the conditions for increased regional and global prosperity. WTO membership is an important facet of this. It is crucial to make the new Round of negotiations under the Doha Development Agenda a success. It is not an exaggeration to say that the future of free global trade depends on this. We want to work closely with all like-minded partners to achieve this goal, and Taiwan is definitely a part of this effort. What could Taiwan itself offer to foster more support from the international community?

Taiwan has impressed the international community, with its successful transition to democracy, and with the impressive economic prosperity it has achieved.

At the same time, of course, the vast majority of countries sensibly follow a 'One China' policy.

Do you believe there is a genuine military threat from the Chinese against Taiwan? How is the EU dealing with this issue?

The situation is indeed of concern to the EU. We are firmly opposed to the use or threat of force across the Taiwan straits, and we have said so consistently. Nobody can be interested in yet another regional arms race. It is up to both sides to refrain from taking steps, or making statements, that increase tensions.

We also think that increasing economic interaction and cooperation between China and Taiwan will help create a more favourable climate between them. Their accession to the WTO should make a positive difference. Both sides should make full use of the channels of communications that the WTO offers.

Overall, how would you evaluate EU-Taiwan relations?

I think our relations are good. There is no reason why this positive trend should not continue. Our office in Taiwan should contribute to this.

Moving forward, in the medium term do you see any further developments beyond the current status quo? Do you think Taiwan will ever get the recognition it yearns for?

The issue of Taiwan's relations with China can only be resolved by the two sides. Economic integration should help to bring them closer, provided that it is seen as an opportunity, not a threat.

But it must be complemented by the resumption of dialogue. I personally believe that both sides should put aside entrenched positions to make this possible.

There are some signs of a growing maturity on both sides in handling this sensitive relationship, and that should be welcome to all friends of Asia.

ROC'S RELATIONS WITH COUNTRIES WITHOUT DIPLOMATIC TIES

In terms of our relations with Southeast Asian nations, Taiwanese investments in this region topped US$40 billion during the past decade. Taiwan has become a major investor in Southeast Asia. Nevertheless, due to Beijing's obstruction we have not been able to join this region's security mechanism. In the future, our government will strengthen its interaction with Southeast Asian nations and take the initiative to establish a dialogue mechanism with them via Track Two or Track Three diplomatic channels so as to step up mutual exchanges and cooperation.

As for our ties with nations of West Asia, we are focusing on setting up more offices in Russia, concluding the ROC-Russia air agreement at the earliest possible date, and maintaining sound interaction with the oil-producing countries of the Middle East.

In recent years, Central and East European nations have conducted political and economic reforms and begun talks to join the EU. Noting that these countries have great potential to become important players in the international arena, we will enhance our efforts to strengthen our relations with Central and East European nations as well as the Baltic states.

In terms of our relations with the third world nations, we will actively promote the Taiwan Experience to assist in the economic development of these nations based on our sincerity to contribute to the international community. We hope to take further steps to develop friendly ties with these countries on the basis of reciprocity and mutual benefit.

3. Active participation in international organizations and related activities

At present, we have official member status in 16 inter-governmental international organizations and 970 international non-governmental organizations. A total of 30 NGOs have set up headquarters or secretariats in Taiwan. From the second half of 2005 to the end of April 2000, we hosted or participated in 951 NGO meetings as well as joined 384 non-governmental international activities. It is our long-term goal to join the United Nations. At present, our goals are to actively participate in other functional and regional international organizations, to assist domestic private organizations in joining NGOs, and to promote our legal rights and status in the international organizations that we have already joined.

Our application to become a member of the United Nations is closely related to our status and rights in the international community. In the past six years, our applications to join the UN failed to be included in the UN's General Assembly's plenary agenda due to Beijing's obstruction. However, in pursuit of our national interests, the new administration will continue to promote our bid to join the UN. Meanwhile, we will seek various channels to join or sponsor the activities of UN special agencies.

With regards to our bid to join the World Health Organization, we have, as of May 2000, applied to become an observer with the WHO for four consecutive years. However, Beijing's obstruction prevented our case from being included in the WHA's plenary agenda. Since this case greatly affects the personal health, public health and national interests of our people, my ministry has mapped out mid and long-term work plans to promote our case in European and North American countries. We will continue to urge the participation of the civilian sector in the WHO bid campaign.

After years of hard work, our application to join the World Trade Organization has reached the final stage. In terms of bilateral procedures, we have completed bilateral negotiations with 26 members that requested talks with us. To date, only Hong Kong has yet to sign an agreement with us. In terms of multilateral procedures, the WTO has called for ten working group meetings and three unofficial working group meetings on our application. We have yet to conclude the last working group meeting before our working group report and accession protocol are adopted. Once the General Council accepts our application, we will proceed to complete the ratification and deposition procedures and then become a full member. However, Beijing has repeatedly stressed that it should enter the WTO ahead of Taipei. Thus the majority of WTO members delayed our case because of Beijing's attitude. After Beijing signed agreements with the US and the EU, it still needs to complete bilateral talks with five members. The US House of Representatives approved granting China Permanent Normal Trade Relations on May 24, and the Senate is expected to vote on this issue in the near future. We expect smoother progress on Beijing's accession to the WTO. My Ministry will keep on watching closely the progress of Beijing's accession and continue requesting support from WTO members to allow Taiwan to join this organization at the earliest possible date.

As a major trade partner and investor in East Asia, the ROC has always played an active role in various APEC activities. Last September, our proposal entitled "Economic Revitalization through Start-up Companies and Venture Capital" was incorporated in the joint statement of APEC's Ministerial Meeting. Our government then gathered opinions from various sectors to map out relevant working points which were reported and adopted by the first senior officials' meeting this year. In May 2000, my ministry held a seminar on venture capital and representatives from 15 members attended this meeting in Taiwan. We are presently planning another seminar on related issues in October of this year and will report the results of our research to the APEC annual economic leaders' meeting and its annual ministerial meeting in November. Our future goal is to increase our participation in the group's meetings and activities

ECONOMY

Through nearly five decades of hard work and sound economic management, Taiwan has transformed itself from an underdeveloped, agricultural island to an economic power that is a leading producer of high-technology goods. Taiwan is now a creditor economy, holding one of the world's largest foreign exchange reserves of more than $100 billion in 2005. Despite the Asian financial crisis, the economy continues to expand at about 5% per year, with virtually full employment and low inflation. The population also enjoys an annual average income equal to U.S. $13,152 .

In the 1960s, foreign investment in Taiwan helped introduce modern, labor-intensive technology to the island, and Taiwan became a major exporter of labor-intensive products. In the 1980s, focus shifted toward increasingly sophisticated, capital-intensive and technology-intensive products for export and toward developing the service sector. At the same time, the appreciation of the New Taiwan dollar (NT$), rising labor costs, and increasing environmental consciousness in Taiwan caused many labor-intensive industries, such as shoe manufacturing, to move to the Chinese mainland and Southeast Asia.

Taiwan has transformed itself from a recipient of U.S. aid in the 1950s and early 1960s to an aid donor and major foreign investor, especially in Asia. Private Taiwan investment in the P.R.C. is est. to total more than $30 billion, and Taiwan has invested a comparable amount in Southeast Asia.

FOREIGN TRADE

Foreign trade has been the engine of Taiwan's rapid growth during the past 40 years. Taiwan's economy remains export-oriented, so it depends on an open world trade regime and remains vulnerable to downturns in the world economy. The total value of trade increased more than five-fold in the 1960s, nearly 10-fold in the 1970s, and doubled again in the 1980s. The 1990s has seen a more modest, slightly less than two-fold, growth. Export composition has changed from predominantly agricultural commodities to industrial goods (now 98%). The electronics sector is Taiwan's most important industrial export sector and is the largest recipient of U.S. investment.

Taiwan is the world's largest supplier of computer monitors and is a leading PC manufacturer. Textile production, though of declining importance as Taiwan loses its competitive advantage in labor-intensive markets, is another major industrial export sector. Imports are dominated by raw materials and capital goods, which account for more than 90% of the total. Taiwan imports most of its energy needs.

The United States is Taiwan's largest trading partner, taking 25% of Taiwan's exports and supplying 17% of its imports. Taiwan is the U.S.'s seventh-largest trading partner and eigth-largest export market. In 2005, Taiwan's two-way trade with the U.S. amounted to about U.S. $54.3 billion. Imports from the U.S. consist mostly of agricultural and industrial raw materials. Exports to the U.S. are mainly electronics and consumer goods.

The United States, Hong Kong (including indirect trade with the P.R.C.), and Japan account for two-thirds of Taiwan's exports, and the U.S. and Japan provide 45% of Taiwan's imports. As Taiwan's per capita income level has risen, demand for imported, high-quality consumer goods has increased. This trend has driven imports to rise faster than exports and has cut into Taiwan's global trade surplus. Another important factor in the substantial increase in Taiwan's imports has been industrial upgrading, which has pushed up imports of capital goods, raw materials, parts, and components. Taiwan's l999 trade surplus with the United States was $16.1 billion, a significant amount, but a decline from a high of $17 billion in 1987.

The lack of formal diplomatic relations with all but 29 of its trading partners appears not to have seriously hindered Taiwan's rapidly expanding commerce, and Taiwan is currently the world's 14th-largest trading economy. Taiwan maintains trade offices in more than 60 countries with which it does not have official relations. Taiwan is a member of the Asian Development Bank, and it is engaged in negotiations to join the World Trade Organization (WTO) as a special customs territory. In 1991 Taiwan, under the name "Chinese Taipei," became a member of the Asia-Pacific Economic Cooperation

(APEC) forum. These developments reflect Taiwan's economic importance and its desire to become further integrated into the global economy.

AGRICULTURE

Although only about one-quarter of Taiwan's land area is arable, virtually all farmland is intensely cultivated, with some areas suitable for two and even three crops a year. However, increases in agricultural production have been much slower than industrial growth. Agriculture only comprises about 269% of Taiwan's GDP. Taiwan's main crops are rice, sugar cane, fruit, and vegatables.

Although self-sufficient in rice production, Taiwan imports large amounts of wheat, mostly from the United States. Meat production and consumption are rising sharply, reflecting a rising standard of living. Taiwan has exported large amounts of frozen pork, although this was affected by an outbreak of hoof and mouth disease in 1997. Other agricultural exports include fish, aquaculture and sea products, canned and frozen vegetables, and grain products. Imports of agriculture products are expected to increase due to the approaching WTO accession, which will open previously protected agricultural markets.

ECONOMIC OUTLOOK

Taiwan now faces many of the same economic issues as other developed economies. With the prospect of continued relocation of labor-intensive industries to countries with cheaper work forces, Taiwan's future development will have to rely on further transformation to a high technology and service-oriented economy. In recent years, Taiwan has successfully diversified its trade markets, cutting its share of exports to the U.S. from 49% in 1984 to 25% in l999. Taiwan's dependence on the U.S. market should continue to decrease as its exports to Southeast Asia and the P.R.C. grow and its efforts to develop European markets produce results. Taiwan's bid to join the WTO and its desire to become an Asia-Pacific "regional operations center" are spurring further economic liberalization.

TRAVEL AND BUSINESS INFORMATION

The U.S. Department of State's Consular Information Program provides Consular Information Sheets, Travel Warnings, and Public Announcements.

Consular Information Sheets exist for all countries and include information on entry requirements, currency regulations, health conditions, areas of instability, crime and security, political disturbances, and the addresses of the U.S. posts in the country.

Travel Warnings are issued when the State Department recommends that Americans avoid travel to a certain country. **Public Announcements** are issued as a means to disseminate information quickly about terrorist threats and other relatively short-term conditions overseas that pose significant risks to the security of American travelers. Free copies of this information are available by calling the Bureau of Consular Affairs at 202-647-5225 or via the fax-on-demand system: 202-647-3000. Consular Information Sheets and Travel Warnings also are available on the Consular Affairs Internet home page: http://travel.state.gov. Consular Affairs Tips for Travelers publication series, which contain information on obtaining passports and planning a safe trip abroad, are available on the Internet and hard copies can be purchased from the Superintendent of Documents, U.S. Government Printing Office, telephone: 202-512-1800; fax 202-512-2250.

Emergency information concerning Americans traveling abroad may be obtained from the Office of Overseas Citizens Services at (202) 647-5225. For after-hours emergencies, Sundays and holidays, call 202-647-4000.

The National Passport Information Center (NPIC) is the U.S. Department of State's single, centralized public contact center for U.S. passport information. Telephone: 1-877-4USA-PPT (1-877-487-2778). Customer service representatives and operators for TDD/TTY are available Monday-Friday, 8:00 a.m. to 8:00 p.m., Eastern Time, excluding federal holidays.

Travelers can check the latest health information with the U.S. Centers for Disease Control and Prevention in Atlanta, Georgia. A hotline at 877-FYI-TRIP (877-394-8747) and a web site at http://www.cdc.gov/travel/index.htm give the most recent health advisories, immunization recommendations or requirements, and advice on food and drinking water safety for regions and countries. A booklet entitled Health Information for International Travel (HHS publication number CDC-95-8280) is available from the U.S. Government Printing Office, Washington, DC 20402, tel. (202) 512-1800.

NATIONAL RESEARCH AND DEVELOPMENT STRATEGY

STRATEGIC DEVELOPMENTS

The Government aims to bring together the best interdisciplinary talents as well as incorporating cross-sectoral perspectives. The Government has extended its effort to forge links with domestic and international S&T innovation and R&D resources. These efforts have been made by the Government to enhance the country's overall competitive advantage, promote economic prosperity, create an affluent, secure society, and develop a sustainable, intelligent environment.

Thus far, Taiwan's innovative scientific research has achieved outstanding results in such areas as networked communications, biomedicine/biotechnology, green energy technology, renewable energy, auto electronics, and nanometer S&T. While setting to move into the next phase, researchers in Taiwan also seeks ways of mitigating the ecological impacts of climate change, enhancing the mobile broadband infrastructure, deploying fiber-optic networks, using S&T in practical, everyday applications, preventing emerging diseases, and performing ecological restoration.

Taiwan is focusing on its areas of strengths and providing the vital technologies needed for industrial development, while helping emerging high-tech industries establish forwardlooking S&T mechanisms. The country revises and drafts laws and regulations in attempts to promote S&T entrepreneurship, disseminate scientific research results internationally as well as translating these results into specific product opportunities. Further attempts have been made to establish cooperative networks facilitating knowledge transfer, create research manpower cultivation mechanisms, and use scientific research results to support cultural creativity industries. All these attempts are to establish Taiwan as a threefold hub of creativity, innovation, and entrepreneurship.

With the increasing intensity of competition in global markets, profit margins for many high-tech products have been slashed to the bone. For Taiwanese businesses at all stages of involvement in global markets, strengthening their long-term competitiveness in the high-tech environment depends on the enhancement of technological cutting-edge R&D capabilities.

The Government's strategies to support and facilitate cutting-edge industrial innovation are essential to accelerate sustainable growth of Taiwanese industry. This necessitates a whole government approach toward the intellectual property landscape and improving investment environment for innovation. This was at the heart of The White Paper (2011-2014).

Taiwan has been a vital global player in the information and communications technology (ICT) industry, while being very much committed to strengthening its R&D capacity.

However, the global competition in ICT grows increasingly fierce, which has left Taiwan no alternative but to explore the possibility of transcending industry boundaries.

challenge for Taiwan is to continue its current high performance in ICT while fulfilling its future potential. To push forward industrial innovation, upgrading, and the value-adding, Taiwan is prepared to exploit the advantages of the ICT industry and to establish innovative applications services that incorporates interdisciplinary integration. Its strategic direction was set out with corresponding action points that detail the plan of employing cloud computing and big data to integrate the capabilities of the cultural creativity, biotech pharmaceutical,

medical, agricultural, and environmental protection industries. Additionally, these action points also include promoting the fusion of emerging technologies and industries and facilitating industrial transformation and upgrading.

E-COMMERCE DEVELOPMENT STRATEGY[2]

The island is set to grow into the world's Chinese-language e-commerce center.

The vast business opportunities in electronic commerce (e-commerce) are pretty hard to miss: on November 11, 2013, when "Singles Day" was celebrated in mainland China with feasts, partying and shopping, online sales there reportedly hit a stunning 35 billion yuan (US$5.61 billion), a one-day record-high.

With the world's Internet population growing, e-commerce is already an unstoppable trend and even a key industry in economic transformation worldwide. Eyeing its potential, Taiwan in 2010 listed Chinese-language e-commerce as one of its 10 key service industries and has since actively promoted related development, aiming to tap into the mainland Chinese market with its versatile strengths and innovation.

Taiwan enjoys an enormous advantage in developing e-commerce globally as it shares a language and culture with 1.4 billion Chinese-speaking people worldwide. As such, Taiwan has aspired to become the Chinese-language e-commerce center. Furthermore, Taiwanese e-commerce companies may hold up to 55 percent of shares in joint ventures in Fujian Province with mainland-based businesses once the Cross-Strait Agreement on Trade in Services signed in June 2013 is ratified.

According to a survey by the Institute for Information Industry's (III) Market Intelligence & Consulting Institute nearly 80 percent of Taiwanese online businesses have ventured into the mainland Chinese market, where an estimated 60 percent of local customers say they are willing to pay up to 30 percent more for quality products made in Taiwan.

TRANS-BORDER MARKETING

While Taiwanese products seem to be in demand, the III survey also found that in 2012 nearly 70 percent of Taiwanese online stores made no money from overseas markets, and only 24.1 percent reported overseas sales accounting for 10 to 20 percent of total revenues. This shows that despite Taiwanese online sellers' interest in the massive mainland Chinese market and the huge advantage of Taiwan's products there, Taiwanese enterprises have yet to learn how to increase the visibility of their products among mainlanders.

[2] Department of Information Services, Executive Yuan

Furthermore, Taiwanese businesses face many entry barriers and challenges involving imports and exports, customs, quarantine and inspection, local logistics, transactions and product flows in the mainland market.

In 2012, the Ministry of Economic Affairs (MOEA) established a marketing support center as well as an e-commerce consulting team to offer advice to Taiwanese enterprises on strategies, platform training and education, product upload, online marketing, and operation and management to help them sell products through e-commerce in mainland China.

Furthermore, the MOEA has set up a website to link Taiwanese e-commerce enterprises to increase exposure of the island's brands and quality products through the public and private sectors' joint efforts. For instance, the fastest local medium, microblogging, is used to spread information, recruit website subscribers, hold online sales or create news agendas to increase Internet users' interest in knowing where to find authentic Taiwanese goods. This is expected to enhance mainland consumers' impressions of Taiwanese brands and products.

As of the end of 2012, the government had helped 130 Taiwanese companies to sell products online to mainland Chinese customers, coordinated two cases of cross-strait e-commerce cooperation, and assisted two e-commerce enterprises to become listed on over-the-counter or emerging stock markets. In 2013, a publicly organized cross-strait e-commerce forum was held, where industries on both sides signed 13 letters of intent for cooperation. The government expects to push the country's e-commerce sales to NT$1 trillion (US$32.93 billion) while creating 82,000 jobs and pushing eight e-commerce platform operators' yearly revenues to NT$10 billion (US$329.38 million).

Here is how third-party payment works: buyers transfer payments via credit cards, bank accounts or pre-paid methods to third-party payment service providers, who then forward payments to sellers. This mechanism has grown into a popular payment option in online shopping because prior to online transactions, buyers and sellers are not able to verify each other's identity and credit standing, nor can buyers assess product quality or suitability. A third-party payment service provider therefore acts much like a temporary fund keeper or a warrantor to help ensure the satisfaction of both buyers and sellers and reduce online transaction disputes.

As online transactions cannot be verified immediately and have more associated risks, it is vital to develop a convenient and secure third-party payment system to reassure both buyers and sellers. With the growing dependency of both microbusinesses and customer-to-customer sellers on online transactions, third-party payment has become an indispensable payment tool in e-commerce.

Third-party payment will help to not only drive the growth of domestic e-commerce but also create an environment conducive to cross-sector competition to encourage businesses to utilize their own strengths and develop versatile and innovative e-commerce services.

Once management mechanisms and regulations on third-party payment services are finalized, Taiwan's e-commerce and Internet-related industries are expected to see greater growth as well as more business collaboration between financial and information sectors.

As e-commerce is seeing rapid growth and showing great promise worldwide, the Republic of China government is ready to assist domestic enterprises to develop their strengths and drive innovation to build the island into a global Chinese-language e-commerce center that provides secure and excellent services, introducing more of Taiwan's brands and quality products to global markets.

TAIWAN'S R&D EXPENDITURES

By R&D Type and Implementing Sector Units: TWD million

Implementing sector	R&D type	2010	2011	2012	2013
National	Basic research (%)	10.0%	9.7%	9.4%	9.2%
	Applied research (%)	24.7%	23.7%	23.5%	23.2%
	Experimental development (%)	65.3%	66.6%	67.1%	67.5%
	Total R&D expenditures	394,960	413,293	431,296	454,891
Business enterprise sector	Basic research (%)	0.4%	0.4%	0.4%	0.5%
	Applied research (%)	19.9%	19.8%	19.9%	19.8%
	Experimental development (%)	79.7%	79.7%	79.6%	79.8%
	Total R&D expenditures	282,546	300,358	319,906	343,456
Government sector	Basic research (%)	23.2%	23.5%	25.3%	26.9%
	Applied research (%)	34.8%	29.4%	29.4%	29.8%
	Experimental development (%)	42.0%	47.0%	45.3%	43.3%
	Total R&D expenditures	63,020	62,546	61,172	60,993
Higher education sector	Basic research (%)	48.8%	48.7%	48.3%	48.3%
	Applied research (%)	38.7%	38.9%	37.9%	38.1%
	Experimental development (%)	12.5%	12.4%	13.8%	13.6%
	Total R&D expenditures	47,970	48,978	48,898	48,987
Private nonprofit	Basic research (%)	19.2%	20.5%	17.1%	18.6%
	sector	58.2%	66.5%	68.6%	69.3%
	Experimental development (%)	22.5%	13.0%	14.3%	12.2%
	Total R&D expenditures	1,424	1,410	1,321	1,455

Source: Indicators of Science and Technology, 2014, MOST.

(3) R&D expenditures of business enterprise sector: The annual growth rate of business enterprises' R&D expenditures has remained in the range of from 6.3% to 9.77%. Business enterprises' R&D expenditures as a share of industrial added value has risen from 2.72% in 2010 to 3.09% in 2013, which indicates that Taiwan's companies are devoting increasing effort to

TELECOMMUNICATIONS AND INTERNET DEVELOPMENT

BASIC INFORMATION

TW - 23,464,787 population (2016) - Area: 36,175 sq km
Capital City: Taipei - population 2,618,720
19,666,364 Internet users as of Dec/2014, 83.8% penetration, per ITU.
18,000,000 Facebook subscribers on Nov/2015, 76.7% penetration

The number of Internet users aged 12 and above in Taiwan reached 15.94 million, up 3.57 percent year on year, accounting for 77.25 percent of the island's population. Of these, 74.18 percent use broadband devices as their primary mode of connectivity, the study found.

Around 6.52 million Taiwan households, or 81 percent, have access to the Internet, with Taipei City topping the list at 89.02 percent.

Around 80 percent of all households in Taiwan have broadband access, up 12.65 percent from a year ago. Over 97 percent report a monthly income of over NT$100,001 (US$3,390).

Abour 60 percent of web surfers shop online, with the 20-44 age group recording the highest buying frequency. Nearly a third of purchases ranged from NT$2,001 to NT$5,000.

Close to 40 percent of online gamers cut back on visiting other websites, while half of online shoppers steer clear of frequenting real-world stores.**Communications in Taiwan** comprise the following communication media, deployed in the Taiwan Area of the **Republic of China** and regulated by the National Communications Commission of the Executive Yuan.

Since the mid-1970s there has been an accelerating shift from traditional personal services (small shops and restaurants) to modern personal services (department stores and hotels) and modern commercial services (finance and communications).

Domestic television has long carried many foreign programs, and liberalization of import restrictions in the 1980s brought more.

There are about 30 daily newspapers and thousands of periodicals, many of the latter house organs of various political and non-political organizations. The government sets general guidelines for the political and cultural content of newspapers and periodicals. There are three television stations and about 30 radio broadcasting companies with more than 180 stations.

TRENDS AND OPPORTUNITIES

Taiwan's reputation as an advanced ICT country is supported by international surveys ranking the country as a leader in various categories for ICT performance. The World Economic Forum ranks Taiwan at 14 out of 148 nations in 2014 for network readiness, highlighting Taiwan's global competitiveness. Other measures similarly underscore the extent of Taiwan's progress in developing ICT capabilities.

In 2014, the internet popularisation rate in Taiwan was over 81.6 per cent, the number of mobile/wireless internet users in Taiwan increased rapidly to over 19.7 million and the number of regular users had reached over 5.38 million. (Source: Institute for Information Industry, 2014 Taiwan's Internet and Mobile Environment, Nov 2014)

Taiwan's market growth can be attributed to several factors:

The growing importance and awareness of international e-commerce.

Taiwan's position as a major procurement centre for global ICT companies.

The heightened use of information technology, particularly in the areas of web-based applications and e-commerce.

Recognition of the attributes of the B2B EC business model and its capabilities.

The Taiwan Government's promotional plans and strategies for ICT development.

The global logistics and supply chain management system requirements of foreign business partners of Taiwan hi-tech manufacturers.

The necessity of appropriate information systems to manage migration of various industries to mainland China.

As Taiwan strives to keep abreast of changes to requirements in ICT hardware, the focus on information/appliance products and wireless/WAN application products is expected to intensify.

The Taiwanese Government has a strong push and focus on e-commerce development. The online integrated supply chain management system between major OEMs and hardware manufacturers has now been extended to include full vertical integration of smaller component and systems suppliers to Taiwanese OEMs. Taiwanese manufacturers in China establishing efficient management systems.

In general, output is generated by three main software categories:

industry-specific computer software

key software tools and components embedded software.

In recent times, Taiwan has seen an accelerated development of locally-developed software by Taiwanese companies, particularly in the multimedia sectors. Taiwanese game companies are now the biggest players in the Greater China region with increased local development in global logistics where locally developed software has better mirrored internal management systems and practices.

OPPORTUNITIES

Gaming, digital animation and e-learning are expected to be the major drivers of the industry in the future in Taiwan. Opportunities exist for Foreign companies to provide and create digital content with and/or for broadcasters, mobile and wireless platforms, Internet platforms and multimedia software firms. In addition to cooperative arrangements, there are opportunities in human resource development.

The best opportunities in Taiwan's ICT industry for Foreign exporters are:

Innovative software applications, particularly in games and management application software.

E-commerce and digital content for e-commerce, e-security, e-government and e-learning

Mobile games, content and applications.

Intelligent transport systems.

E-learning projects in Third World countries – Taiwan is keen to work with Foreign software players as a consortium to bid for international projects sponsored by the United Nations or other international banking organisations.

Competitive Environment

Over the past few years, Hewlett-Packard, NEC, Fujitsu, Dell, Microsoft and Sony have all announced the establishment of Research and development (R&D) centres in Taiwan. Currently 20 of the world's top ICT original equipment manufacturer (OEM) and original design manufacturer (ODM) operate international procurement offices in Taiwan. Significant orders have been placed by OEMs for notebooks and a wide range of peripherals including mobile phones, wireless access cards and scanners.

Capturing these opportunities will require strong links with local players in the market and there is already intense competition from established local and global vendors for major business opportunities in this national strategy.

MARKETING PRODUCTS AND SERVICES

Emerging small-to-medium sized companies in other Asia-Pacific nations are actively emulating the development model of Taiwanese firms. A joint venture with a Taiwanese software manufacturer is certain to help make the most of market opportunities.

The two most important issues to be addressed in marketing IT products and services in Taiwan are to customise the products for Chinese consumers and have brochures, catalogues, a company profile, capability statement and other promotional materials printed in traditional Chinese. In software, it is important to offer a two-byte character capability if localisation is to be easily achieved.

Foreign companies in the ICT sector are best advised to offer:

flexible and competitive pricing strategies

scalable capabilities

strong local support and after-sales service, while working closely with a qualified local partner who can offer Mandarin speaking support

All the leading computer players work very closely with Taiwan's ICT hardware manufacturers. Companies provide both OEM and ODMs – including product design and manufacture service for the world leading ICT brands. Foreign players will compete with global software companies in bundling their software/application into the hardware manufacture.

Among the most notable of Taiwan's ongoing business-to-business (B2B) projects is the formation of supply-chain systems linking leading international IT firms and their domestic suppliers, together with the supply chains connecting leading domestic IT firms and their supporting factories. Those systems are being built up with subsidies from the Industrial Development Bureau of the Ministry of Economic Affairs.

Some e-marketplaces that have started up include:

com2B.com – established by Compaq, with a number of leading local firms, with the goal to develop an e-marketplace for a number of Taiwan's major industries

e2Open – with a capital of US$200 million, it was established in mid-2000 as a joint venture between Acer Inc., IBM, Nortel, Toshiba, Hitachi, LG, Seagate, Lucent, and Solectron, which together boast a trading volume of US$700 billion annually (Source: E2Open, Company, Nov 2014)

Converge (formerly known as eHitex.com) – set up as a joint venture with a capital of US$100 million by Mitac, Tatung, Compaq, AMC, Gateway, Infineon Technology, NEC and Samsung, which among them have a total trading volume of US$650 billion a year.

Many of Taiwan's IT firms are expected to join at least one of these marketplaces to take advantage of the rich business opportunities they will offer.

INTERNET REGULATIONS

The major modes of internet access service are ADSL, FTTx and cable modem. Chunghwa Telecom is the largest provider of ADSL/FTTx and acquires about 70% of the market share; the leading cable modem operators are Kbro and CNS, acquiring about 20% of the market share. In the mobile market, an official statistic suggests that at the end of 2014, 2G, 3G and 4G services had a total of 29,328,000 users. The penetration of 3G service has been growing fast, with almost 25 million subscribers, while little progress has been made in WiMAX available for Wireless Broadband Access License with around 12,000 subscribers.

4G LTE licences for mobile broadband services in the frequency bands of 700MHz, 900MHz and 1800MHz were released by auction in the fourth quarter of 2013. Six operators – Chunghwa Telecom, Taiwan Mobile, FarEasTone, Asia Pacific Telecom, Ambit Microsystems Corporation and Taiwan Star – won the bids and since the first three major incumbents launched new 4G LTE services in June 2014 the 4G market has been in fierce competition. There were 3.45 million subscribers to the LTE-Advance service until the end of 2014, and the number continues to grow due to the National Communications Commission's aggressive number portability policy and the "all-you-can-eat" fee plan heavily marketed by the operators.

The most important legislation which applies to the:

(a) telecoms;

(b) audio-visual media distribution; and

(c) internet, sectors in Taiwan.

The Fundamental Communications Act was created in January 2004 to address the goals to be achieved in the course of digital convergence. Functionally, there is the Telecommunications Act, the Radio and Television Law, the Cable Radio and Television Law, and the Satellite Broadcasting Law respectively, which draw lines in between respective transmission platforms though the National Communications Commission (NCC) has been exercising its exclusive power granted by the Fundamental Communications Act to have regulatory reform by converging all of the above platform regulations in a single legislation.

There is no specific regulation for the internet. It is noted, however, that the internet, in relation to audio-visual content distribution, remains a grey area in NCC's policy.

Government ministries, regulators, other agencies and major industry self-regulatory bodies which have a role in the regulation of the:

(a) telecoms;

(b) audio-visual media distribution; and

(c) internet sectors in Taiwan.

The National Communications Commission (NCC) is the authority on telecoms and audio-video media distribution, and the internet, except for the following:

1. The Ministry of Transportation and Communications (MOTC) has exclusive power on spectrum allocation, the numbering plan and any relevant policy planning, such as IP addresses based on a decision entered into by the Executive Yuan in 2007.

2. The Ministry of Culture is the co-regulator in the fields of radio and television regardless of transmission types.

3. The NCC has been appointed by the Executive Yuan as the regulator for personal data protection in relation to internet matters. However, in November 2011 the NCC officially refused to take such responsibility even though it does regulate internet businesses in the form of Type II telecoms operators subject to the Telecommunications Act.

4G MOBILE BROADBAND - IMPORTANT REGULATIONS[3]

STATUS OF MOBILE MARKET

With the wide range of mobile broadband application services being driven forward with the ubiquity of smart phones and tablets, people continually require more bandwidth and higher speeds to meet their needs.

With view to ensuring a sound mobile communications environment, facilitating high-speed, high-quality and diverse telecommunications services, NCC, on October 30, 2013, released 270MHz of bandwidth in the 700 MHz, 900 MHz, and 1800 MHz bands.

This release ushered in a new milestone in the development of telecommunications services in Taiwan, and from the end of May 2014, operators began providing 4G services.

Moving forward to the end of September 2015, the number of 4G subscribers in Taiwan had already reached 9.33 million and has show explosive growth since then..

SPECTRUM PLAN

In this light, we can clearly see demand for bandwidth increasing in the future. According to estimates from the ITU, demand for mobile broadband bandwidth in each country is expected to reach around 1000MHz by 2020. In response, NCC plans to continuously release mobile broadband spectrum. Currently, 540MHz of bandwidth has been planned. Nearer the end of 2015, the 2500MHz and 2600MHz bands will be released to enable mobile broadband operators to promote high-speed mobile network bandwidth and to satisfy the public's demands.

POLICIES FOR BETTER 4G SERVICES

With the objective of enabling the public to enjoy ubiquitous high quality mobile broadband services, deployment of the 4G network infrastructure will be accelerated while the public's awareness of its benefits will be enhanced. Promotional policies include:

l inter-ministerial awareness campaigns concerning electromagnetic waves;

l continual promotion of the co-location of mobile communications platforms;

l release of public land for base stations;

l establishment of next generation electric wave monitoring system, and;

[3] Taiwan National Communication Commission Materials

l continual spectrum planning for the future.

Moreover, while assisting the industry to promote the development of mobile broadband service, NCC endeavors to facilitate a secure environment so as to ensure security is strengthened, as well as economic development. Promotional policies include:

l improving the general quality of 4G network services;

l strengthening cyber security inspection and authentication mechanisms;

l enhancing the public's understanding of electromagnetic waves and building sustainable environments;

l reinforcing services for the minorities, those in remote or offshore-island areas, and;

l establishing an effective mobile broadband network disaster prevention notification and response system.

SPECTRUM MANAGEMENT POLICY

First, the significance of spectrum management of radio frequencies for the necessary conditions for a variety of wireless communications, mobile communications in today's era of vigorous development, plays an important role. With the liberalization of telecommunications open to competition, the number of users of radio services and applications continues to increase, the overall impact on national security and the economy is very significant. Because radio frequencies exclusivity in the use of radio frequencies should be how to allocate, how to exert their effects, are important issues of spectrum management in China. Countries in the world have developed spectrum management policy, which aims to maintain the order of frequency of use, frequency of use to enhance efficiency and ensure communication quality, a further positive development of the economic value inherent in the spectrum. Therefore, spectrum management in today's information age, represents not only a sense of communication on media management, and more actively promote the information society functions.

Second, the international norms of the International Telecommunication Union (International Telecommunication Union, ITU) for the communications management organization under the United Nations, to deal specifically with the establishment of the inter-governmental rules of communication, coordination and management, and the development of many communications protocol (such as the International Radio Regulations , Radio Regulations), as the basis for countries to use the frequency allocation. ITU to ensure the appropriate use of radio frequencies and avoid interference occurs between countries impede radio station, the world is divided into three areas (in the third district of), depending on the characteristics of various types of radio communications business is divided into fixed, mobile, broadcasting and so on ... thirty-seven kinds of business, and implement distribution and registration of radio frequency assignments with the radio frequency for countries to develop their national rules by reference. Withdrawal of the United Republic of China in six decades, has also quit Telecommunication Union organization. At present, though not the ITU Member States, but the international affairs involving radio-based and based on considerations of the international community, it is still in line with the relevant principles of international technical regulations, the third regional frequency allocation provisions of the Radio Regulations referring to the preparation of radio frequency allocation table, of making use of radio frequencies in harmony with the world.

Third, the spectrum management scope and objectives of spectrum management including: (a) the frequency allocation: Frequency assignment means under certain conditions, a given frequency band, assigned to one or more terrestrial or space radio services. (B) frequency assignments: frequency assignment means under certain conditions, to give the approval process of a specified channel stations. (C) Spectrum Planning: Spectrum planning is in order to achieve the goal of spectrum management to make use of frequency resources can take into account national development and security, to meet the demand for ever-increasing frequency. (Iv) Spectrum Monitoring: Measures to order the use of the airwaves adopted the spectrum monitoring system maintenance, such as the implementation of "radio detection energy plan" setting telecommunications supervisors and telecommunications police force to enhance our ability to monitor radio waves, protect the legitimate, ban illegal use of radio waves, radio waves use to maintain order. (V) the frequency and costs: by "charging mechanism" to reflect the efficient use of limited resources, the implementation of "user pays" concept, the radio frequencies to promote equitable distribution and effective use of frequency resources. With free and open competition in telecommunications, the number of radio frequency users of services and applications have continued to increase, the frequency of the use of increasingly crowded spectrum management work Yuxing important. How to use the limited spectrum resources to achieve maximum efficiency in the use of frequencies, is indeed engaged in the actual frequency management worker biggest challenge, our target frequency management as follows: (a) improve efficiency and meet market demand. (Ii) to assist industrial development, promote economic prosperity. (3) to encourage research and development, promotion of the use of resources. (Iv) transparent management mechanisms, equitable distribution.

Fourth, spectrum planning principles frequency is a limited resource of high-value, advanced countries attach great importance to how to effectively plan frequency resources to meet the demand for new technology and services produced, and appropriate fit national development and security objectives. To achieve these goals, the spectrum planning job, you must understand the changes in the environment, to master the correct use of information, and follow the following spectrum planning principles: (a) based on the international community, and the provisions of international technical and protocol. (Ii) the public interest to determine the priority, the establishment of major, minor business spirit. (Iii) the frequency sharing and redistribution in order to play the maximum efficiency in the use of limited resources. (Iv) to meet market demand, the development of domestic industries and provide free market competition environment. (E) reserve space for development of new technologies and expansion of future demand. (Vi) to encourage the development of high-frequency, wireless technology instead of a wired network.

Fifth, the principle of frequency assignments with the growth of the sustainable development of wireless communication technology and a wide range of wireless applications, the frequency of use will become increasingly congested, in the case of radio frequency planning international organizations continue to evolve, our future frequency assignments of work except in special assessment techniques focusing on trends and demand, and in an open and transparent procedure of obtaining a consensus, follow these frequency assignments six principles , as a basis for the review of the frequency of demand: (a) whether or not essential (Have other alternatives such as cable, etc.). (B) the maintenance of public order of life and property security preferred. (Iii) for most uses maximum effectiveness. (D) whether it has a practical device and the necessity of the public. (V) should be done according to the radio frequency characteristics of the most appropriate application. (Vi) the active frequency should regularly review the feasibility of redistribution of deliberation, the priorities should be in line with the progress of science and technology.

Sixth, the effective use of the frequency with the overall telecommunications technology advances, resulting in the use of radio frequencies towards the popularization of various people's lives at stake communication product innovation, and the use of increasingly crowded radio frequency, this time to improve the efficient use of radio spectrum and frequency resources development use has become an important issue. In order to promote the efficient use of frequencies, radio equipment users should employ advanced technology in order to save the required number of channels and bandwidth to improve frequency usage efficiency in a manner such as: (a) restrict the use of frequency diversity (frequency diversity), spatial / pole of diversity (space / polarization diversity) technology to save on frequency of use. (B) restrictions on the use of electric power, and encouraging the use of directional antennas to transmit to a specific area, increasing the frequency re-use times. (C) the use of low-frequency band is quite crowded, encourage the use of higher frequency bands. (Iv) modulation using the latest technology, with minimal bandwidth maximum amount of information transmitted. (E) Whenever possible, use a wired circuit (such as cable) or satellite circuits to replace radio channels.

INFORMATION REGULATIONS

In recent years, due to the rapid development of digital technology, communication, spread two field factor became increasingly digitized bus service continues to introduce new faces. In response to this technological trends and effective balance between national interests, the interests of consumers and industry, the Government announced the development of the Basic Law on National Communications Republic of China 93 years and in Article 3 of the Act set out for the effective dissemination of communication handle management issues, the government should Let communications Commission (hereinafter referred to as the Council), independent exercise of powers. In all walks of life efforts, the Republic of China will be in 95 years February 22 established National Communications enumerate dual management plan on a period of ten years, the development of Taiwan's National Communications under the pilot will be unified by the digital convergence era.

The policy will serve for the majority of citizens and consumers, as well as dissemination of business communications. On the concept of communication and communication services enjoy the rights of citizens is an important part of the construction is the basic medium of civil society (civil society) of. National Communications market order is currently an urgent need to reform regulatory practice, the organization of the supervisory authority and role must also be re-architecting and positioning. Therefore, in practice, to nationals and consumer services, this will be the specific policy issues for the protection of consumers and respect for minorities' rights, and promote the balanced development of multiculturalism; the National Communications services industry, particularly the Council of the policy directions In an effort to maintain professional media freedom, the effective implementation of National communications supervision matters and to ensure fair competition in the communication market spread. This was scheduled to be next National Communications Act Article 1 Organization and the Council of Article 1, that is the purpose of this will be set up where.

This will be set up to reflect the purpose of the strategy, in response to the trend of technology convergence needs to shape the new order, this newsletter will spread the Basic Law as a standard, phased legal convergence preparedness. On goal setting, this will set the current four major policy objective is "to promote the effectiveness of digital convergence competition; improve communication propagation supervision system; safeguard the interests of consumers and citizens; promotion of cultural diversity and minorities' rights." On governance practices, the Council is committed to creating a highly transparent information, administrative and legislative procedures and decision-making open to participation. One of the important features of this would WWW, namely the outside world with one of this platform will be an exchange of views, the construction period can become online deliberative democracy (online deliberative democracy) policy forum. The community may, by further understanding of this Council, or provide timely policy suggestions. All walks of life support and correction of this Council, to be performance-oriented governance of the important help. We will wholeheartedly welcome this Council to join with the Council reached Qi "Construction of a digital convergence, fair competition and healthy development, high-quality content National Communications Environment" policy of vision.

IMPORTANT TRENDS AND OPPORTUNITIES

IOT DEVELOPMENTS STRATEGY

BASIC INFORMATION

The **internet of things** (**IoT**) is the network of physical devices, vehicles, buildings and other items—embedded with electronics, software, sensors, actuators, and network connectivity that enable these objects to collect and exchange data. In 2013 the Global Standards Initiative on Internet of Things (IoT-GSI) defined the IoT as "the infrastructure of the information society."

The IoT allows objects to be sensed and/or controlled remotely across existing network infrastructure,[3] creating opportunities for more direct integration of the physical world into computer-based systems, and resulting in improved efficiency, accuracy and economic benefit. When IoT is augmented with sensors and actuators, the technology becomes an instance of the more general class of cyber-physical systems, which also encompasses technologies such as smart grids, smart homes, intelligent transportation and smart cities. Each thing is uniquely identifiable through its embedded computing system but is able to interoperate within the existing Internet infrastructure. Experts estimate that the IoT will consist of almost 50 billion objects by 2020.

British entrepreneur Kevin Ashton coined the term in 1999 while working at Auto-ID Labs (originally called Auto-ID centers, referring to a global network of objects connected to radio-frequency identification, or RFID). Typically, IoT is expected to offer advanced connectivity of devices, systems, and services that goes beyond machine-to-machine (M2M) communications and covers a variety of protocols, domains, and applications. The interconnection of these embedded devices (including smart objects), is expected to usher in automation in nearly all fields, while also enabling advanced applications like a smart grid,[13] and expanding to the areas such as smart cities.

"Things," in the IoT sense, can refer to a wide variety of devices such as heart monitoring implants, biochip transponders on farm animals, electric clams in coastal waters,[16] automobiles with built-in sensors, DNA analysis devices for environmental/food/pathogen monitoring[17] or field operation devices that assist firefighters in search and rescue operations.[18] Legal scholars suggest to look at "Things" as an "inextricable mixture of hardware, software, data and service".[19] These devices collect useful data with the help of various existing technologies and then autonomously flow the data between other devices.[20] Current market examples include smart thermostat systems and washer/dryers that use Wi-Fi for remote monitoring.

As well as the expansion of Internet-connected automation into a plethora of new application areas, IoT is also expected to generate large amounts of data from diverse locations, with the consequent necessity for quick aggregation of the data, and an increase in the need to index, store, and process such data more effectively. IoT is one of the platforms of today's Smart City, and Smart Energy Management Systems

APPLICATIONS

According to Gartner, Inc. (a technology research and advisory corporation), there will be nearly 20.8 billion devices on the internet of things by 2020.[38] ABI Research estimates that more than 30 billion devices will be wirelessly connected to the internet of things by 2020.[39] As per a recent survey and study done by Pew Research Internet Project, a large majority of the technology experts and engaged Internet users who responded—83 percent—agreed with the notion that the Internet/Cloud of Things, embedded and wearable computing (and the corresponding dynamic systems[40]) will have widespread and beneficial effects by 2025.[41] As such, it is clear that the IoT will consist of a very large number of devices being connected to the Internet.[42] In an active move to accommodate new and emerging technological innovation, the UK Government, in their 2015 budget, allocated £40,000,000 towards research into the internet of things. The British Chancellor of the Exchequer George Osborne, posited that the internet of things is the next stage of the information revolution and referenced the inter-connectivity of everything from urban transport to medical devices to household appliances.[43]

Integration with the Internet implies that devices will use an IP address as a unique identifier. However, due to the limited address space of IPv4 (which allows for 4.3 billion unique addresses), objects in the IoT will have to use IPv6 to accommodate the extremely large address space required.[44][45][46][47][48] Objects in the IoT will not only be devices with sensory capabilities, but also provide actuation capabilities (e.g., bulbs or locks controlled over the Internet).[49] To a large extent, the future of the internet of things will not be possible without the support of IPv6; and consequently the global adoption of IPv6 in the coming years will be critical for the successful development of the IoT in the future.[45][46][47][48]

The ability to network embedded devices with limited CPU, memory and power resources means that IoT finds applications in nearly every field.[50] Such systems could be in charge of collecting information in settings ranging from natural ecosystems to buildings and factories,[49] thereby finding applications in fields of environmental sensing and urban planning.[51]
On the other hand, IoT systems could also be responsible for performing actions, not just sensing things. Intelligent shopping systems, for example, could monitor specific users' purchasing habits in a store by tracking their specific mobile phones. These users could then be provided with special offers on their favorite products, or even location of items that they need, which their fridge has automatically conveyed to the phone.

Additional examples of sensing and actuating are reflected in applications that deal with heat, electricity and energy management, as well as cruise-assisting transportation systems. Other applications that the internet of things can provide is enabling extended home security features and home automation.[55] The concept of an "internet of living things" has been proposed to describe networks of biological sensors that could use cloud-based analyses to allow users to study DNA or other molecules. All these advances add to the numerous list of IoT applications. Now with IoT, you can control the electrical devices installed in your house while you are sorting out your files in office.

Your water will be warm as soon as you get up in the morning for the shower. All credit goes to smart devices which make up the smart home. Everything connected with the help of Internet.

However, the application of the IoT is not only restricted to these areas. Other specialized use cases of the IoT may also exist. An overview of some of the most prominent application areas is provided here. Based on the application domain, IoT products can be classified broadly into five different categories: smart wearable, smart home, smart city, smart environment, and smart enterprise. The IoT products and solutions in each of these markets have different characteristics.[58]

MEDIA

In order to hone the manner in which things, media and big data are interconnected, it is first necessary to provide some context into the mechanism used for media process. It has been suggested by Nick Couldry and Joseph Turow that practitioners in media approach big data as many actionable points of information about millions of individuals.

The industry appears to be moving away from the traditional approach of using specific media environments such as newspapers, magazines, or television shows and instead tap into consumers with technologies that reach targeted people at optimal times in optimal locations. The ultimate aim is of course to serve, or convey, a message or content that is (statistically speaking) in line with the consumer's mindset. For example, publishing environments are increasingly tailoring messages (advertisements) and content (articles) to appeal to consumers that have been exclusively gleaned through various data-mining activities.[59]

The media industries process big data in a dual, interconnected manner:

- Targeting of consumers (for advertising by marketers)
- Data-capture

Thus, the internet of things creates an opportunity to measure, collect and analyse an ever-increasing variety of behavioural statistics. Cross-correlation of this data could revolutionise the targeted marketing of products and services.[60] For example, as noted by Danny Meadows-Klue, the combination of analytics for conversion tracking with behavioural targeting has unlocked a new level of precision that enables display advertising to be focused on the devices of people with relevant interests.[61] Big data and the IoT work in conjunction. From a media perspective, data is the key derivative of device interconnectivity, whilst being pivotal in allowing clearer accuracy in targeting. The internet of things therefore transforms the media industry, companies and even governments, opening up a new era of economic growth and competitiveness.[62] The wealth of data generated by this industry (i.e. big data) will allow practitioners in advertising and media to gain an elaborate layer on the present targeting mechanisms used by the industry.

ENVIRONMENTAL MONITORING

Environmental monitoring applications of the IoT typically use sensors to assist in environmental protection[63] by monitoring air or water quality, atmospheric or soil conditions,[64] and can even include areas like monitoring the movements of wildlife and their habitats.[65] Development of resource constrained devices connected to the Internet also means that other applications like earthquake or tsunami early-warning systems can also be used by emergency services to provide more effective aid. IoT devices in this application typically span a large geographic area and can also be mobile.[49] It has been argued that the standardization IoT brings to wireless sensing will revolutionize this area.[66]

INFRASTRUCTURE MANAGEMENT

Monitoring and controlling operations of urban and rural infrastructures like bridges, railway tracks, on- and offshore- wind-farms is a key application of the IoT.[67] The IoT infrastructure can be used for monitoring any events or changes in structural conditions that can compromise safety and increase risk. It can also be used for scheduling repair and maintenance activities in an efficient manner, by coordinating tasks between different service providers and users of these facilities.[49] IoT devices can also be used to control critical infrastructure like bridges to provide access to ships. Usage of IoT devices for monitoring and operating infrastructure is likely to improve incident management and emergency response coordination, and quality of service, up-times and reduce costs of operation in all infrastructure related areas.[68] Even areas such as waste management can benefit from automation and optimization that could be brought in by the IoT.[69]

MANUFACTURING

Network control and management of manufacturing equipment, asset and situation management, or manufacturing process control bring the IoT within the realm on industrial applications and smart manufacturing as well.[70] The IoT intelligent systems enable rapid manufacturing of new products, dynamic response to product demands, and real-time optimization of manufacturing production and supply chain networks, by networking machinery, sensors and control systems together.

Digital control systems to automate process controls, operator tools and service information systems to optimize plant safety and security are within the purview of the IoT.[67] But it also extends itself to asset management via predictive maintenance, statistical evaluation, and measurements to maximize reliability.[71] Smart industrial management systems can also be integrated with the Smart Grid, thereby enabling real-time energy optimization. Measurements, automated controls, plant optimization, health and safety management, and other functions are provided by a large number of networked sensors.

National Science Foundation established an Industry/University Cooperative Research Center on intelligent maintenance systems (IMS) in 2001 with a research focus to use IoT-based predictive analytics technologies to monitor connected machines and to predict machine degradation, and further to prevent potential failures.[72] The vision to achieve near-zero breakdown using IoT-based predictive analytics led the future development of e-manufacturing and e-maintenance activities.

The term IIOT (industrial internet of things) is often encountered in the manufacturing industries, referring to the industrial subset of the IoT. IIoT in manufacturing would probably generate so much business value that it will eventually lead to the fourth industrial revolution, so the so-called Industry 4.0. It is estimated that in the future, successful companies will be able to increase their revenue through internet of things by creating new business models and improve productivity, exploit analytics for innovation, and transform workforce.[74] The potential of growth by implementing IIoT will generate $12 trillion of global GDP by 2030.

IoT devices can be used to monitor and control the mechanical, electrical and electronic systems used in various types of buildings (e.g., public and private, industrial, institutions, or residential)[49] in home automation and building automation systems.

TRANSPORTATION

The IoT can assist in integration of communications, control, and information processing across various transportation systems. Application of the IoT extends to all aspects of transportation systems (i.e. the vehicle, the infrastructure, and the driver or user). Dynamic interaction between these components of a transport system enables inter and intra vehicular communication, smart traffic control, smart parking, electronic toll collection systems, logistic and fleet management, vehicle control, and safety and road assistance.[49]

LARGE SCALE DEPLOYMENTS

There are several planned or ongoing large-scale deployments of the IoT, to enable better management of cities and systems. For example, Songdo, South Korea, the first of its kind fully equipped and wired smart city, is near completion. Nearly everything in this city is planned to be wired, connected and turned into a constant stream of data that would be monitored and analyzed by an array of computers with little, or no human intervention.[]

Another application is a currently undergoing project in Santander, Spain. For this deployment, two approaches have been adopted. This city of 180,000 inhabitants, has already seen 18,000 city application downloads for their smartphones. This application is connected to 10,000 sensors that enable services like parking search, environmental monitoring, digital city agenda among others. City context information is used in this deployment so as to benefit merchants through a spark deals mechanism based on city behavior that aims at maximizing the impact of each notification.[89]

Other examples of large-scale deployments underway include the Sino-Singapore Guangzhou Knowledge City;[90] work on improving air and water quality, reducing noise pollution, and increasing transportation efficiency in San Jose, California;[91] and smart traffic management in western Singapore.[92] French company, Sigfox, commenced building an ultra-narrowband wireless data network in the San Francisco Bay Area in 2014, the first business to achieve such a deployment in the U.S.[93][94] It subsequently announced it would set up a total of 4000 base stations to cover a total of 30 cities in the U.S. by the end of the 2016, making it the largest IoT network coverage provider in the country thus far.[95][96]

Another example of a large deployment is the one completed by New York Waterways in New York City to connect all their vessels and being able to monitor them live 24/7. The network was designed and engineered by Fluidmesh Networks, a Chicago-based company developing wireless networks for critical applications. The NYWW network is currently providing coverage on the Hudson River, East River, and Upper New York Bay. With the wireless network in place, NY Waterway is able to take control of its fleet and passengers in a way that was not previously possible. New applications can include security, energy and fleet management, digital signage, public Wi-Fi, paperless ticketing and others.[97]

CONSUMER APPLICATION

A growing portion of IoT devices are created for consumer use. Examples of consumer applications include connected car, entertainment, residences and smart homes, wearable technology, quantified self, connected health, and smart retail. Consumer IoT provides new opportunities for user experience and interfaces.

Some consumer applications have been criticized for their lack of redundancy and their inconsistency, leading to a popular parody known as the “Internet of Shit.”[98] Companies have been criticized for their rush into IoT, creating devices of questionable value,[99] and not setting up stringent security standards.[100]

THINGS ADDRESSABILITY

The original idea of the Auto-ID Center is based on RFID-tags and unique identification through the Electronic Product Code however this has evolved into objects having an IP address or URI.

An alternative view, from the world of the Semantic Web[101] focuses instead on making all things (not just those electronic, smart, or RFID-enabled) addressable by the existing naming protocols, such as URI. The objects themselves do not converse, but they may now be referred to by other agents, such as powerful centralized servers acting for their human owners.

The next generation of Internet applications using Internet Protocol version 6 (IPv6) would be able to communicate with devices attached to virtually all human-made objects because of the extremely large address space of the IPv6 protocol. This system would therefore be able to scale to the large numbers of objects envisaged.[102]

A combination of these ideas can be found in the current GS1/EPCglobal EPC Information Services[103] (EPCIS) specifications. This system is being used to identify objects in industries ranging from aerospace to fast moving consumer products and transportation logistics.[104]

TRENDS AND CHARACTERISTICS

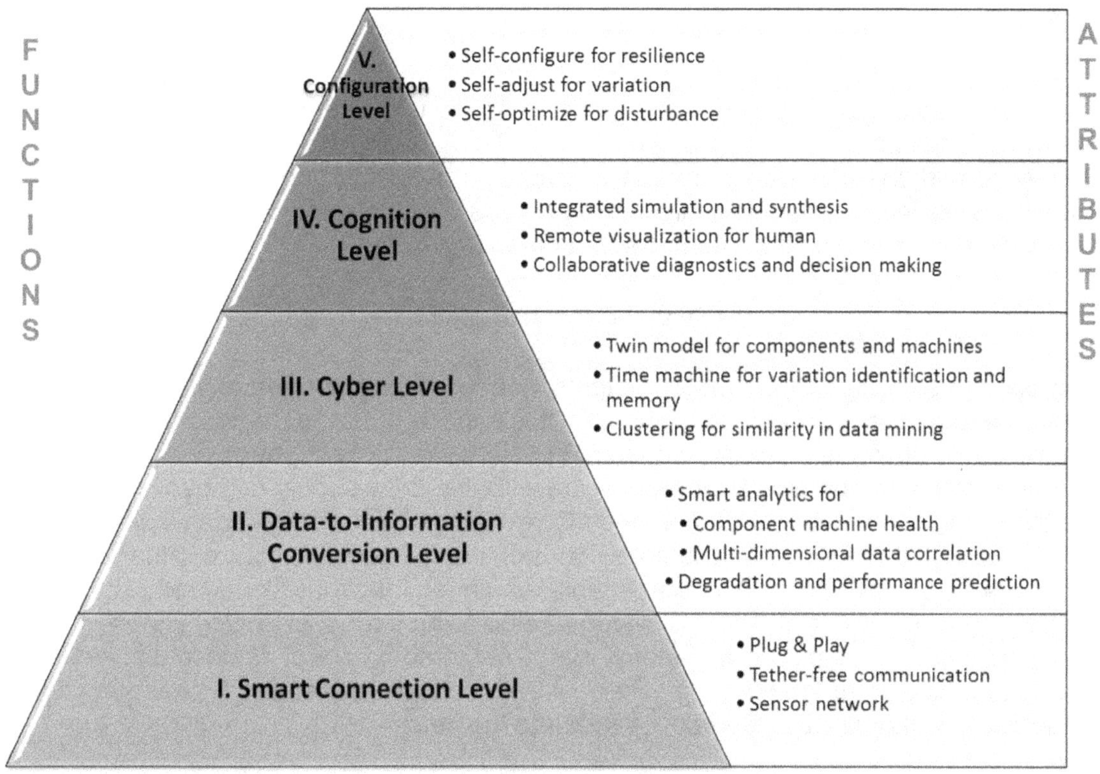

Design architecture of cyber-physical systems-enabled manufacturing system

While connectivity and data acquisition are imperative for IIoT, they should be the foundation and path to something bigger but not the purpose. Among all the technologies, predictive maintenance is probably a relatively "easier win" since it is applicable to existing assets and management systems. The objective of intelligent maintenance systems is to reduce unexpected downtime and increase productivity. And to realize that alone would generate around up to 30% over total maintenance costs.

Industrial big data analytics will play a vital role in manufacturing asset predictive maintenance, although that is not the only capability of industrial big data.[78][79] Cyber-physical systems (CPS) is the core technology of industrial big data and it is will be an interface between human and the cyber world. Cyber-physical systems can be designed by following the *5C* (connection, conversion, cyber, cognition, configuration) architecture,[76] and it will transform the collected data into actionable information, and eventually interfere with the physical assets to optimize processes.

An IoT-enabled intelligent system of such cases has been demonstrated by the NSF Industry/University Collaborative Research Center for Intelligent Maintenance Systems (IMS) at University of Cincinnati on a band saw machine in IMTS 2014 in Chicago.[80] Band saw machines are not necessarily expensive, but the band saw belt expenses are enormous since they degrade much faster. However, without sensing and intelligent analytics, it can be only determined by experience when the band saw belt will actually break.

The developed prognostics system will be able to recognize and monitor the degradation of band saw belts even if the condition is changing, so that users will know in near real time when is the best time to replace band saw. This will significantly improve user experience and operator safety, and save costs on replacing band saw belts before they actually break. The developed analytical algorithms were realized on a cloud server, and was made accessible via the Internet and on mobile devices.

ENERGY MANAGEMENT

Integration of sensing and actuation systems, connected to the Internet, is likely to optimize energy consumption as a whole.[49] It is expected that IoT devices will be integrated into all forms of energy consuming devices (switches, power outlets, bulbs, televisions, etc.) and be able to communicate with the utility supply company in order to effectively balance power generation and energy usage.[81] Such devices would also offer the opportunity for users to remotely control their devices, or centrally manage them via a cloud based interface, and enable advanced functions like scheduling (e.g., remotely powering on or off heating systems, controlling ovens, changing lighting conditions etc.).[49] In fact, a few systems that allow remote control of electric outlets are already available in the market, e.g., Belkin's WeMo, Ambery Remote Power Switch,[83] Budderfly,[84] Telkonet's EcoGuard,[85] WhizNets Inc., etc.

Besides home based energy management, the IoT is especially relevant to the Smart Grid since it provides systems to gather and act on energy and power-related information in an automated fashion with the goal to improve the efficiency, reliability, economics, and sustainability of the production and distribution of electricity.[81] Using advanced metering infrastructure (AMI) devices connected to the Internet backbone, electric utilities can not only collect data from end-user connections, but also manage other distribution automation devices like transformers and reclosers.[49]

MEDICAL AND HEALTHCARE SYSTEMS

IoT devices can be used to enable remote health monitoring and emergency notification systems. These health monitoring devices can range from blood pressure and heart rate monitors to advanced devices capable of monitoring specialized implants, such as pacemakers, Fitbit electronic wristbands or advanced hearing aids.[49] Specialized sensors can also be equipped within living spaces to monitor the health and general well-being of senior citizens, while also ensuring that proper treatment is being administered and assisting people regain lost mobility via therapy as well.[87] Other consumer devices to encourage healthy living, such as, connected scales or wearable heart monitors, are also a possibility with the IoT. More and more end-to-end health monitoring IoT platforms are coming up for antenatal and chronic patients, helping one manage health vitals and recurring medication requirements.

BUILDING AND HOME AUTOMATION

INTELLIGENCE

Ambient intelligence and autonomous control are not part of the original concept of the internet of things. Ambient intelligence and autonomous control do not necessarily require Internet structures, either. However, there is a shift in research to integrate the concepts of the internet of things and autonomous control, with initial outcomes towards this direction considering objects as the driving force for autonomous IoT.

In the future the internet of things may be a non-deterministic and open network in which auto-organized or intelligent entities (Web services, SOA components), virtual objects (avatars) will be interoperable and able to act independently (pursuing their own objectives or shared ones) depending on the context, circumstances or environments. Autonomous behavior through the collection and reasoning of context information as well as the objects ability to detect changes in the environment, faults affecting sensors and introduce suitable mitigation measures constitute a major research trend,[105] clearly needed to provide credibility to the IoT technology. Modern IoT products and solutions in the marketplace use a variety of different technologies to support such context-aware automation but more sophisticated forms of intelligence are requested to permit sensor units to be deployed in real environments.

ARCHITECTURE

The system will likely be an example of event-driven architecture,[106] *bottom-up* made (based on the context of processes and operations, in real-time) and will consider any subsidiary level. Therefore, model driven and functional approaches will coexist with new ones able to treat exceptions and unusual evolution of processes (multi-agent systems, B-ADSc, etc.).

In an internet of things, the meaning of an event will not necessarily be based on a deterministic or syntactic model but would instead be based on the context of the event itself: this will also be a semantic web.[107] Consequently, it will not necessarily need common standards that would not be able to address every context or use: some actors (services, components, avatars) will accordingly be self-referenced and, if ever needed, adaptive to existing common standards (*predicting everything* would be no more than defining a "global finality" for everything that is just not possible with any of the current *top-down* approaches and standardizations). Some researchers argue that sensor networks are the most essential components of the internet of things.[108]

Building on top of the internet of things, the web of things is an architecture for the application layer of the internet of things looking at the convergence of data from IoT devices into Web applications to create innovative use-cases. In order to program and control the flow of information in the internet of things, a predicted architectural direction is being called BPM Everywhere which is a blending of traditional process management with process mining and special capabilities to automate the control of large numbers of coordinated devices.

NETWORK ARCHITECTURE[EDIT]

[109]

The internet of things requires huge scalability in the network space to handle the surge of devices. IETF 6LoWPAN would be used to connect devices to IP networks.With billions of devices[38] being added to the internet space, IPv6 will play a major role in handling the network layer scalability. IETF's Constrained Application Protocol, MQTT and ZeroMQ would provide lightweight data transport.

Fog computing is a viable alternative to prevent such large burst of data flow through Internet. The edge devices' computation power can be used to analyse and process data, thus providing easy real time scalability.

COMPLEX SYSTEM[EDIT]

In semi-open or closed loops (i.e. value chains, whenever a global finality can be settled) it will therefore be considered and studied as a complex system[110] due to the huge number of different links and interactions between autonomous actors, and its capacity to integrate new actors. At the overall stage (full open loop) it will likely be seen as a chaotic environment (since systems have always finality).

SIZE CONSIDERATIONS

The Internet of objects would encode 50 to 100 trillion objects, and be able to follow the movement of those objects. Human beings in surveyed urban environments are each surrounded by 1000 to 5000 trackable objects.[111]

SPACE CONSIDERATIONS

In an internet of things, the precise geographic location of a thing—and also the precise geographic dimensions of a thing—will be critical. Therefore, facts about a thing, such as its location in time and space, have been less critical to track because the person processing the information can decide whether or not that information was important to the action being taken, and if so, add the missing information (or decide to not take the action). (Note that some things in the internet of things will be sensors, and sensor location is usually important).

The GeoWeb and Digital Earth are promising applications that become possible when things can become organized and connected by location. However, challenges that remain include the constraints of variable spatial scales, the need to handle massive amounts of data, and an indexing for fast search and neighbor operations. If in the internet of things, things are able to take actions on their own initiative, this human-centric mediation role is eliminated, and the time-space context that we as humans take for granted must be given a central role in this information ecosystem. Just as standards play a key role in the Internet and the Web, geospatial standards will play a key role in the internet of things.

SECTORS

There are three core sectors of the IoT: enterprise, home, and government, with the enterprise internet of things (EIoT) being the largest of the three. By 2019, the EIoT sector is estimated to account for nearly 40% or 9.1 billion devices.

A "BASKET OF REMOTES"

According to the CEO of Cisco, the commercial opportunity for "connected products ranging from cars to household goods" is expected to be a $USD 19 trillion.[115] Many IoT devices have a potential to take a piece of this market. Jean-Louis Gassée (Apple initial alumni team, and BeOS co-founder) has addressed this topic in an article on *Monday Note*, where he predicts that the most likely problem will be what he calls the "basket of remotes" problem, where we'll have hundreds of applications to interface with hundreds of devices that don't share protocols for speaking with one another.

There are multiple approaches to solve this problem, one of them called the "predictive interaction",[117] where cloud or fog based decision makers [clarification needed] will predict the user's next action and trigger some reaction.

For user interaction, new technology leaders are joining forces to create standards for communication between devices. While AllJoyn alliance is composed the top 20 World technology leaders, there are also big companies that promote their own protocol like CCF from Intel.

This problem is also a competitive advantage for some very technical startup companies with fast capabilities.

- AT&T Digital Life provides one solution for the "basket of remotes" problem. This product features home-automation and digital-life experiences. It provides a mobile application to control their closed ecosystem of branded devices;

- Nuve has developed a new technology based on sensors, a cloud-based platform and a mobile application that allows the asset management industry to better protect, control and monitor their property.[118]

Manufacturers are becoming more conscious of this problem, and many companies have begun releasing their devices with open APIs. Many of these APIs are used by smaller companies looking to take advantage of quick integration.

SUB SYSTEMS

Not all elements in an internet of things will necessarily run in a global space. Domotics running inside a smart home, for example, might only run and be available via a local network.

FRAMEWORKS

Internet-of-things frameworks might help support the interaction between "things" and allow for more-complex structures like distributed computing and the development of distributed applications. Currently, some internet-of-things frameworks seem to focus on real time data logging solutions like Jasper Technologies, Inc. and Xively (formerly Cosm and before that Pachube): offering some basis to work with many "things" and have them interact. Future developments might lead to specific software-development environments to create the software to work with the hardware used in the internet of things. Companies are developing technology platforms to provide this type of functionality for the internet of things. Newer platforms are being developed, which add more intelligence. Foremost, IBM has announced cognitive IoT, which combines traditional IoT with machine intelligence and learning, contextual information, industry-specific models and even natural language processing. The XMPP standards foundation XSF is creating such a framework in a fully open standard that isn't tied to any company and not connected to any cloud services. This XMPP initiative is called Chatty Things.[119] XMPP provides a set of needed building blocks and a proven distributed solution that can scale with high security levels.

The independently developed MASH IoT Platform was presented at the 2013 IEEE IoT conference in Mountain View, CA. MASH's focus is asset management (assets=people/property/information, management=monitoring/control/configuration). Support is provided for design through deployment with an included IDE, Android client and runtime. Based on a component modeling approach MASH includes support for user defined things and is completely data-driven.[120]

REST is a scalable architecture which allows for things to communicate over Hypertext Transfer Protocol and is easily adopted for IoT applications to provide communication from a thing to a central web server. MQTT is a publish-subscribe architecture on top of TCP/IP which allows for bi-directional communication between a thing and a MQTT broker.

ENABLING TECHNOLOGIES FOR THE IOT

There are many technologies that enable IOT. A key foundation piece is the network used to communicate between nodes of an IOT installation, a role that several wireless and/or wired technologies may fulfill:

RFID and near-field communication – In the 2000s, RFID was the dominant technology. Later, NFC became dominant (NFC). NFC have become common in smartphones during the early 2010s, with uses such as reading NFC tags or for access to public transportation.

Rapid developments in the Optical technologies like Li-Fi, Cisco's 40 Gbit/s bidirectional optical technology (BiDi[125]) may aid the development of IoT.

Optical tags and quick response codes – This is used for low cost tagging. Phone cameras decode QR code using image-processing techniques. In reality QR advertisement campaigns gives less turnout as users need to have another application to read QR codes.

Bluetooth low energy – This is one of the latest tech. All newly releasing smartphones have BLE hardware in them. Tags based on BLE can signal their presence at a power budget that enables them to operate for up to one year on a lithium coin cell battery.

Low energy wireless IP networks – embedded radio in system-on-a-chip designs, lower power WiFi, sub-GHz radio in an ISM band, often using a compressed version of IPv6 called 6LowPAN and relying on dedicated routing protocols such as LOADng[126] standardized by the ITU under the recommendation ITU-T G.9903 and RPL.[127]

ZigBee – This communication technology is based on the IEEE 802.15.4 2.4 GHz-band radio protocol to implement physical and MAC layer for low-rate wireless Private Area Networks. Some of its main characteristics like low power consumption, low data rate, low cost, and high message throughput make it an interesting IoT enabler technology.

Z-Wave – is a communication protocol that is mostly used in smart home applications. It uses a radio protocol in the 900 MHz-band.

Thread – Like ZigBee, this IoT communication technology relies on the IEEE 802.15.4 2.4 GHz-band radio protocol. A key difference is that its networking protocol is IPv6-compatible.

LTE-Advanced – LTE-A is a high-speed communication specification for mobile networks. Compared to its original LTE, LTE-A has been improved to have extended coverage, higher throughput and lower latency. One important application of this technology is Vehicle-to-Vehicle (V2V) communications.

WiFi-Direct – It is essentially WiFi for peer-to-peer communication without needing to have an access point. This feature attracts IoT applications to be built on top of WiFi-Direct to get benefit from the speed of WiFi while they experience lower latency.

HomePlug – This networking standard can be used to enable IOT communication over a home or building's power lines

MoCA – This networking standard can be used to enable IOT communication over CATV-type coaxial cable

Ethernet – This general purpose networking standard can be used to enable IOT communication over twisted pair or fiber network links

SIMULATION

IOT modeling and simulation (and emulation) is typically carried out at the design stage before deployment of the network. Network simulators like OPNET, NetSim and NS2 can be used to simulate IOT networks.

POLITICS AND CIVIC ENGAGEMENT

Some scholars and activists argue that the IoT can be used to create new models of civic engagement if device networks can be open to user control and inter-operable platforms. Philip N. Howard, a professor and author, writes that political life in both democracies and authoritarian regimes will be shaped by the way the IoT will be used for civic engagement. For that to happen, he argues that any connected device should be able to divulge a list of the "ultimate beneficiaries" of its sensor data, and that individual citizens should be able to add new organizations to the beneficiary list. In addition, he argues that civil society groups need to start developing their IoT strategy for making use of data and engaging with the public.[128]

PRIVACY, AUTONOMY AND CONTROL

The concern over the privacy was led many to consider the possibility that Big Data infrastructures such as the IoT and Data Mining are inherently incompatible with privacy.[130] Writer Adam Greenfield claims that these technologies are not only an invasion of public space but are also being used to perpetuate normative behavior, citing an instance of billboards with hidden cameras that tracked the demographics of passersby who stopped to read the advertisement.

The Council of the Internet of Things compared the increased prevalence of digital surveillance due to the Internet of Things to the conceptual panopticon described by Jeremy Bentham in the 18th Century.[132] The assertion was defended by the works of French philosophers Michel Foucalt and Gilles Deleuze. Foucalt wrote in his novel Discipline and Punish: The Birth of the Prison that the panopticon was a central element of the discipline society developed during the Industrial Era.[133] Foucalt also argued that the discipline systems established in factories and school reflected Bentham's vision of panopticism. In his 1992 paper "Postscripts on the Societies of Control," Delueze wrote that the discipline society had transitioned into a control society, with the computer replacing the panopticon as an instrument of discipline and control while still maintaining the qualities similar to that of panopticism.

A research team of the National Science Foundation and University of Arkansas at Little Rock discovered that the privacy of households using smart home devices could be compromised by analyzing network traffic.[135][136]

Peter-Paul Verbeek, a professor of philosophy of technology at the University of Twente, Netherlands, writes that technology already influences our moral decision making, which in turn affects human agency, privacy and autonomy. He cautions against viewing technology merely as a human tool and advocates instead to consider it as an active agent.

Justin Brookman, of the Center for Democracy and Technology, expressed concern regarding the impact of IoT on consumer privacy, saying that "There are some people in the commercial space who say, 'Oh, big data — well, let's collect everything, keep it around forever, we'll pay for somebody to think about security later.' The question is whether we want to have some sort of policy framework in place to limit that."[138]

Tim O'Reilly believes that the way companies sell the IoT devices on consumers are misplaced, disputing the notion that the IoT is about gaining efficiency from putting all kinds of devices online and postulating that "IoT is really about human augmentation. The applications are profoundly different when you have sensors and data driving the decision-making."

Editorials at WIRED have also expressed concern, one stating "What you're about to lose is your privacy. Actually, it's worse than that. You aren't just going to lose your privacy, you're going to have to watch the very concept of privacy be rewritten under your nose."

The American Civil Liberties Union (ACLU) expressed concern regarding the ability of IoT to erode people's control over their own lives. The ACLU wrote that "There's simply no way to forecast how these immense powers – disproportionately accumulating in the hands of corporations seeking financial advantage and governments craving ever more control – will be used. Chances are Big Data and the Internet of Things will make it harder for us to control our own lives, as we grow increasingly transparent to powerful corporations and government institutions that are becoming more opaque to us."

Researchers have identified privacy challenges faced by all stakeholders in IoT domain, from the manufacturers and app developers to the consumers themselves, and examined the responsibility of each party in order to ensure user privacy at all times. Problems highlighted by the report[142] include:

- User consent – somehow, the report says, users need to be able to give informed consent to data collection. Users, however, have limited time and technical knowledge.
- Freedom of choice – both privacy protections and underlying standards should promote freedom of choice.
- Anonymity – IoT platforms pay scant attention to user anonymity when transmitting data, the researchers note. Future platforms could, for example, use TOR or similar technologies so that users can't be too deeply profiled based on the behaviors of their "things".

In response to rising concerns about privacy and smart technology, in 2007 the British Government stated it would follow formal Privacy by Design principles when implementing their smart metering program. The program would lead to replacement of traditional power meters with smart power meters, which could track and manage energy usage more accurately.[143] However the British Computer Society is doubtful these principles were ever actually implemented.[144] In 2009 the Dutch Parliament rejected a similar smart metering program, basing their decision on privacy concerns. The Dutch program later revised and passed in 2011.[144]

SECURITY

Concerns have been raised that the internet of things is being developed rapidly without appropriate consideration of the profound security challenges involved[145] and the regulatory changes that might be necessary.[146] According to the Business Insider Intelligence Survey conducted in the last quarter of 2014, 39% of the respondents said that security is the biggest concern in adopting internet-of-things technology.[147] In particular, as the internet of things spreads widely, cyber attacks are likely to become an increasingly physical (rather than simply virtual) threat.

In a January 2014 article in *Forbes*, cybersecurity columnist Joseph Steinberg listed many Internet-connected appliances that can already "spy on people in their own homes" including televisions, kitchen appliances,[149] cameras, and thermostats.[150] Computer-controlled devices in automobiles such as brakes, engine, locks, hood and truck releases, horn, heat, and dashboard have been shown to be vulnerable to attackers who have access to the onboard network. In some cases, vehicle computer systems are internet-connected, allowing them to be exploited remotely.

By 2008 security researchers had shown the ability to remotely control pacemakers without authority. Later hackers demonstrated remote control of insulin pumps [152] and implantable cardioverter defibrillators.[153] David Pogue wrote[154] that some recently published reports about hackers remotely controlling certain functions of automobiles were not as serious as one might otherwise guess because of various mitigating circumstances; such as the bug that allowed the hack having been fixed before the report was published, or that the hack required security researchers having physical access to the car prior to the hack to prepare for it.

The U.S. National Intelligence Council in an unclassified report maintains that it would be hard to deny "access to networks of sensors and remotely-controlled objects by enemies of the United States, criminals, and mischief makers... An open market for aggregated sensor data could serve the interests of commerce and security no less than it helps criminals and spies identify vulnerable targets. Thus, massively parallel sensor fusion may undermine social cohesion, if it proves to be fundamentally incompatible with Fourth-Amendment guarantees against unreasonable search." In general, the intelligence community views internet of things as a rich source of data.

As a response to increasing concerns over security, the Internet of Things Security Foundation (IoTSF) was launched on 23 September 2015. IoTSF has a mission to secure the internet of things by promoting knowledge and best practice. Its founding board is made from technology providers and telecommunications companies including BT, Vodafone, Imagination Technologies and Pen Test Partners.

DESIGN

Given widespread recognition of the evolving nature of the design and management of the internet of things, sustainable and secure deployment of internet-of-things solutions must design for "anarchic scalability."[159] Application of the concept of anarchic scalability can be extended to physical systems (i.e. controlled real-world objects), by virtue of those systems being designed to account for uncertain management futures. This "hard anarchic scalability" thus provides a pathway forward to fully realize the potential of internet-of-things solutions by selectively constraining physical systems to allow for all management regimes without risking physical failure.

Brown University computer scientist Michael Littman has argued that successful execution of the internet of things requires consideration of the interface's usability as well as the technology itself. These interfaces need to be not only more user-friendly but also better integrated: "If users need to learn different interfaces for their vacuums, their locks, their sprinklers, their lights, and their coffeemakers, it's tough to say that their lives have been made any easier."

ENVIRONMENTAL IMPACT

A concern regarding IoT technologies pertains to the environmental impacts of the manufacture, use, and eventual disposal of all these semiconductor-rich devices.[161] Modern electronics are replete with a wide variety of heavy metals and rare-earth metals, as well as highly toxic synthetic chemicals. This makes them extremely difficult to properly recycle. Electronic components are often incinerated or placed in regular landfills. Furthermore, the human and environmental cost of mining the rare-earth metals that are integral to modern electronic components continues to grow. With production of electronic equipment growing globally yet little of the metals (from end-of-life equipment) being recovered for reuse, the environmental impacts can be expected to increase.

Also, because the concept of IoT entails adding electronics to mundane devices (for example, simple light switches), and because the major driver for replacement of electronic components is often technological obsolescence rather than actual failure to function, it is reasonable to expect that items that previously were kept in service for many decades would see an accelerated replacement cycle, if they were part of the IoT. For example, a traditional house built with 30 light switches and 30 electrical outlets might stand for 50 years, with all those components still original at the end of that period. But a modern house built with the same number of switches and outlets set up for IoT might see each switch and outlet replaced at five-year intervals, in order to keep up-to-date with technological changes. This translates into a ten-fold increase in waste requiring disposal.

INTENTIONAL BRICKING OF DEVICES

The Electronic Frontier Foundation has raised concerns that companies can use the technologies necessary to support connected devices to intentionally disable or "brick" their customers' devices via a remote software update or by disabling a service necessary to the operation of the device. In one example, home automation devices which were sold with the promise of a "Lifetime Subscription" were rendered useless after Nest Labs acquired Revolv and made the decision to shut down the central servers the Revolv devices had used to operate.[162] As Nest is a company owned by Alphabet (Google's parent company), the EFF argues this sets a "terrible precedent for a company with ambitions to sell self-driving cars, medical devices, and other high-end gadgets that may be essential to a person's livelihood or physical safety."[163]

Owners should be free to point their devices to a different server or collaborate on improved software. But such action violates the United States DMCA section 1201, that only has an exemption for "local use". This forces tinkerers that want to keep using their own equipment into a legal grey area. EFF thinks buyers should refuse electronics and software that prioritize the manufacturer's wishes above their own.[

INTERNET OF THINGS GLOBAL STANDARDS INITIATIVE

IoT-GSI aimed to promote a unified approach in ITU-T for development of technical standards (Recommendations) enabling the Internet of Things on a global scale. ITU-T Recommendations developed under the IoT-GSI by the various ITU-T Questions - in collaboration with other standards developing organizations (SDOs) – will enable worldwide service providers to offer the wide range of services expected by this technology. IoT-GSI also aimed to act as an umbrella for IoT standards development worldwide.

The Internet of Things (IoT) has been defined in Recommendation ITU-T Y.2060 (06/2012) as a global infrastructure for the information society, enabling advanced services by interconnecting (physical and virtual) things based on existing and evolving interoperable information and communication technologies.

Study Group 20 is working to address the standardization requirements of Internet of Things (IoT) technologies, with an initial focus on IoT applications in smart cities and communities (SC&C).

SG20 develops international standards to enable the coordinated development of IoT technologies, including machine-to-machine communications and ubiquitous sensor networks. A central part of this study is the standardization of end-to-end architectures for IoT, and mechanisms for the interoperability of IoT applications and datasets employed by various vertically oriented industry sectors.

The deployment of IoT technologies is expected to connect an estimated 50 billion devices to the network by year 2020, impacting nearly every aspect of our daily lives. IoT is contributing to the convergence of industry sectors, and SG20 provides the specialized IoT standardization platform necessary for this convergence to rest on a cohesive set of international standards.

An important aspect of SG20's work is the development of standards that leverage IoT technologies to address urban-development challenges.

IoT is a key enabler of the Information Society and offers an opportunity to transform city infrastructure, benefiting from the efficiencies of intelligent buildings and transportation systems, and smart energy and water networks. SG20 will assist government and industry in capitalizing on this opportunity, providing a unique platform to influence the development of international IoT standards and their application as part of urban-development master plans.

ITU put forward a vision of IoT in the landmark "Internet of Things" report published in 2005 as part of a series of ITU reports on the Internet. The foundations of the new Study Group are provided by ITU-T's experience in the development of IoT standards and the findings of the ITU-T Focus Group on Smart Sustainable Cities (FG-SSC), which concluded its activities in May 2015 with the release of 21 technical reports and specifications.

The decision to create SG20 was made by the Telecommunication Standardization Advisory Group (TSAG) at its meeting at ITU Headquarters in Geneva, 2-5 June 2015, exercising TSAG's authority to modify ITU-T's structure and work programme between quadrennial World Telecommunication Standardization Assemblies.

IOT IN TAIWAN

IoT is usually divided into three forms of interaction among different entities via a communication network: People-to-Machine (P2M), People-to-People (P2P), or Machine to Machine (M2M). Among these entities, data is being transmitted and processed either by centralized computing or distributed nodes. Supporting this data communication is a wide spectrum of technologies encompassing cloud computing, communications protocols, human-machine interface, wireless sensor networks, big data, Cyber Physical Systems, artificial intelligence, flexible displays, and many others.

While most market forecasts focus on how big the device-related opportunities will be for smart watches or smart home meters, less attention is being paid to how to collect and analyze data. In this regard, all companies pursing IoT-related business opportunities need to be reminded that "People-centric" should be the focal point of all business models and technology development. "Machine-centric" or "Data analytics" are important elements in the IoT value web, but should be utilized only to support the provision of innovative services to satisfy the unmet needs of "People" in Business-to-Consumer (B2C) or Business-to-Business (B2B) business models. By emphasizing People-to-Services (P2S) and integrating it into the offering of IoT applications, the Internet of Minds (IoM) will be established as a critical success factor for IoT.

As a case in point, iRobot is famous for developing household robots for vacuuming and floor-washing purposes. These products already have certain user-friendly features that users find appealing, such as automatic return to the home-base charging dock when running out of battery life, and sensors to detect when the robot is approaching a wall. In the future, similar new household robots will be connected to the internet via a wireless network to enable them to carry out IoT functions such as allowing caretakers to monitor the security of elderly patients or making it possible for the robot to carry on small talk with lonely elderly users. These are appropriate P2S features that connect the minds of people (unmet needs, wish lists) with the minds of machine (artificial intelligence, friendly user interface) to establish IoM.

As mentioned above, since no one knows which of today's many emerging IoT applications will become tomorrow's killer apps, thus putting Taiwan companies on the same starting line with all global competitors. For capturing IoT business opportunities, it would be best for Taiwan to adopt an approach similar to that of a Special Operations Force (SOF) in unconventional military operations. SOF usually refers to a small, elite military force trained to perform unconventional missions. The U.S. military has many such units for different purposes. For example, the Army has its Green Berets, Rangers, and Delta Force, etc.; the Navy is known for its Navy SEALs, and the Air Force has Special Operations Squadrons and others. Unlike conventional warfare, an SOF unit often needs to conduct operations with quick deployment and surgical precision around targets. Rather than involving synchronized massive planning across different military units which would be time consuming, operations by an SOF would typically require comprehensive support within the same military unit for self-sustaining operations. For example, Navy Seals will need air strike support from Navy's air force during operations. An SOF is designed to quickly conquer target beachheads and establish defendable fortress, before the arrival of regular battle forces to continue with conventional battles.

Internet of Minds (IoM) as Critical Success Factor for IoT

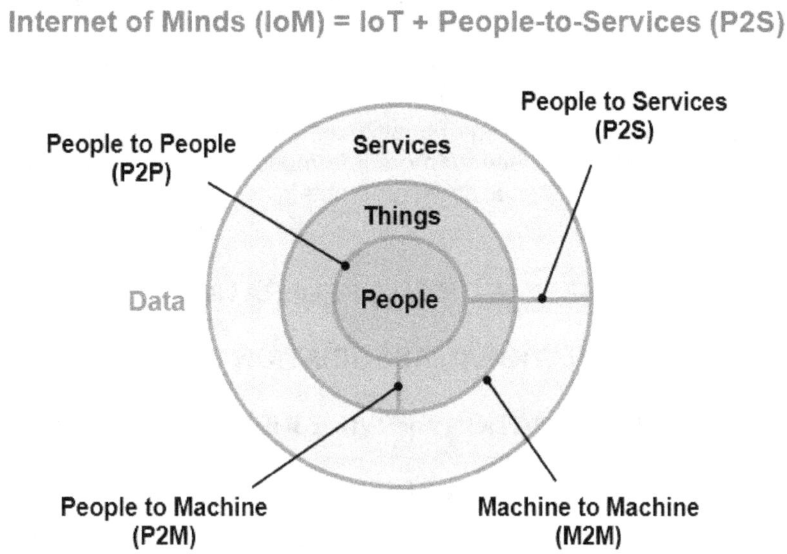

Source: ITRI/EK(2014/08)

The Taiwan government and industries consider forming similar "Beachhead Special Ops Teams" to swiftly conquer the beachheads of target IoT applications. Each such target application would be strategically chosen for its high impact with regard to potential market size, yet also carrying a high degree of uncertainty in terms of risks associated with technological maturity or potential substitution by other technology. As a result, it would be preferable to make a small but early investment in exploring breakthrough technology or innovative business-model for each IoT application, rather than making a massive effort that requires complex cross-disciplinary coordination which often slows down product development speed. The aim is to fast-develop some target IoT applications to pilot test in a new ecosystem, then adjust the design of the product or service based on early feedback. While not all target IoT applications will become future winners, hopefully some selected few can attain early success outcome.

PRACTICAL INFORMATION FOR BUSINESS AND INVESTMENT OPPORTUNITIES IN TAIWAN

INVESTMENT REGISTRATION

Different requirements apply for each type of business entities. Therefore, we provide a comparison list for various business entities, and then an overall introduction to investment registration depending on the type(s) of business entity identified by the investor(s). Please click directly to link to the related website for more information, if you are interested in establishing a business entity in any of the special zones and obtaining information on related investment incentives.

CNFI(CHINESE NATIONAL FEDERATION OF INDUSTRIES)

CNAIC(THE CHINESE NATIONAL ASSOCIATION OF INDUSTRY AND COMMERCE)

CISA(INFORMATION SERVICE INDUSTRY ASSOCIATION)

PIDA(PHOTONICS INDUSTRY & TECHNOLOGY DEVELOPMENT ASSOCIATION)

ROCCPA(CERTIFIED PUBLIC ACCOUNTANT)

ROCCOC(THE GENERAL CHAMBER OF COMMERCE)

TBA(TAIPEI BAR ASSOCIATION)

TAITRA(TAIWAN EXTERNAL TRADE DEVELOPMENT COUNCIL)

TAMI(TAIWAN ASSOCIATION OF MACHINERY INDUSTRY)

TEEMA(TAIWAN ELECTRICAL AND ELECTRONIC)

TCOC(TAIWAN CHAMBER OF COMMERCE)

TIEC(TAIWAN IMPORTERS & EXPORTERS CHAMBER OF COMMERCE)

BUSINESS TYPE

A company and a firm

Business Type Items	Company	Firm
Minimum capital requirement	No minimum requirement, but the capital still needs to be examined and certified by a local CPA and covers at least the incorporation	Not required.

	cost (Note 1)	
Extent of shareholders/responsible person/partners' liability	Shareholders are liable to the extent of their capital contribution to the company.	The responsible person or partners of the business are liable for any liabilities arising from the business operation.
Business expansion	A registered company name is approved by the Ministry of Economic Affairs. This name is legally protected and its usage is nationwide. It is advantageous for business expansion.	A registered business name is approved by a local (county or city) government. The name protection and usage are limited.
Qualification of being a juristic person	A company is qualified as a juristic person.	Not qualified as a juristic person.
Requirement for accounting books and vouchers.	Must keep complete set of accounting books and accounting records to document its operating results.	Not compulsorily required. The profit and loss is reflected directly in income individually reported by the responsible person or partners.

Note 1: If the business entity engages in activities that require a special permit or approval, the authorities may set a higher capital requirement.

COMPARISON OF A SUBSIDIARY, A BRANCH OFFICE AND A REPRESENTATIVE OFFICE

Business Type Items	Company (Company Limited by Shares/Limited Company)	Branch Office of a Foreign Company	Representative Office
Permitted activities	General trading, sales and manufacturing	General trading, domestic sales and manufacturing	Legal acts and liaison activities
Profit-Seeking Enterprise Income Tax(T)	I: Taxable income; T:Tax liability . If I≦NTD120,000, T=0 . If NTD120,000 < I≦NTD181,818, T=(I-120,000)*1/2 . if I > NTD181,818,T=I*17%	Same as a company	Not applicable
Profit remittance tax	Withholding tax of 20%; however, the 10% surtax paid	None	Not applicable

	by the company on its undistributed profits may be credited against the withholding tax.		
Tax incentives under the Statute for Industrial Innovation	Applicable	Not applicable	Not applicable
Extent of the liability of a shareholder/head office	Shareholders are liable to the extent of their capital contribution to the company.	Foreign head office is liable for any liabilities unsettled by the branch.	Not applicable
Requirement for shareholder(s)/responsible person	Must have at least 1 corporate shareholder or 2 individual shareholders (1 or more individual or corporate shareholders in the case of a limited company). All shareholders may be foreign nationals residing outside of Taiwan	Not required to have shareholders but required to register a responsible person	Not required
Requirement for director(s)	Must have at least 3 directors (between 1 and 3 in the case of a limited company). All directors can be foreign nationals residing outside of Taiwan.	Not required	Not required
Requirement for supervisor(s)	Must have at least 1 supervisor (no requirement in the case of limited company) who can be a foreign national residing outside of Taiwan.	Not required	Not required
Minimum capital requirement or minimum operating capital requirement	No minimum requirement, but the capital still needs to be examined and certified by a local CPA and covers at least the incorporation cost (Note 1)	No minimum requirement, but the capital still needs to be examined and certified by a local CPA and covers at least the incorporation cost (Note 1)	Not required

Sources of capital contribution	Capital contribution can be made in cash or thru capitalization of retained earnings or capital surplus.	Initial operating capital must be remitted in Taiwan from the offshore head office. Subsequent contribution of additional operating capital can be made through remittance from offshore head office or thru capitalization of the branch retained earnings.	Not applicable
Filing of annual income tax return	Required	Required	Not required
Withholding tax on salaries, rental income, professional fees, and other income payments.	Required	Required	Required
Allocation of administrative expenses by parent / head office	Subject to a 20% withholding tax. The deductibility of this allocation for tax reporting purposes will depend on the adequacy of the supporting documents thereon.	Normally not subject to 20% withholding tax and can be treated as a tax deductible item if certain criteria are met.	Not applicable
Keeping of accounting books and records	Required	Required	Required
Liquidation of the entity following completion of dissolution	Required	Required	Not Required
Purchase of real property and automobiles in the	Permitted	Permitted	Not Permitted

name of subsidiary / branch / representative			

Note 1. If the business entity engages in activities that require a special permit or approval, the authorities may set a higher capital requirement

PROCEDURES FOR COMPANY REGISTRATION

For Local Investor(s)

Option 1: Setting up a General Company

Apply for search and reservation of company name and business scope. Please provide 1 to 5 company names in Chinese in their order of priority and proposed business scope, the company names will be surveyed by the competent authority in the order of priority and only one name will be reserved if it is available .(Please click here to link to Company and Business One-stop Service Request website)

Apply for company registration.

A pre-approval is required before applying for company registration if the company intends to conduct restrictive business which is subject to additional requirements and regulations ruled by the competent authority.

Apply for business registration.

Apply for factory registration (note- this is not applicable to non-manufacturing business)

Apply for registration of importer/exporter (note -for trading business only). (Please click here to link to BOFT's online application website or click here to link to Company and Business One-stop Service Request website for online application)

Option 2: Setting up a firm

Apply for search and reservation of firm name and business scope.

Apply for firm registration.

A pre-approval is required before applying for firm registration if the firm intends to conduct restrictive business which is subject to additional requirements and regulations ruled by the competent authority.

Apply for business registration.

Apply for registration of importer/exporter (note -for trading business only. (Please click here to link to BOFT's online application website or click here to link to Company and Business One-stop Service Request websitefor online application).

FOR OVERSEAS CHINESE AND FOREIGN INVESTOR(S)

Foreign Investment is subject to the "Negative List for Investment by Overseas Chinese and Foreign Nationals" issued by the investment Commission, MOEA. (Please click here to link to the website)

Option 1: Setting up a General Company

Apply for search and reservation of company name and business scope. Please provide 1 to 5 company names in Chinese in their order of priority and proposed business scope, the company names will be surveyed by the competent authority in the order of priority and only one name will be reserved if it is available . (Please click here to link to the website)

Apply for Overseas Chinese/ Foreign investment approval. (Please click here to link to the website to apply for Identification Certificate of Overseas Chinese. Note - This is only applicable to Overseas Chinese investor(s))

Processing time

Investment in nonrestrictive industries and the investment amount or capital increase is not more than NT$500 million--- 2 to 4 days.

Investment in nonrestrictive industries and the investment amount (or capital increase) is not more than NT$1500 million---3 to 5 days.

Investment in restrictive industries and the investment amount (or capital increase) is more than NT$1500 million or mergers, acquisitions and spin-offs ---10 to 20 days.

Investment in Mergers and Acquisition or extraordinary case----20 to 30 days.

Apply for approval for examination of investment capital.

Apply for company registration.

A pre-approval is required before applying for company registration if the company intends to conduct special business which is subject to additional requirements and regulations ruled by the competent authority.

Apply for business registration.

Apply for factory registration.(Note-This is not applicable to a non-manufacturing business)

Apply for registration of importer/exporter -for trading business only. (Please click here to link to BOFT's online application website or click here to link to Company and Business One-stop Service Request websitefor online application).

Option 2: Setting up a firm (for individual investor(s) only)

Foreign Investment is subject to the "Negative List for Investment by Overseas Chinese and Foreign Nationals" issued by the investment Commission, MOEA. (Please click here to link to the website)

Apply for search and reservation of firm name and business scope.

Apply for Overseas Chinese/ Foreign Investment Approval (Please click here to link to the website to apply for Identification Certificate of Overseas Chinese. Note - This is only applicable to Overseas Chinese investor(s))

Processing time

Investment in nonrestrictive industries and the investment amount (or capital increase) is not more than NT$500 million---2 to 4 days.

Investment in nonrestrictive industries and the investment amount (or capital increase) is not more than NT$1500 million---3 to 5 days.

Investment in restrictive industries and the investment amount (or capital increase) is more than NT$1500 million or mergers, acquisitions and spin-offs ---10 to 20 days.

Investment in Mergers and Acquisition or extraordinary case----20 to 30 days.

Apply for approval for examination of investment capital.

Apply for firm registration.

A pre-approval is required before applying for firm registration if the firm intends to conduct special business which is subject to additional requirements and regulations ruled by the competent authority.

Apply for business registration.

Apply for registration of importer/exporter-for trading business only (Please click here to link to BOFT's online application website or click here to link to Company and Business One-stop Service Request website for online application).

Option 3: Setting up a Representative Office of a Foreign Company

Apply for reporting designated representative of a foreign company for handling legal matters in the R.O.C.

Apply for a tax code.

Option 4: Setting up a Branch of a Foreign Company

The proposed business scope of a Branch Office of a Foreign Company is subject to the "Negative List for Investment by Overseas Chinese and Foreign Nationals" issued by the investment Commission, MOEA. (Please click here to link to the website)

Apply for search and reservation of company name and business scope. Please provide 1 to 5 company names in Chinese in their order of priority and proposed business scope, the company names will be surveyed by the competent authority in the order of priority and only one name will be reserved if it is available. (Please click here to link to Company and Business One-stop Service Request website)

Apply for Investment Approval and Recognition of Foreign Company and Registration of a Branch Office.

A pre-approval is required before applying for branch registration if the branch intends to conduct special business which is subject to additional requirements and regulations ruled by the competent authority.

Apply for business registration.

Apply for factory registration(Note- This is not applicable to a non-manufacturing business).

Apply for registration of importer/exporter -for trading business only. (Please click here to link to BOFT's online application website or click here to link to Company and Business One-stop Service Request websitefor online application).

SPECIAL ZONES

HSINCHU SCIENCE PARK

* Address : No.2, Xin'an Rd., East Dist., Hsinchu City 300
* TEL : 886-3-577-3311
* FAX : 886-3-577-6222

The Ministry of Science and Technology set up the Hsinchu Science Park (HSP), the first establishment of its kind in Taiwan, on December 15, 1980. By ushering in technologies and talent from abroad, bringing about the transformation of domestic conventional industry, and fostering the upgrade of industrial technology across the board, the park is intended to help high-tech industry take off in Taiwan.

Straddling the city and county of Hsinchu, the 6.5-square kilometer HSP now mainly houses semiconductor and optoelectronics ventures. More than 520 tenant companies employ more than 150,000 people. For the past three years, HSP companies posted an annual average of more than NT$1 trillion in revenue, which tends to fluctuate in tandem with the ups and downs in the global economy. Over the years HSP companies have been approved to invest more than NT$1 trillion. The close dependence of tenant companies on the Industrial Technology Research Institute, National Tsing Hua University and National Chiao Tung University can be easily illustrated by the fact that more than 50 of them have emerged as spinoffs from the aforementioned institutions. The high concentration of high-caliber talent at the HSP is only to be expected. Those who are devoted to R&D and technology development account for 40% of the HSP's overall workforce, with the remaining 60% taken by people engaged in production, management, marketing, etc. In terms of educational levels, around 75% of HSP employees have junior college or higher degrees, which compares with 18% registered by Taiwan's overall manufacturing sector. Some 63% of HSP employees own a university above diploma while the ratio is only 7% for the broader manufacturing sector. Additionally, more than 43,000 master's degree holders and 3,500 with doctorate degrees now work at the HSP. Of the total, more than 4,000 have returned from abroad to start their own businesses in Taiwan.

Imaging that a piece of land sharing less than 0.04% of land in Taiwan but creating global high-tech industry records from times to times, the Hsinchu Science Park generates an annual revenue of more than 33 billion USD over the past five years and enjoys its global reputation as a brilliant science park. The Hsinchu Science Park has cultivated a number of high-tech talent and global flagship IT enterprises over the past three decades, e.g. the largest IC foundry provider TSMC, the second largest IC foundry provider UMC, the third largest TFT-LCD maker CHIMEI INNOLUX, the fourth largest TFT-LCD maker AUO, the second largest mobile phone chipset maker and the fourth largest IC designer MediaTek, the third largest NOR Flash IC maker Macronix, and the largest Polymeric Positive Temperature Coefficient (PPTC) components manufacturer Polytronics Technology Corp., which solidifies the position of the Hsinchu Science Park in global IT industries. Besides, the Park also includes a number of renowned foreign companies, e.g. the largest plasma etching equipment maker Lam Research, the second largest IC equipment maker TEL, the third largest optical lens maker HOYA, etc. The Hsinchu Science Park is constantly extending its industry capacity as well as competence in semiconductor, opto-electronics, information, and telecommunications industries. Thus, more than 70% of global IT industry products are initiated from companies at the Hsinchu Science Park. As a venue full of chances, the Hsinchu Science Park has turned out to be the first choice of high-tech industry investment globally.

The past three decades have seen the HSP attain the strategic goal of luring high-tech investments. By putting in place an internationally competitive environment for Taiwan's high-tech industry, it has helped induce an across-the-board upgrade of domestic industry and foster expansion of the national economy. In addition to stimulating R&D on the science and technology front, benefits are enjoyed in many other respects—creating clusters of industrial ventures, cultivating talent, brining prosperity to local communities and enhancing the nation's overall cultural awareness. Furthermore, the success of the HSP is now being copied at the CTSP and STSP as well as its various satellite parks.

JHUNAN SCIENCE PARK

* Address : 1F., No.10, Kedong 3rd Rd., Zhunan Township, Miaoli County 350
* TEL : 886-037-585588
* FAX : 886-037-586588

The site of the Jhunan Science Park, at Dingpu Village, Jhunan Township, Miaoli County, was accorded its current status by the Executive Yuan in July 1997. Construction on the 123-hectare Jhunan base as a satellite park of the HSP began in July 1999. To date it has accommodated biotechnology, telecommunications and optoelectronics ventures. The establishment of the Jhunan site as a multipurpose science and technology park has proven effective in fostering the region's industry upgrade and sustainable development. That is, the cultivation of high-tech industry here has gone a long way toward attaining balanced development across the board.

The Jhunan Science Park is fitted with well-rounded infrastructure and public facilities. To date 80 standardized plants meant for high-tech companies have been built, including 40 designed specifically to cater to biotechnology ventures. In terms of pollution control, the park has a sewage system that handles rainwater and wastewater separately. Furthermore, there is a Class III sewage treatment plant with a daily capacity for handling 60,000 cubic meters of wastewater. With its operations consigned to a Class A environmental engineering firm, the plant was accorded by the Environmental Protection Administration an Excellence Award after its "Evaluation of Sewage and Drainage Systems at Industrial Parks" for three consecutive years from 2005 to 2007. On the other hand, the park is equipped with a 24,000-cubic meter distribution reservoir, a 35,000-cublic meter storage reservoir and two primary distribution substations, allowing it to provide tenant companies with top-quality water supply. Other establishments catering to daily needs include banks, telecom operators, police, restaurants, employment service providers, etc. Alongside an activity center and a park, an exclusive bike path has been installed to serve both park employees and residents of nearby communities.

LONGTAN SCIENCE PARK

* Address : No.1, Longyuan 1st Rd., Longtan Township, Taoyuan County 325
* TEL : 886-3-4709323
* FAX : 886-3-4709326

The Longtan Science Park is located at the juncture of three townships in Taoyuan County—Longtan, Pingzhen and Yangmei. On January 28, 2004, the Executive Yuan decided that the Longtan project would be run as a science park. A total of 106.94 hectares would be developed in two stages: 76.11 hectares in the first and 30.83 hectares in the second.

Current development status:

Phase I (existed development zone): Covering 76.11 hectares, land use priority is given to retaining original uses. With some public facilities left as they are, larger expanses of land are reserved for prospective tenants.

Phase II (Area to Be Developed): Spanning 30.83 hectares, it mainly comprises hilly lands. With excavation and filling kept to a minimum, the area is mostly meant as green lots and open spaces.

At present, the Longtan Science Park already accommodates such tenants as AU Optronics Corp., BenQ Materials Corp. Hsinchu Science Park Branch, Forhouse Corporation Longtan Park Branch, Formosa Epitaxy Inc., which are in business operation, Qualcomm Panel Manufacturing Ltd., Wafer Works Corp., Hsinchu Science Park Branch, HIROSE Tech Co., Ltd., and Novatech Co., Ltd., Nikko Metals Taiwan Co., Ltd. Anor Precision Ceramic Industrial Co., Ltd.

The park is mainly intended to house optoelectronics ventures and those spanning the entire spectrum of the solar energy industry. In so doing, it expects to help the revamping of local industry and create jobs, thus giving a boost to local economy.

TONGLUO SCIENCE PARK

TEL : 886-3-5773311-2522

1.Purpose

To meet land use demands from domestic high-tech industries, the government launched the fourth phase of science park expansion program, where Jhunan site and Tongluo site were selected as the designate extended science park.

2.Location

The Tongluo Science Park is located in Gio-Hu Village of Tongluo Township, Miaoli County, adjacent to Tongluo city plan zone in east and Tongshio Township in west. The Tongluo Science Park is next to Sun Yat-Sen Freeway, near its 140-km mileage sign. It is 42 kilometers from the Hsinchu Science Park to its north, 30 kilometers from the Jhunan Science Park, 20 kilometers from the Houli base of the Central Taiwan Science Park (CTSP), and 33 kilometers from the CTSP's Taichung base. The National Freeway Bureau has completed a new Tongluo Interchange that offers direct access to Sun Yat-Sen Freeway in mid 2012, providing a sound links to the Central Taiwan Science Park and the Hsinchu Science Park and facilitating regional high-tech industry development and industry technology diffusion.

3.Geographical Properties

Locating on a plateau, the Tongluo Science Park ranges from 220-380 meters high from sea level covered with gravel and sand, with a sound foundation.

4. Land Use Plan

The Tongluo Science Park covers an area of 349.7 hectares, with 96.2 hectares, or 27.5%, of industry zone, 130.3 hectares, or 37.3%, of public facilities, 118.9 hectares, or 34%, of conservation zone, 4.3 hectares, or 1.2%, of service facilities.

Building coverage ratio accounts 50% at the Park, where floor area ratio accounts 200% and building height limits to 25 meters. Tenants renting more than 2 hectares are required to build dormitories for singles and floor area of dormitories can not exceed 10% of the total fab floor area.

5. Industry Solicitation

Focus industries to bring in

(1) Advanced SiP zone: the Tongluo Science Park locates between two semiconductor industry clusters, namely the Hsinchu Science Park and Central Taiwan Science Park. Most fabs have engaged in advanced production technology , pushing System in Package, SiP, as future technology trend. The Tongluo Science Park holds niches and turns out to be an ideal site for SiP industry development.

(2) Clean energy and solar industries: to cope with global energy development trend, the Tongluo Science Park is expected to bring in clean energy industry, high opto-electronic transfer efficiency poly-silicon solar panel industries, and thin-film solar industries.

(3) Telecommunications knowledge-based industries and aero-electronics industries: solicitation of knowledge-based and low energy consumption industries, e.g.

telecommunications knowledge-based industries, aero-electronics, and aero-space industries, so as to incorporate with high-tech industries at the Park.

6. Miaoli Hakka Cultural Center

Located in southern part of the first development phase of the Tongluo Science Park, the Miaoli Hakka Cultural Center belongs to a national Hakka Cultural Center, focusing on Hakka cultural data survey, document archives, and exhibition. The Center is expected to cooperate with academia in northern Taiwan to carry out long-term systemic operation mechanism and promote Hakka culture, turning out to be a global Hakka research center. The Center started construction in February 2009 and was completed in May 2012.

7. Expected goals

The Tongluo Science Park is expected to form as a Park with technology, environmental protection, and humanity and to pilot domestic science parks via bring-in of potential, low pollution, and energy-saving industries.

YILAN SCIENCE PARK

* TEL : 886-3-5773311-2610
* FAX : 886-3-5772591

If there is a high-tech wonderland with terrific landscape, diversified lifestyles, Foreword and cordial cultural characteristics, then the Yilan Science Park will absolutely take the crown. The Executive Yuan in Taiwan approved the preparatory plan of the Yilan Science Park on May 16, 2005, giving the park a legal standpoint for follow-up development. Necessary infrastructure and public utilities in the first phase of park development have been completed and the first tenant, OMNI Calibration Laboratory Ltd., has moved in the park on April 24, 2013. With strengths of local industrial and cultural elements, together with scenic surroundings, the Yilan Science Park will certainly act as a piloting science park in east Taiwan guiding development of local digital content industries.

*II. Strengths of the Yilan Science Park

1.Government policy support of fostering knowledge-based telecommunications and digital content industries development at the park as core mission.

Strengths of the Yilan Science Park

2.Brilliant supports from the Hsinchu Science Park in terms of superior ICT industries and technologies, as well as unique development experiences.

3.Taipei-Yilan National Freeway literally extends the high-tech corridor in western Taiwan to Yilan. It is now only a 30-minute drive from Taipei to Yilan. As such, the county and city of Taipei and the counties of Taoyuan, Hsinchu and Yilan can all be perceived as participants in a common community for people to work and spend their leisure time.

4.The park is conveniently located, with the Yilan Sports Park (27 hectares, venue of national sport and festival events) to its north, Yilan Science Parkthe Yilan County Government Complex (site of the Yilan county government and council) to its south, and downtown with 5 minutes drive. Superior scenic environment offers a creative working venue for those who work at the park.

5. Cheaper land prices, 22.97NTD/m2/month at present, and an abundant pool of human resources go a long way toward bringing down operating costs.

6. In its southwest, the park borders on the site meant for the Yilan branch of National Tsing Hua University, together with a number of academia, e.g. National Ilan University, Fo Guang University, Tamkang University Lanyang Campus, and Lan Yang Institute of Technology. Cooperation across industry, government and academia going forward will greatly facilitate the cultivation and utilization of high-caliber talent. Security units, pipelines, wastewater treatment facilities, and experimental schools are well allocated, offering a superior living and working environment. Ilan University

7. Given its appealing natural surroundings, Yilan County makes a fine choice for high-tech professionals as both their workplace and home. Intended as an outfit specializing in knowledge-based services, the park is expected to attract establishments of such varieties to form a unique cluster, thereby enabling other industries in Yilan and eastern Taiwan to move on to higher grounds.

8. One-stop administrative services offered by the Science Park Bureau, which make tenant away from time-consuming application procedures services offered

*III. Development profile of the Yilan Science Park (Chen-Nan Base)

1. The first science park in Taiwan focusing on development of digital contents and knowledge-based telecommunications industries.

2. Area: 71 hectares. A total of34.8 hectares of industry zone will be available after completed.

Building coverage ratio

3. Building coverage ratio: 60%. Floor area ratio: 200%. Tenancy: 20 years and renewable. The total area for housing should not exceed 10% of the area for industrial land.

4. Incubators and labs at the park will be soon available.

*IV. Incentives for investors:

1. Corporate income tax: 17%

2. R&D expenditure tax deduction up to 15% without exceeding 30% of corporate tax to be paid

3. The Yilan Science Park is a bonded area where all the imported machines could enjoy five-year of free customs duties.

4. Following the standards and specifications of the HSP, related underground pipelines for utilities and optical fibers have been well prepared. To-chen ocean telecommunications cable is nearby, providing superior quality of network services.

5. R&D grant is given up to 10 million NTD for each project.

*V. Rental and related costs:

A. Land(NTD/m2/month, with adjustment every 3 years) 22.97 NTD / m2 /month

B.Standard Factory

138.84 NTD/m2 /month (special price 97 NTD/m²/month from 7/1/2016 to 6/30/2019)

C.Management Fee

Accounting on 0.19% out of sales revenue or based on land area leased, choosing the higher one for charging.

D.Power Cost: Each degree: 2-3 NTD depending on power used.

E.Water Cost: Each degree: 7-11 depending on to us used.

*VI. Target industries to usher in

1. Telecommunications knowledge-based industries: related network software and knowledge service applications.

2. Digital contents: animation, games, video, learning, publication, SoLoMo and related software industries, etc.

3. Innovative and R&D-based industries: pioneering product R&D centers or innovative startups incubators.

BIOMEDICAL PARK

* ADD : 385, Sec.2,Wenhsin Rd., Zhubei City, Hsinchu County, Taiwan 30261, R.O.C.
* TEL : +886-3-667-6489
* FAX : +886-3-667-6465

According to the successful examples of the overseas developmental process of biomedical industry and biotechnology park, the developmental model for the establishment of biomedical science park cluster in Taiwan was integrated with the concept of one-stop shop for biotechnology integrated incubation mechanism, in order to develop the R&D potential of biomedical business. Biomedical industry can also develop product with market value through the verification of clinical trial platforms. Furthermore, the advantages over ICT design and manufacturing of HSP can be integrated with biomedical industry at the Park to trigger new development of biomedical technology in Taiwan, to put into practice the development of knowledge economy by the government and to enhance national competitiveness.

1.Base Location

The base of “HBSP” is on the 38.1 hectares of industrial area of “HSR Hsinchu Station Special District Project” in Jhubei City, Hsinchu County. Hsinchu City is approximately 8 km southwest of the base, and Jhubei City and Hsinchu County Government are approximately 3 km northwest. The County 120 Expressway to the north is the main traffic artery of the base. The Taiwan Rail (TR) Liujia Line (co-constructed with the High Speed Rail) is in its vicinity, and National Highway No. 1 and Second Freeway are at its two sides. It will take only 10 minutes to get to the park from Jhubei Interchange of National Highway No. 1 or Jhulin Interchange of Second Freeway.

The operation of High Speed Rail (HSR) has significantly reduced the traveling time between the Park and Taipei City. The HSR connects to the Taoyuan International Airport and Metropolitan Taipei to the north and Metropolitan Taichung City, the central Taiwan and the southern Taiwan to the south. The traffic of the Park is extremely convenient.

The Park is in the vicinity of academic institutions such as National Chiao Tung University, National Tsing Hua University and Industrial Technology Research Institute, as well as Hsinchu County Government and Hsinchu City. Moreover, the Park, HSP and Jhunan Biotech Industrial Area (mainly led by National Health Research Institute) jointly constitute the “Biotechnology Development Belt,” which is beneficial to the formation of industrial cluster.

2. Industry Focus

The Park is one of the major national construction projects. The R&D information sharing of three major centers of the Park aggressively attract internationally well-known biomedical industrial and research units. Moreover, the Park is integrated with HSP and the industrial advantage over ICT to form a cluster effect. The Park is the platform focusing on the establishment of innovative technology and industrial value adding, and is the pioneer leading the development of biotechnology industry in Taiwan.

According to the policy instruction of "strengthening industrial incubation" of biotechnology industry promotion strategy in Taiwan, the industrial objectives of the Park emphasize the industrial incubation and developmental planning of industries concerning "advanced medical devices" and "pharmaceuticals."

3. Functions

The Park is the science park for the cultivation of knowledge innovation and will play the role as the important site of biomedical industrialization and clinical trial development. In addition to providing the functions of general parks, it also provides business planning, instructional research (research facilities and personnel), clinical trial subjects, research and clinical trial-related hardware facilities, human resource, business and legal affairs-related services and industrial investment opportunities. The Park will significantly reduce the industrial R&D cost, increase the successful rate of biotechnology corporations and ensure the formation of biomedical industry in Taiwan by providing business platform, resource sharing, knowledge exchange and clinical trial-related hardware/software.

4. Layout

The Park covers an area of approximately 38.1 hectares, including the layout of medical complex area, incubation R&D area, industrial area and required service facilities. The most significant characteristic is the central green belt penetrating the whole Park, and its strong visual effect in the overall landscape makes it an eye-catching landmark in Hsinchu.

CENTRAL TAIWAN SCIENCE PARK

Tel : During office hours, please call representative number : 886-4-25658588
Emergency Call : 886-4-25658088
Or please call the Second Special Police Corps : 886-4-25605768
Fax : 886-4-25658288
Address : No.2, Jhongke Rd., Situn District, Taichung City 407, Taiwan (R.O.C.)
E-mail : ctsp00@ctsp.gov.tw

Industrial Specialties

The six major industries of CTSP are based on Nano- technology, which covers Optoelectronics, Integrated Circuit, Biotechnology, Precision Machinery, Computer Peripherals, and Green Energy. The mass production of the 12-inch wafer is available in all eight 12-inch wafer GIGAFAB. Furthermore, more 12-inch and 18-inch wafer GIGAFAB™ facilities will be expanded while enhancing the manufacturing process. Therefore, CTSP will be the powerhouse for semiconductor industries.

Future Prospects

(1)Promoting Taichung Science Park Expansion Development Plan: To build up basic technology in Taiwan's IC industry and help businesses leave their roots in Taiwan in order to secure Taiwan's leading position in the IC industry, urban planning and environment impact assessments have been completed for the expansion plan, and the space can be expected to be made available to manufacturers on schedule in 2015 Q2

(2)Science parks represent one of the driving forces behind industry upgrading and transformation and economic growth in a country. Faced with challenges of a constantly changing high tech industry, the park is always trying to inject creative momentum. The CTSP Bureau will work with the Ministry of Science and Technology (MOST) to promote innovation and entrepreneurship, academia-industry cooperative research, and training programs. Efforts will continue to be devoted to improving quality of the parks, supporting startups, helping manufacturers invest in R&D and innovation, facilitating academia-industry cooperative programs, and ensure effective product realization of R&D results so that the parks shift from efficiency-oriented to being innovation- oriented and facilitate transformation and upgrade of domestic industries.

(3)Efforts will be made to accelerate the second stage of environmental impact assessments for Phase 3 and Phase 4 of CTSP development and the corresponding review processes in order to make the space available to manufacturers.

SOUTHERN TAIWAN SCIENCE PARK

The Southern Taiwan Science Park (STSP) includes the Tainan Science Park and the Kaohsiung Science Park. The Tainan Science Park is situated between Xinshi, Shanhua and Anding District of Tainan City with a total area of 2,578 acres. The Kaohsiung Science Park is situated between Luzhu, Gangshan and Yong'an District of Kaohsiung City with a total area of 1,409 acres.

On July 1, 1993, the 2,388th executive meeting of the Executive Yuan approved an Economic Revitalization Project in which the establishment of a Science Park in southern Taiwan was proposed. The STSP Development Plan (which covered the Phase I Site of the Tainan Science Park) by National Science Council was approved by the Executive Yuan in May 1995 to mark the beginning of southern Taiwan's high-tech development.

In 2000 with the economy booming, over 80% of the industrial land available for the Phase I Site of the Tainan Science Park was leased out, and requests for more industrial land continued to pour in. In response to the demand from the Integrated Circuits (IC) and TFT-LCD industries for large tracts of factory land, the Executive Yuan agreed in May 2000 to designate the Intellectual Industrial Park developed in Luzhu by Taiwan Sugar Corporation as the site for the Luzhu Science Park. The project was officially approved on April 6, 2001. The Luzhu Science Park was renamed as the Kaohsiung Science Park on July 27, 2004.

To help the Park enterprises within 1 kilometer of the High Speed Rail deal with the impact of vibrations, former Premier Chun-Hsiung Chang during his inspection of STSP on May 17, 2001 ordered that the Phase II Site of the Tainan Science Park be accelerated. The expansion plan was approved by the Executive Yuan on September 19, 2001.

With the establishment of Ministry of Science and Technology, we have restructured and renamed as Southern Taiwan Science Park Bureau, Ministry of Science and Technology since March 3rd ,2014.

On March 3 ,2014, in coordination with the establishment of Ministry of Science and Technology, the STSP Administration was restructured as the "Southern Taiwan Science Park Bureau" (STSPB).

EXPORT PROCESSING ZONE

AGRICULTURAL BIOTECHNOLOGY PARK

THE ENVIRONMENTAL SCIENCE AND TECHNOLOGY PARKS IN TAIWAN

FREE TRADE ZONE

OPERATING LOCATIONS

Taiwan provides suitable operating environment. With respect to land cost, the commercial office rental in Taiwan is lower than in Hong Kong and in Singapore, which provides a lot of cost saving for enterprises in Taiwan. Take the top office building as an example, the rental in Hong Kong in 2013 is NT$23,200/ping (1 ping=3.3 square meters) while the rental in the Taipei 101 building is only NT$3,400 to NT$4,600/ping. In addition to the land cost per se, Taiwan government has continued to improve the administrative procedures for land acquisition, establishment of software companies, logistic and production facilities for both local and foreign companies. In this regard, the government has actively developed new science parks, ordinary industrial parks and free trade zones. Currently, there are 181 industrial parks, 10 export processing zones, three science parks, 7 free trade zones, agricultural biotechnology parks and environmental science and technology parks in Taiwan. Also, the government provides quality and low cost business environment.

Industrial development is the main force of Taiwan's economic development. Along with the rapid industrial development, factories of all kinds have been established throughout Taiwan. In early days, factories were located along the major highways or scattered all over the island. Therefore, the use of land and environment was not efficient. For this reason, the government designated the Industrial Development Bureau of the MOEA in 1970 to organize development teams for planning and developing the use of industrial parks/zones. Land is made available for factory establishment in the industrial parks. It has greatly influenced Taiwan's industrial development and the usage and planning of land. With the change of eras, the traditional industrial zones can not anymore fulfill the needs of the Taiwan industry. In response to the clamor of the industry, multi-purpose parks are planned to help form industrial clusters and accelerate integration of industries. The following types of industrial parks are available in Taiwan for different usages:

Types of Industrial Parks	Descriptions
Industrial Parks	Industrial Parks are the fundamental for Taiwan industrial development and the path to economic growth success, which provides manufacturers with sufficient lands, avoiding the disturbances from the surrounding environment, boosting local economic development with industrial clusters economic effect and creating high add value production environment.
Export Processing Zones	Have centralized administration, simplified and efficient system; play an important role in national economic development; provide great contributions to the accumulation of Taiwan's foreign exchange reserves and introduction of technologies.
Science Parks	Locations for development of high-tech industries; endeavor to create sound environment for quality R&D, production, work and leisure activities; promote Taiwan industry upgrade.
Agricultural Biotechnology Parks	Intended for the development of agricultural technologies; introduction of talents of agricultural technologies; creation of industrial clusters of agricultural technologies; promotion of transformation of agricultural industry; advancement of product R&D, innovation, cultivation, production and marketing capabilities; assurance of sustainable operations of the agricultural industry.
Environmental Science and Technology Parks	Intended for the prevention, improvement, or solutions for current environmental threats; provision of sufficient energy and resources to sustain living environment; creation of environment friendly society to assure the sustainability of energy and resources.
Free Trade Ports	Intended for the development of global logistics and operations management; promotion of trade liberalization and internationalization; increase of national competitiveness and improvement of national economy.

With the rapid industrial development, the environmental issue has been of great importance. The Environmental Protection Administration of Taiwan has implemented the environmental assessment measure to prevent or reduce the negative impact on the environment caused by land development. To create clustering effects and improve regional development, most of the operating locations in Taiwan, including ordinary offices, industrial parks, export processing zones, science parks, free trade ports, agricultural biotechnology parks and environmental protection parks have to undergo and to pass the environmental assessments. Therefore, entities establishing operations in the parks will save costs for environmental protection. As the Parks have existing infrastructure and convenient administration, and provide various incentives, they are the number one choice for both local and foreign companies to establish production and R&D facilities and operating headquarters.

HIGH TECH, TELECOM AND INTERNET COMPANIES

NO. Title Of Company Tel

A0004 UNITED MICROELECTRONICS CORP. (03)5782258
*

A0006 MICROTEK INTERNATIONAL INC. 03-5772155
*

A0007 QUARTZ FREQUENCY TECHNOLOGY LTD. (03)5779000
*

A0008 SINO-AMERICAN SILICON PRODUCTS INC. (03)5772233
*

A0009 FLOW ASIA CORPORATION 03-5772102
*

A0010 TECOM CO. LTD. 03-5775141
*

A0022 MITAC INTERNATIONAL CORP 03-5779250
*

A0026 KEST SYSTEMS & SERVICE LTD. (03)5772107
*

A0038 MICROELECTRONICS TECHNOLOGY, INC. 03-5773335
*

A0043 SYNTEK SEMICONDUCTOR CO., LTD. 02-26590055
*

A0049 GENERAL BIOLOGICALS CORP. (03)5779221
*

A0050 PRINCO CORP. (03)5773177
*

A0053 OPTO TECH CORPORATION (03)5638951
*

A0054 NEW MICROPORE,INC. 03-5773385
*

A0065 MOSEL VITELIC INC. (03)5795888

A0069 EPISIL TECHNOLOGIES INC. (03)5779245
*

A0071 EVERNEW BIOTECH INC. (03)5772191
*

A0076 CADENCE TAIWAN INC. (03)5778951
*

A0082 UNITED FIBER OPTIC COMMUNICATION INC. (03)5779211
*
A0084 LOGITECH FAR EAST LTD. 03-5778241
*
A0098 TAIWAN SEMICONDUCTOR MFG CO. LTD. 886-3-563-6688
*
A0102 ADVANCED MICROELECTRONIC PRODUCTS INC (03)5770033
*
A0107 GRAND BIOTECHNOLOGY CO.,LTD. (03)5780446
*
A0112 TAIWAN HI-TECH CORP. (03)5774600
*
A0117 NIPRO DIAGNOSTICS TAIWAN, INC. (03)5770259
*
A0119 K LASER TEHCNOLOGY INC. (03)5770316
*
A0121 TYNTEK CORPORATION (037)582997
*
A0122 ACCTON TECHNOLOGY CORP. (03)5770270
*
A0125 VATE TECHNOLOGY CO., LTD. (03)5770345
*
A0128 TAIWAN MASK CORPORATION 03-5634370

A0132 UNITED INDUSTRIAL GASES CO., LTD. (03)5783876 or 5783878
*
A0133 SINONAR CORP. (037)585599
*
A0139 E-CMOS CORPORATION 03-5783622
*
A0141 MIRLE AUTOMATION CORPORATION 03-5783280
*
A0145 REALTEK SEMICONDUCTOR CORP. (03)5780211
*
A0146 MUSTEK SYSTEM INC. (03)5779373
*
A0148 WELTREND SEMICONDUCTOR INCORPORATED (03)5780241
*
A0149 MITAC TECHNOLOGY CORPORATION (03)5782280
*
A0152 MACRONIX INTERNATIONAL CO., LTD. (03)5786688
*
A0160 ATOP TECHNOLOGIES INC. (03)5508137
*
A0163 TREND TONE IMAGING, INC. (03)5783620
*
A0168 SHOWA DENKO HD TRACE CORP. 03-5770777

*

A0176 TRANSYSTEM INC. 03-5780393
*

A0177 HEXAWAVE INC. (03)5785100
*

A0183 ETRON TECHNOLOGY INC.(03)5782345

A0184 MICRO LITHOGRAPHY, INC. (TAIWAN) (03)5785168
*

A0185 PROMISE TECHNOLOGY INC. 03-5782395
*

A0188 ACTiSYS International Corp. (03)5785161
*

A0189 AVISION INC. (03)5782388
*

A0190 SUCCESS PRIME CORPORATION (037)586999
*

A0191 Myson Century INC. (03)5784866
*

A0195 LOOP TELECOMMUNICATION INTERNATIONAL INC (03)5787696
*

A0196 CYNTEC CO., LTD. (03)5799829
*

A0197 STARTEK ENGINEERING INC. (03)5785389
*

A0198 ORIENTAL SYSTEM TECHNOLOGY INC. 03-5785177
*

A0201 SYNTEST TECHNOLOGIES INC. TAIWAN 03-5789880
*

A0207 ANALOG INTEGRATIONS CORP. (03)5772500
*

A0209 E INK HOLDINGS INC. (03)5643200
*

A0210 OPNET TECHNOLOGIES CO., LTD. (03)5788693
*

A0211 FARADAY TECHNOLOGY CORPORATION (03)5787888

A0212 CORETRONIC CORPORATION 03-5772000
*

A0216 WINCOMM CORPORATION (03)5780000
*

A0219 HITRON TECHNOLOGIES INC. HSINCHU SBIP SUBSIDIARY (03)5786658
*

A0221 RADIANTECH INCORPORATION 03-5777818
*

A0223 UNITED ORTHOPEDIC CORP. (03)5773351
*

A0238 APPLIED MATERIALS TAIWAN (03)5798888
*
A0240 TAIWAN BIOTECH CO., SCIENCE PARK BRANCH (03)5789060
*
A0242 SUNPLUS TECHNOLOGY CO., LTD. (03)578-6005
*
A0243 BAYCOM OPTO-ELECTRONICS TECH. CO.,LTD. (03)5786178
*
A0250 LUREN PRECISION CO., LTD. (03)5786767
*
A0252 ELAN MICROELECTRONICS CORPORATION (03)5639977
*
A0253 TM TECHNOLOGY INC. (03)5787720
*
A0256 NEXCELL BATTERY CO., LTD. (03)5783800
*
A0257 TAISIL ELECTRONIC MATERIALS CORPORATION (03)5783131
*
A0260 Fitipower Integrated Technology Inc. 03-5799255

A0264 ADVANCED COMBUSTION TTECHNOLOGY CO.,LTD. (03)5788508
*
A0267 VANGUARD INTERNATIONAL SEMICONDUCTOR COR (03)5770355
*
A0270 Z-COM, INC. (03)5777364
*
A0274 Powerchip Technology Corporation (03)5795000
*
A0275 ASIX ELECTRONICS CORP. LTD. (03)5799500
*
A0276 SHIN-ETSU OPTO ELECTRONIC CO., LTD. (03)5784566
*
A0283 UTAC (Taiwan) Corporation (03)5788780
*
A0284 SILICON BASED TECHNOLOGY, CORP. (03)5777897
*
A0286 FOCI FIBER OPTIC COMMUNICATIONS, INC. (03)5770099
*
A0287 Uwin Technologies Co.,Ltd. (03)5788690
*
A0288 LUST TECHNOLOGY CO., LTD. 03-5795188
*
A0292 SHIN-ETSU HANDOTAI TAIWAN CO., LTD. (03)5771188
*
A0293 LAM RESEARCH CO., LTD. (03)5798666
*
A0297 AVID ELECTRONICS CORP. (03)5795222

*
A0298 RORZE TECHNOLOGY INCORPORATED (03)5776482
*
A0299 INTECH TAIWAN COMPANY (03)5678199
*
A0305 ITE Tech. Inc. (03)5798658
*
A0311 AIRWAVE TECHNOLOGIES, INC. (03)5778099
*
A0313 EXPLORE MICROELECTRONICS INC. (03)5643595
*
A0316 GLOBAL MIXED-MODE TECHNOLOGY INC. (03)5788833
*
A0317 AU OPTRONICS CORP. 03-5008800
*
A0320 DAVICOM SEMICONDUCTOR, INC. (03)5798797
*
A0321 EPISTAR CORPORATION (03)5783078
*
A0322 LIGHTWAVE LINK, INC. 03-5785574
*
A0325 PROMOS TECHNOLOGIES INC. 03-5798308
*
A0327 SOURCE PHOTONICS TAIWAN, INC. (03)5790177
*
A0328 EUTREND TECHNOLOGY INC. (03)5633328
*
A0329 EXCELLENCE OPTOELECTRONICS INC. (03)5679000
*
A0332 XAC AUTOMATION CORP. (03)5772738
*
A0334 PHOENIX SILICON INTERNATIONAL CORP. (03)5641888

A0338 ABOCOM SYSTEMS, INC. (03)5789090
*
A0340 INNOMEDIA TECHNOLOGY INC. (03)5641299
*
A0342 NOVATEK MICROELECTRONICS CORP. (03)5670889
*
A0343 MEDIATEK INC. 03-5670766
*
A0348 AMIC Technology Corporation (03)5679966
*
A0349 CHIPBOND TECHNOLOGY CORPORATION (03)5678788
*
A0350 ALTEK CORPORATION (03)5784567
*

A0353 KINGSTON TECHNOLOGY FAR EAST CO. (03)5641539
*
A0361 NUTEX COMMUNICATIONS CORP. (03)5223035
*
A0362 DOMEX TECHNOLOGY CORPORATION (03)5772115
*
A0363 CHIPMOS TECHNOLOGIES INC. (03)5770055
*
A0364 Photronics DNP Mask Corporation (03)5679933
*
A0370 Metrodyne Co., Ltd. 03-5632161
*
A0371 SILICON TOUCH TECHNOLOGY INC. (03)5645656
*
A0372 EVERMORE TECHNOLOGY INC. (03)5642062

A0377 MICROJET TECHNOLOGY CO., LTD. 886-3-5794766
*
A0378 SYNERGY SCIENTECH CORP. (03)5643700
*
A0379 APEX BIOTECHNOLOGY CORPORATION (03)5641952
*
A0381 ANPEC ELECTRONICS CORPORATION (03)5642000
*
A0386 ELITE SEMICONDUCTOR MEMORY TECHNOLOGY IN (03)5781970
*
A0391 AERO VISION AVIONICS, INC. (03)5643912
*
A0392 TRUELIGHT CORPORATION. (03)5780080
*
A0396 POLYTRONICS TECHNOLOGY CORP. (03)5643931
*
A0400 HOLTEK SEMICONDUCTOR INCORPORATION (03)5631999
*
A0402 Chingis Technology Corporation (03)5780333
*
A0403 Episil-Precision Inc. (03)5632255
*
A0405 TELESYNERGY TECHNOLOGY INC. (03)5635858
*
A0407 GLOBAL UNICHIP CORP. 03-5646600
*
A0410 CHAMPION MICROELECTRONIC CORP. (03)5679979
*
A0413 M/A-COM TECH ASIA INC. (03)5679680

A0414 HANDLINK TECHNOLOGIES INC. (03)5645166
*

A0420 AIPTEK INTERNATIONAL INC. (03)5678138
*

A0424 CHANGING INFORMATION TECHNOLOGY INC. (03)5630688
*

A0437 PIXART IMAGING, INC. 03-5795317
*

A0444 RAYSON TECHNOLOGY CO., LTD. HSIN-CHU SCIENCE PARK BRANCH (03)5633666
*

A0446 VXIS TECHNOLOGY CORPORATION (03)5630888
*

A0447 BROWAVE CORPORATION (03)5630099
*

A0448 CyberTAN TECHNOLOGY INC. (03)5777777
*

A0449 FIBER LOGIC COMMUNICATIONS, INC. (03)5638889
*

A0451 Glory Praise Photronics Corp. (03)5637218
*

A0457 UNISVR GLOBAL INFORMATION TECHNOLOGY COR (03)5632456
*

A0458 MACHVISION INC. (03)5638599
*

A0459 YODA COMMUNICATIONS, INC. (03)5632323
*

A0460 TYSON BIORESEARCH INC. (037)585988
*

A0462 RDC SEMICONDUCTOR CO., LTD. 03-6662866

A0463 PROSCEND COMMUNICATIONS INC. (03)5639000
*

A0471 KOPIN TAIWAN CORPATION 03-5798181
*

A0475 ENE TECHNOLOGY INC. (03)666-2888
*

A0477 ORGCHEM TECHNOLOGIES, INC. (03)5782200
*

A0480 SILICONWARE PRECISION INDUSTRIES INDUSTR (03)5785599
*

A0487 GIGACOMM CORPORATION (03)6668850
*

A0488 SYNCMOS TECHNOLOGIES INTERNATIONAL,INC. (03)5789988
*

A0489 BIOPTIK TECHNOLOGY INC. SCIENCE-BASED IN (03)5782999
*

A0492 EMEMORY TECHNOLOGY INC. 03-5631616
*
A0493 AXCELIS TECHNOLOGIES, LTD. 886+3-564-8000
*
A0495 HC PHOTONICS CORPORATION (03)6662123
*
A0497 SST Taiwan Ltd. (03)5778366
*
A0499 EE SOLUTIONS INC. (03)5678568
*
A0500 GIGA SOLUTION TECHNOLOGY CO., LTD. 03-6116168
*
A0503 DENMOS TECHNOLOGY INC. (03)6669777

A0509 Wistron NeWeb Corporation 03-6667799
*
A0513 INTEGRATED DIGITAL TECHNOLOGIES, INC. 03-6668885
*
A0516 WISTRON CORPORATION 03-5770707
*
A0518 WELKIN TECHNOLOGIES, INC. (03)6667336
*
A0521 LINK-WAVE AEROSPACE TECHNOLOGY INC. (03)6661136
*
A0525 CORETEK OPTO CORPORATION (03)5966007
*
A0526 YOUNG OPTICS INC. (03)5772000
*
A0529 ASIA PACIFIC MICROSYSTEMS, INC. 03-6661188
*
A0534 ELANSAT TECHNOLOGIES INC. (03)5635105
*
A0536 BT BIOTECH CO., LTD. 037-586333
*
A0540 EVEREST DISPLAY INCORPORATION (03)6667350
*
A0541 foxsemicon integrated technology Inc. (037)580088
*
A0542 BENQ CORPORATION HSIN-CHU BRANCH 03-6118800
*
A0548 CORETECH KNOWLEDGE INC. 03-6667448
*
A0551 DIGIWELL TECHNOLOGY INC. 03-5782910

A0552 TOPCO E&M SYSTEMS, INC. 03-6015888
*
A0554 Mycenax Biotech Inc. 037-587-988

*

A0555 AIROHA TECHNOLOGY INC. 03-612-8188

*

A0561 Syntronix Corporation (03)5631986

*

A0570 Innolux Corporation (037)586000

*

A0580 Amersen Bioscience International. Inc. 037-583665

*

A0582 Chiplus Semiconductor Corp. 03-5637887

*

A0584 致茂電子股份有限公司新竹科學園區分公司

*

A0585 RADIANT INNOVATION INC. +886-3-6111666 or 5644185

*

A0586 Asia Pacific Fuel Cell Technologies,Ltd.

*

A0588 Jmicron Technology Corp. 03-5797389

*

A0591 HORTEK CRYSTAL CO., LTD. HSIN CHU SCIENCE PARK BRANCH

*

A0594 CMSC,Inc. (03)5634866

*

A0597 Advanced & Wise Technology Corp. 03-578-0088

*

A0599 Union Biotechnology Co., Ltd. 03-5781168

A0601 INNOCHIP TECHNOLOGY INC. +886(3)666-3077

*

A0602 ZyFLEX Technologies Incorporation (03)5679168

*

A0616 Enova Technology Corporation 03-5772767

*

A0617 Mobile Magic Design Corporation 03-6668188

*

A0619 Agnitio Science &Technology, INC. 03-5631088

*

A0620 Alpha Networks Inc. 03-563-6666

*

A0625 Russel Information System Co.,Ltd.APEX Division (03)5637898

*

A0627 SPIROX CORPORATION HSINCHU SCIENCE PARK BRANCH 5347388

*

A0635 HOYA MICROELECTRONICS TAIWAN CO.,LTD.

*

A0640 HON HAI PRECISION IND. CO., LTD. Hsinchu Science Park Branch Office 03-5784975

*

A0643 Sunext Technology Co., Ltd.

*

A0648 YOUNGTEK ELECTRONICS CORP. SCIENCE-BASED PARK BRANCH 03-5711506

*

A0650 Advanced Ion Beam Technology, Inc. 5678485

*

A0659 FORMOSA EPITAXY INCORPORATIOIN (03)4994555

A0662 Savior Lifetec Corporation 037-580100

*

A0666 Crowningtek inc. 037-586898

*

A0667 Incentia Design Systems Corp. 03-5782868

*

A0668 HOLUX Technology, Inc. 03-6687000

*

A0675 Zentel Electronics Corp. 03-5799599

*

A0677 WALTOP International Corporation 03-5786388

*

A0678 ULVAC, Taiwan Inc., HSP Branch 5795688

*

A0682 ICF Technology Co.,Ltd 037-778898

*

A0688 Asuka Semiconductor Inc.

*

A0690 Hsinchu Science City Logistics Co., Ltd. Branch 03-5783200

*

A0691 LONGTEK SCIENTIFIC CO., LTD. 03-5773398

*

A0693 Optivision Technology Incorporated 03-5776686

*

A0695 LITE-ON SEMICONDUCTOR CORP., HSINCHU BRA

*

A0696 CHENG UEI PRECISION IND., CO., LTD. HSIN 02-22689888

*

A0698 Sumika Technology Co., Ltd. Hsinchu Branch 07-3641316

A0699 VisEra Technologies Company Ltd. 03-6668788

*

A0700 Rohm and Haas Electronic Materials Asia 037-539100

*

A0701 Semi-Photonics Co., Ltd. 037-586788

*

A0704 Sino-American Silicon Products Inc. Chun

*

A0706 Pointec Technology Co., Ltd. 037-585636
*

A0707 Andes Technology Corporation 03-6668300
*

A0708 SINONAR SOLAR CORP. (037)539089
*

A0709 A-Optronics Technology Inc. 03-5779999
*

A0711 ANWELL SEMICONDUCTOR CORPORATION 03-6669898
*

A0713 DuPont Taiwan Limited (Hsin-Chu Branch) 03-5790500
*

A0716 AMIC Communication Corporation
*

A0717 Taiwan Microelectronics Technologies INC.
*

A0718 StarChips Technology Inc. 03-5775767
*

A0720 Materials Analysis Technology Inc. Science Park Branch 03-6116678
*

A0722 Prolific Technology Inc., Hsin-Chu Branch 03-5782011

A0725 Luminescence Technology Corp. 03-6663188
*

A0728 PRIT Biotech Co., LTD. 037-585661
*

A0732 Orise Technology Co.,Ltd (03)6661660
*

A0733 Tear Xtal Technology Corporation 03-6668779
*

A0734 Mars Semiconductor Corp.
*

A0737 Avisonic Technology Corporation 03-5778077
*

A0741 Infomax Communication Co., Ltd. 03-6668866
*

A0742 MioDioTek Co. Ltd.
*

A0743 全宏科技股份有限公司 03-6661778
*

A0744 Key Asic Inc.
*

A0745 Silicon Optronics,Inc 03-5678986
*

A0748 Arch Meter Corporation 03-5631359

A0758 Sunplus mMobile Inc. 03-5799699
*
A0759 Sunplus Innovation Technology Inc. 03-5632822
*
A0762 Raydium Semiconductor Corporation 03-6661818
*
A0766 TacBright Optronics Co., Ltd.
*
A0767 Shinbright Optronics Corporation
*
A0769 GALLANT PRECISION MACHINING CO., LTD. 03-5639999
*
A0774 Tunable Optix Corporation (03)5637699
*
A0775 Ulead Technology Inc.
*
A0776 Neo Solar Power Corporation035780011
*
A0778 Sunplus mMedia Inc. 03-5641600
*
A0785 BenQ Materials Corp. Hsinchu Science Park Branch 03-3748800
*
A0786 APM Communication, Inc. 03-6668315
*
A0787 Generalplus Technology Inc. 03-6662118
*
A0788 TOKYO ELECTRON TAIWAN LIMITED 03-6662266
*
A0789 LIONIC Corp. 03-5789399

A0790 Collamatrix Co., Ltd. 02-7711-329
*
A0795 Laser Life Company HSIP Branch 035525358
*
A0796 Zilltek Technology Corp., 03-5777509
*
A0797 Nolvate Advanced Ltd. 03-5789939
*
A0799 Wafre Works Corp. SBIP Branch 03-4815001
*
A0801 Navisys Technology Corp. 03-5632598
*
A0802 TOP UNION GLOBALTEK INC. 03-6669911
*
A0803 ACTHERM INC. 03-6669596
*
A0805 Grenergy Poto. Inc. 03-5786363

*
A0807 Soundwin Network Inc.
*
A0808 InvenSense Taiwan Company Ltd. 03-6686999
*
A0809 Cheeshin Technology Co., Ltd. 037-585008
*
A0810 ASPEED Technology Inc. 03-5789568

A0815 Wafer MEMS Co., Ltd. 037-778989
*
A0817 Maxchip Electronics Corporation 03-5656000
*
A0819 Camels Vision Technologies Inc.
*
A0821 Nuvoton Technology Corporation 03-5770066
*
A0822 Lof Solar Corp.
*
A0825 Young Lighting Technology Inc. 03 5772000
*
A0826 Silicon Base Development Inc. 03-6661056
*
A0827 Lyontek Inc. 03-6668838
*
A0828 IPworks Technology Corporation 03-5635198
*
A0829 YEEDEX CERATEC CORPORATION 577-1538
*
A0830 VASSTEK INTERNATIONAL CORPORATION 037-580626
*
A0832 Archers System, Inc. 02-23259918
*
A0834 Applied Green Light Taiwan, Inc.
*
A0836 AQUA LOHAS WATER-TECH SERVICE CO., LTD.037-582-486

A0839 Harvatek Corporation Hsinchu Science Park Branch
*
A0846 CN-J Technology Co., Ltd.
*
A0847 WiseChip Semiconductor Inc. 037-587168
*
A0854 J-MEX Inc. 03-6661036
*
A0865 Elite Silicon Technology Inc. 03-5797271

A0875 AXElite Technology Co., Ltd. 03-5776662
*
A0880 Gthink Technology Integration, Inc. 037-580800
*
A0886 成一電子股份有限公司
*
A0888 Garsen Scientech Corp.
*
A0894 Advanced Optoelectronic Technology, Inc-Zhunan Branch 5976988
*
A0896 Unicon Optical Co., Ltd. 03-5775586
*
A0897 North-vision Tech. Inc. 03-5771038
*
A0898 MKD Technology Inc. 03-5781899

NATIONAL STRATEGY FOR CYBERSECURITY DEVELOPMENT PROGRAM[4]

National Information & Communication Security Taskforce, Executive Yuan
Taiwan, R.O.C.
Organization Chart

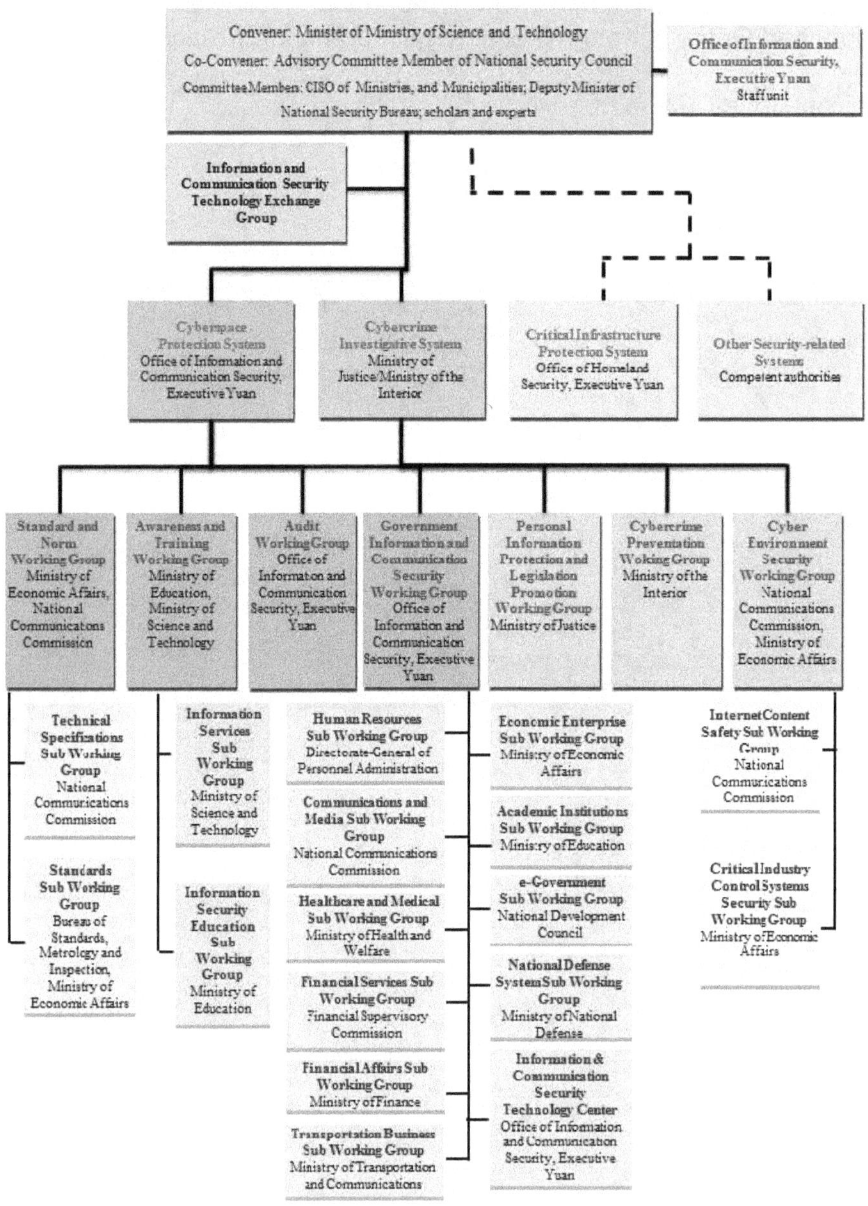

[4] Approved by the Executive Yuan on December 25, 2013

National Information and Communication Security Taskforce, Executive Yuan

CHAPTER 1 INTRODUCTION

With the widespread utilization of information technology and the continuing evolvement of the Internet in the 21st century, information and communication technology (ICT) applications have become ubiquitous and have changed our everyday lives. In tandem with the ICT revolution however ICT-related security issues have become a major issue of growing concern, and as a result in many countries information and communication security is now in the spotlight.

To strengthen Taiwan's capability to deal with information and communication security issues, the Executive Yuan approved the National Information and Communication Infrastructure Security Mechanism Plan (2001-2004) (the Phase 1 Mechanism Plan) at its 2718th meeting on January 17, 2001, and established the National Information and Communication Security Taskforce (the Taskforce), the purpose of which is to actively implement ICT security infrastructure policy.

Between 2005 and 2012, the Executive Yuan carried out the National Information and Communication Infrastructure Security Mechanism Plan (2005-2008) (the Phase 2 Mechanism Plan) and the National strategy for Cybersecurity Development Program (2009-2012) (the Phase 3 Development Program). Consequently, with the collaborative efforts of agencies from central government, special municipalities and local government, the interim objective of "establishing an overall information security protection system and improving information security protection capabilities" has been achieved in the prescribed order.

Taiwan has a unique political and economic environment, and when confronted with a complex and ever-changing global ICT environment and the information security threats, it is imperative that work related to the implementation and refinement of ICT security should be continued. Therefore the Taskforce has conducted the necessary research and is now proposing the National Strategy for Cybersecurity Development Program (2013-2016) (the Program), which is designed to be the basis on which all government agencies implement information and communication security plans in the current phase.

CHAPTER 2 GLOBAL INFORMATION SECURITY DEVELOPMENT TRENDS

I STATUS OF GLOBAL INFORMATION SECURITY THREATS

The Internet has brought great convenience and speed to our lives. However the prevalence of the Internet and related changes in consumer behavior mean that issues such as cyber crime and protection of personal information and privacy have become a source of great concern affecting national security and social stability. Due to this situation the world is now facing some serious information security threats (see Figure 1).

Figure 1. Global information security threats

A Rampant organized cyber crime

Around the world information security threats have evolved from individual threats that are nothing more than a display of hacking skills to organized and economically or politically motivated intrusions. Recently cybercriminal organizations have become highly specialized. This, coupled with the fact that launch of cyber warfare is not constrained by time or space, means that the first attack can

now become the decisive battle, implying that the concept and scope of national security have fundamentally and substantially changed.

B Theft of personal information and financial fraud incidents abound

Hackers embed malicious code into victims' computers via e-mail social engineering or employ methods such as exploiting web application vulnerabilities and implanting Trojan horse viruses into web pages in order to steal private personal information. They even conspire with criminal organizations to perpetrate financial fraud. For example, Japan's Play Station Network (PSN) was attacked, resulting in 80 million personal records being leaked in April 2011.

C Critical information infrastructures facing increasing information security risks

In the age of the digital economy, destruction of important information and communication facilities will inevitably impact the economy, people's livelihoods and overall government operations. The Supervisory Control And Data Acquisition (SCADA) of various types of Critical Infrastructures (CIs) usually lack robust information security protection designs, and as a result both are major targets for hackers.

D Intensification of Advanced Persistent Threat

Advanced Persistent Threat (APT) attacks are characterized by having specific targets, being inconspicuous, covert, employing diverse tactics and being customizable. Recently government systems in the U.S., Britain, France, Germany, New Zealand and Australia were reportedly breached by APT attacks seeking to steal important confidential and sensitive data.

E Zero-day Attack resulting in difficulties in information security defense

A "Zero-day Attack" refers to an attack that exploits an unknown vulnerability in a computer software, one that developers have had no time to address and patch. Hackers often use a fake identity to send e-mail with intriguing subject and content, combined with file attachments containing zero-day attacks, to carry out e-mail social engineering attacks. Once the recipient opens the attachment of the

e-mail, zero-day malware is implanted.

II INFORMATION SECURITY POLICY DEVELOPMENT IN MAJOR COUNTRIES

In recent years, major countries and regions have actively implemented new information security policies to respond to the current global status of information security threats. Below a list of evolving trends are provided as a reference source for information security policymakers and strategists in Taiwan:

A Raising information security issues to the level of national security

After taking office in 2009, U.S. President Obama solicited the opinions and point of view of various experts and scholars to undertake a comprehensive assessment of the past and present status of U.S. cybersecurity policies. Obama expressed his commitment to establishing a reliable and robust information and communication infrastructure. He also announced a new plan to strengthen cybersecurity in the U.S. by upgrading cybersecurity to the level of national security.

In South Korea, the government initiated the "e-Korea Vision 2006" policy to promote high-speed broadband Internet services, and in response to the impact of information security threats, the government also incorporated information security into the basic national policy "Broadband IT Korea Vision 2007."

In Japan, for the purposes of enhancing national competitiveness and sustaining social and economic development, information security policies have focused on enhancing national security and systems security, improving information security education and promoting international cooperation in recent years.

During the Fourth Plenary Session of the 16th Communist Party of China Central Committee held in 2008, China recognized information security as a major component in national security and unequivocally proposed a policy of "strengthening national security awareness and perfecting national security strategy" to ensure "the country's political, economic, cultural and information security."

B Emphasizing the importance of protecting citizens' rights, in

particular protection of personal information and privacy

In 2011, the U.S. released the National Strategy for Trusted Identities in Cyberspace (NSTIC), designed to advance the development of technologies or platforms for making online transactions at as high a trust level as possible.

In 2008, the Singapore government initiated a five-year information and communication security roadmap to provide a secure environment to enable high-speed Internet and ICT security infrastructures to create more value-added services, such as area-based marketing, logistics tracking and Internet services with higher adaptability, which can be applied to the banking, education and healthcare industries.

In Japan, the Japanese Personal Information Protection Act (JPIPA) was passed in 2005, which expressly stipulates that enterprises that retain personal information have an obligation to protect data and prevent it from being leaked. The government also listed specific measures on enhancing protection of citizens and users and promotion of personal information protection in *Information Security 2011*.

C Increasing emphasis on security issues related to cloud computing

The U.S. Federal Government implemented cloud computing technologies and services for the websites of government agencies in late 2009 as an important basis for the Obama Administration to carry out budget cuts, enhance administrative efficiency and create a greener environment. The administration also appointed Vivek Kundra as the new Federal Chief Information Officer and launched a series of Government Cloud restructuring programs. In late 2011, the U.S. National Institute of Standards and Technology (NIST) issued a series of special documents, which stressed the importance, issues and recommended practices regarding cloud computing technology, including SP 800-144 (Draft Guidelines on Security and Privacy in Public Cloud Computing), SP 800-145 (The NIST Definition of Cloud Computing), SP 800-146 (Draft Cloud Computing Synopsis and Recommendations) and SP 500-293 Volume I & Volume II (US

Government Cloud Computing Technology Roadmap).

In Japan, policies and measures concerning the importance of cloud computing security were emphasized in Secure Japan 2010, which included ensuring information security in cloud computing technology, standardization of cloud computing security programs, small and medium enterprise cloud computing security, development of checklists for cloud service levels, development of high reliability/energy conservation network control technology for cloud services, strategic research and development for promoting information security, and research on new-generation information security technologies. In China, the planning of seven strategic emerging industries will be the focus of national development as listed in the Twelfth Five-Year Plan. In particular, the development of cloud computing as a new generation of information technology will be an area of major importance.

D Emphasizing government/private sector or industry-academic cooperation issues

In the U.S., 85% of all CIs are operated by the private sector. For this reason the government has proposed a national policy on substantive protection of the country's CIs, which will provide a model on which cooperation and alliances between the government, CI operators, civil organizations and individuals can be based. The national policy provides specific strategies to enhance national security.

Japan released the Information Security Strategy for Protecting the Nation program in 2010 and continued the model of cooperation between the public and private sector, which focuses on enhancing planning directions and implementation institutions from the perspectives of security protection and crisis management in order to achieve better policy results.

China's National Medium- to Long-range Program for Scientific and Technological Development proposes that the "information industry and modern service industries" be given priority as major industries for long-term development. In "Facing information

security for core applications," the directions for key information security technologies are pointed out, and measures to encourage development in four areas (i.e. tax breaks on research and development, government procurement, civilian-military collaboration and international cooperation) are designed to advance the development of China's information security technologies.

In South Korea, major enterprises enjoy collaboration with academic institutions, and they have invested large sums of capital in achieving the country's own important information technologies and results.

E Importance of international cooperation on protection and exchange

In the U.S., President Obama announced the government initiative International Strategy for Cyberspace in 2011, which outlines the government's international cyberspace strategies, covering full integration and cooperation between the public and private sector, spanning domestic to international and international to global strategies, as well as combining traditional values and Internet technology applications associated with America's democratic and free-market ideals, thus laying a foundation for a post-911 new order in cyberspace.

South Korea is also in close cooperation with international organizations, including development areas in collaboration with these international organizations, and has provided policy advice to governments in other countries, as well as carried out administrative measures associated with e-government and the training of civil servants.

In Singapore, the government announced the Intelligent Nation 2015 (iN2015) Master Plan in June 2006, the main purposes of which are to achieve innovation, integration and internationalization. The government hopes that by 2015 the country will be able to "establish an intelligent nation and global city with ICT technology," making information and communication technologies pervasive and an integral part of daily life, work and leisure activities, as well as developing Singapore into a smart city based on four elements,

"technology," "infrastructure," "enterprise" and "manpower."

In Japan, Information Security 2011 was introduced to strengthen the country's information security policy in order to adapt to the changing security landscape and to strengthen international cooperation, e.g. improving alliances with the U.S., ASEAN countries and the EU. Japan also aims to implement specific measures through international forums and conferences such as the Asia-Pacific Economic Cooperation (APEC), ASEAN Regional Forum (ARF), International Telecommunication Union (ITU), Meridian and International Watch and Warning Network (IWWN).

In China, the Eleventh Five-Year Plan for National Information Security Standardization focuses on research of information security strategies and basic theory, development of information security standards and promotion, and participation in international standardization activities on a regular basis.

CHAPTER 3 ANALYSIS OF CURRENT STATUS OF INFORMATION SECURITY

I. ORGANIZATION

Pursuant to the Guidelines for Establishing the National Information and Communication Security Taskforce, Executive Yuan, which was amended in January 2013, the Taskforce is responsible for developing national information and communication security policy and notification and response mechanisms, review and consultation on major programs, and coordination and supervision of inter-ministerial affairs concerning information and communication security. Two systems have been established under the Taskforce: Internet Protection and Cybercrime Investigation and Prevention (refer to Figure 2 for the detailed organizational structure of the Taskforce).

Figure 2. Structure of National Information and Communication Security Taskforce, Executive Yuan

The Taskforce was established in January 2001, and in earlier years the Science and Technology Advisory Group (STAG) took on an advisory role. Subsequently, in consideration of a deteriorating information security situation, the Executive Yuan amended the Guidelines for Establishing the National Information and Communication Security Taskforce in March 2011 and set up the Office of Information and Communication Security in order to enhance national information security policy planning, improve efficiency of information security notification and contingency planning, and expedite implementation of major information security programs. In coordination with Executive Yuan restructuring on January 1, 2012, the Office of Information and Communication Security became a permanent taskforce of the Executive Yuan. In accordance with the Guidelines for Establishing the Office of Information and Communication Security, the Office is charged with the following responsibilities in addition to serving as advisor to the Taskforce:

A Development and promotion of national information security policy and measures.

B Notification, response, and review of national information security incidents.

C Promotion and review of major national information security programs.

D Coordination, liaison and promotion of national information security-related legislation and regulations.

The following lists the subsystems and groups within the Taskforce and their corresponding responsible agencies and tasks:

A Cyberspace protection system: Headed by the Office of Information and Communication Security, Executive Yuan, responsible for the integration of information security protection resources and promotion of information security policy; it comprises the following working groups:

(1) Standard and Norm Working Group: Headed by the Ministry of Economic Affairs, responsible for developing certification and verification standards and systems for

information security products and management systems; promoting technical standards of information security technology; and carrying out control, development and maintenance of government agencies' information security operating standards and reference guidelines.

(2) Audit Working Group: Headed by the Office of Information and Communication Security, Executive Yuan, responsible for promoting and implementing information security audit systems and providing assistance to government agencies in strengthening the integrity and effectiveness of information security protection responsibilities; the Office is also responsible for reducing information security risks through continuous improvement.

(3) Awareness and Training Working Group: Headed by the Ministry of Education, responsible for promoting basic education in information security, strengthening information security in the educational system, raising national information security knowledge and awareness, providing information security services, and establishing an information security personnel training system.

(4) Government Information and Communication Security Working Group: Headed by the Office of Information and Communication Security, responsible for planning and promoting security mechanisms of various e-government services, providing guidance to government agencies on information security technical services, information security protection and contingency planning, and integrating and improving information security manpower utilization within government agencies.

B Cybercrime Investigative System: Co-organized by the Ministry of Justice and Ministry of the Interior, responsibilities of which include preventing cybercrime, protecting citizens' privacy, and establishing information and communication infrastructure security; comprises the following working groups:

(1) Personal Information Protection and Legislation Promotion Working Group: Headed by the Ministry of Justice, responsible for reviewing and amending laws and regulations concerning protection of citizens' privacy and prevention and control of cybercrime; and establishing a legal environment that fosters trust and reliability.

(2) Cybercrime Preventation Woking Group: Headed by the Ministry of the Interior, responsible for conducting cybercrime investigations and preventing computer-related crimes.

(3) Cyber Environment Security Working Group: Headed by the National Communications Commission, responsible for promoting Internet content security, cybercrime prevention, enhancing control system security of critical industries, and establishing secure and trustworthy information and communication infrastructure mechanisms.

In order to be kept abreast of the latest trends in information security technologies and enhance information security capability, the Taskforce established the Information Security Technology Exchange Group in August 2012. Representatives from industry, government, academic, and research institutions are invited to participate in seminars on a quarterly basis to discuss information security technology and share how specific or major information security incidents are handled, causes of incidents and recommendations for improvement.

II. MAJOR INFORMATION SECURITY POLICY MILESTONES

Since the Taskforce was established in January 2001, major information security plans or programs, each lasting four years, implemented over three phases have been introduced (see Figure 3 for details). These initiatives have effectively achieved a high degree of information security readiness in Taiwan. The highlights of each program or plan are outlined below.

Figure 3. Major information security policy development milestones

1. Phase 1 Mechanism Plan

In order to coordinate and accelerate the introduction of an information security infrastructure, the Executive Yuan approved the Phase 1 Mechanism Plan in 2001, which ran from 2001 to 2004. This phase concentrated on efforts to implement information security protection systems within the 3,713 major government agencies. In practical terms, government agencies were classified into seven categories: National Defense, Administration, Academic, Enterprises - Group 1 (water, electricity, petroleum and gas), Enterprises - Group 2 (transportation, communications, Internet and air traffic control), Enterprises - Group 3 (financial services, securities, tariff and trade) and

Enterprises - Group 4 (medical services). Each category was further divided into Class A (critical core agencies), Class B (core agencies), Class C (major agencies) and Class D (general agencies). Depending on the classification, different levels of information security support were provided. The rationale was to fulfill information security protection responsibilities in a comprehensive manner despite limited resources.

In addition, the Plan also focused on implementing security

management measures on information systems of more than 20 CIs. This required the on-schedule completion of installation of remote backup systems followed by certification to international information security management standards. In terms of information security awareness training, IT staff and supervisors were required to receive information security technical training or enroll in management courses. At the same time, the Security Operation Center (SOC) was established to provide an early warning and incident notification mechanism.

2. Phase 2 Mechanism Plan

To follow up on the effectiveness and results of Phase 1 Mechanism Plan, the Executive Yuan approved the Phase 2 Mechanism Plan in 2004, which ran from 2005 to 2008. To respond to changes in the security landscape, the Plan was amended in February 2007.

The Phase 1 Mechanism Plan was instrumental in establishing the overall information security protection capability of Taiwan. In Phase 2, principal policies included the establishment of the responsibility system though the appointment of a Chief Information Security Officer (CISO) and National-Security Operation Center (N-SOC), enhancement of information security audits, improvement in information security responsibility classification and protection of confidential information, and development of information security key indicators, which had a definite impact on the government's ability to improve information security.

The initial push for the establishment of the CISO responsibility system in government agencies began in 2005. Currently at Executive Yuan headquarters, in 35 ministries, and in 24 special municipality and local governments, each deputy head assumes the role of CISO and is responsible for supervising an Information & Communication Security Management Team and implementing information security-related programs. By reinforcing the CISO responsibility system, information security

protection and management responsibility can be enhanced. This not only reflects the importance of information security specialists but also highlights that fact that information security work is valued more than ever these days.

N-SOC not only provides ordinary surveillance and warning services but also incorporates the systems of major government agencies under a protective umbrella. Depending on actual requirements, different monitoring equipment can be deployed, e.g. intrusion detection systems, Domain Name System (DNS) alarm systems, internal network alert systems, and end-user warning systems. In addition to enhancing the incident notification and response function website and performing regular notification drills, information regarding system vulnerabilities, hacker information update and other security-related messages can be disseminated through the information security contact person in a timely manner. This effectively improves timeliness of notifications and execution of continuity plans.

The Audit Working Group of the Taskforce (whose responsibilities were formerly assumed by the Electronic Data Processing Center of DGBAS) began to conduct external audits on information security on an annual basis in 2001 by selecting 20 to 30 or more major government agencies. The Group provides audit recommendations and assists agencies undergoing audit to reinforce information security with respect to integrity and timeliness. Since 2005, the Group has also initiated efforts to encourage competent authorities to conduct internal audits.

Based on an information security responsibility classification scheme devised in 2003, a new categorization system was established in 2006, the applicability of which was expanded to cover the entire education system. The number of government agencies under its jurisdiction increased from 3,713 to 6,797. According to data of the former Central Personnel Administration regarding the number of agencies subordinate to the Executive Yuan and local government agencies, this has expanded coverage

to over 80% of all agencies.

To prevent users' computers from being hacked by malicious programs via email social engineering attacks, the Taskforce conducted e-mail social engineering drills in 2006 and required government agencies of a critical and confidential nature to adopt effective physical isolation and encryption protection measures in order to provide secure and effective protection for confidential information. These agencies now comply with security requirements.

In addition, in order to assess the status of Taiwan's information security development, the Phase 2 Plan began to adopt key indicators for assessment of information security in 2006. By collecting quantitative data, performance in information security awareness, environment, overall protection and emergency response capability can be easily assessed.

3. Phase 3 Development Program

The implementation of the first two phases of the mechanism plan has brought some success in terms of promoting awareness of information security among government agencies and soliciting participation from the private sector. However, the amount of overall information security resources invested is still limited, which is not conducive to in-depth assessment of information security risks and effective control of these risks within acceptable limits. Given the overall situation and the fact that new information security issues will always arise, it is necessary for the government to continue to devise information security programs and implement information security practices. As a result, the Executive Yuan approved a Phase 3 Development Program in January 2009, which would run from 2009 to 2012. In this phase, policy continuity was taken into consideration so that the vision of the "Secure and Trusted Smart Taiwan, Safe and High Quality Digital Life" can be achieved. The ultimate goals are to attain four major policy objectives: "Strengthening overall response capability," "Providing reliable information services," "Fostering enterprise

competitiveness" and "Building an information security culture-centric development environment." In actual implementation, "demand side" and "supply side" were taken into consideration when planning five information security measures (including 20 action plans) that meet government standards, Critical Information Infrastructure (CII) requirements and enterprise needs. In terms of the environment, four measures (including 10 action plans) that help to shape the information security culture were adopted to facilitate relevant legislation, awareness education, collaboration through innovation and assessment indicators.

By implementing the 30 action plans described above, the following benefits were achieved in late 2012: increased investment in information security resources, improved readiness in information security regulations, enhanced national information security awareness, strengthened overall information security protection capability, increased frequency of information security drills, and reduced severity in information security incidents. Measures implemented in government agencies have been gradually made available to the private sector and enterprises.

III. CURRENT STATUS OF INFORMATION SECURITY INDUSTRY

1. Size of global information security market

The global information security market can be broken down into three areas: software, hardware and services. The software sector grew from US$12.7 billion in total revenue in 2010 to US$18.3 billion in 2014, with a compound annual growth rate (CAGR) of 9.6%. The hardware sector increased from US$7.7 billion in 2010 to US$12 billion in 2014, which represents a CAGR of 11.7%. The services sector grew from US$24.9 billion in 2010 to US$ 41 billion in 2014, a CAGR of 13.3%. The overall global information security market increased from US$45.3 billion in 2010 to US$71.3 billion in 2014, which represents a CAGR of 12.0% (refer to Figure 4).

Figure 4. Size of global information security market, 2010-2014

Overall the information security market exhibits a trend of growth. The main factors driving growth include the ongoing effects of global regulations, increasing level of threats to the environment (new attack types, such as APT), new security vulnerabilities resulting from the integration of smart mobile devices and enterprise systems, and security issues arising from virtualization of cloud computing (e.g. data transmission security, authentication and access control, and audit issues). In particular, regulations and environmental threats remain the main driving factors since the former involves issues of compensation, and the latter is concerned with the fact that enterprises struggle to easily combat threats, especially since comprehensive solutions are not yet available on the market.

In addition, smart mobile devices have resulted in an entire set of security requirements, which has caused the global smartphone information security market to grow from US$400 million in 2010 to US$1.9 billion in 2015, CAGR of 36.6% (see Figure 5).

Figure 5. Global information security market for smartphones, 2010-2014

2. Size of Taiwan's Information Security Market

The information security market in Taiwan includes domestic players and international vendors. Revenue of Taiwanese vendors is expected to grow from NT$6.2 billion in 2010 to NT$12.7 billion in 2014, with a CAGR of 19.6%. Revenue of international vendors is expected to grow from NT$12.3 billion in 2010 to NT$19 billion in 2014, with a CAGR of 11.6%. The overall information security market in Taiwan will grow from NT$21.1 billion in 2011 to NT$36.3 billion in 2015, which represents a CAGR of 14.6% (see Figure 6 for details).

Note: in NT$ billion Source: MIC, February 2013

Figure 6. Size of Taiwan's information security market, 2011-2015

In response to the rapidly changing social environment and for the purpose of enhancing the protection of personal data, the Personal Information Protection Act expanded the scope of the law from protecting personal data stored and processed by computers to include all personal information. In addition, the Act now allows mechanisms such as class actions to be filed in order to increase the amount of compensatory damages and the severity of criminal liability. More importantly, the industries to which the Act is applicable have increased from the original governmental agencies and eight major industries to include all governmental and non-governmental organizations as well as individuals. The Act came into effect on October 1, 2012, and has subsequently driven the growth of Taiwan's information security market.

With the surge in popularity of smart mobile devices in recent years, the use of mobile devices by company employees to access corporate data or conduct financial transactions has become increasingly widespread. The corporate information security defense perimeter has in turn expanded due to the ensuing increased threats (e.g. personal information leakage, Internet fraud and social engineering) (refer to Figure 7). In the domestic market, although the percentage of corporations in Taiwan that have implemented mobile security was 13.0% in 2011, the proportion of companies with this particular security requirement will be 26.1% within the next three years. Thus demand for mobile security in Taiwan over the next three years is expected to grow.

Figure 7. Implementation status and future mobile security requirements of Taiwanese enterprises, 2011

In addition, with respect to the demand for cloud security in Taiwan, although the cloud computing industry remains in a growth phase, corporate demand and adoption of cloud security products and services have increased over the past three years. Furthermore, there will be changes in the processes and locations associated with cloud-based applications adopted in the past (mostly in-house data storage, transmission, utilization and management). This will affect corporations' data security considerations in every aspect, and the proportion of companies adopting cloud-based information security products and services will clearly rise.

IV. ANALYSIS OF STRENGTHS AND WEAKNESSES OF INFORMATION SECURITY DEVELOPMENT

After three implementation phases of the Mechanism Plan or Development Program and with extensive joint efforts of both

government and citizens, substantial progress in Taiwan's overall information security environment has been made. However, there is much room for improvement before the vision of "Building a secure information security environment and becoming a high quality network society" can be achieved. Given the current situation, the following strengths and weaknesses in the internal environment as well as opportunities and threats in the external environment, as shown in Table 1, should be considered.

Table 1. SWOT analysis of Taiwan's overall information security environment

Strengths (S)	Weaknesses (W)
1. Information and communication technology (ICT) industry in Taiwan is well developed with skilled ICT professionals and experts.	1. Users have not complied with information security standards in terms of usage behavior; room for improvement in terms of awareness and alertness.
2. Access to highly skilled human resources; innovative and highly adaptable to new technologies.	2. Information security regulations not comprehensive enough; further legislative efforts required.
3. The Office of Information and Communication Security has been established under the Executive Yuan to conduct overall planning of government's information security responsibilities.	3. Information security organizations, manpower and budget have yet to be incorporated into legal framework.
4. The Office of National Information and Communication Security has been established under the National Security	

Council to coordinate work associated with the country's information and communication security.

4. Information security governance has been in place for four years, yet effectiveness requires further improvement.

5. Many security vulnerabilities exist in computer applications; information security incidents abound; attacks from hackers are difficult to repel.

6. Demarcation of responsibilities in government's information security duties not clearly defined.

7. Key information security technologies are controlled by more advanced countries and cannot be easily accessed or duplicated.

8. Conditions for developing information security industry are unfavorable.

9. International cooperation in the area of information security is limited.

10. Cloud-related regulatory and legal environment as well as technical capabilities incomplete.

11. Information security defense capability far inferior to that of organized hackers.

Opportunities (O)

1. The government continues to develop ICT applications, optimize public information frameworks and enhance overall information security by taking advantage of the Executive Yuan's organizational restructuring.

Threats (T)

1. Performance evaluation and audits are not easy to conduct, and benefits of these are often overlooked, resulting in inadequate investment in information security resources.

2. Preservation of digital forensic

2. Issues associated with protection of privacy and intellectual property are now given proper attention; the Personal Information Protection Act has also come into effect.

3. Global information security market has grown as information security incidents proliferate and relevant legislation comes into effect.

4. Transformation of the Information and Communication Security Taskforce's Technical Services Center will bring opportunities to the information security industry.

5. In the international community, countries strive to strengthen their international position and influence and seek opportunities for information security cooperation.

evidence is not an easy task; forensic capability is inadequate.

3. The Internet has become an instrument of crime, a location of criminal activity as well as a target of crime.

4. Information security analysis and sharing mechanisms have not been adequately established.

5. Advanced nations have invested heavily in the research and development of information security and digital forensic technologies, which have enabled them to retain the lead in these areas and widen gaps with less advanced countries.

6. Due to the unique cross-strait political and economic situation, Taiwan is restricted in its participation in international organizations and activities.

7. Hackers employ increasingly sophisticated techniques and have evolved into organized crime syndicates, meaning information security is under ever more severe threat.

Under current conditions, the development environment of Taiwan's information security industry does not allow for optimism. The advantages that Taiwan currently enjoys, including excellent ICT and general technology professionals, highly skilled manpower and innovative capabilities, will soon diminish as other countries begin to invest in and build up their own talent pool. At the same time, information security protection experiences and information associated with hacker behavior is time-sensitive and should be utilized in a timely and appropriate manner. Therefore, how to regard, handle and take full advantage of current advantages and strengths so that development can proceed in a positive direction is a critical issue.

The government needs to be fully aware of information security issues as well as possible threats and challenges facing at present, so that it can employ forward-thinking and strategic perspectives to analyze and solve issues. Therefore, to establish a vision and strategic objectives for the Program, it is imperative to address issues faced by the information and communication security at present and to develop effective and appropriate response measures. After all, "the mere existence of law without rigorous enforcement is meaningless." What is more important is the earnest implementation of these measures and the continuing review and improvement of them.

CHAPTER 4 VISION, STRATEGIC GOALS AND DEVELOPMENT ROADMAP

I VISION

With information and communication technologies continuing to evolve, providing a secure and reliable Internet environment, creating information security service value, taking advantage of the cloud computing technology, and migrating to virtualization and integration of information security services have become the most important aspects in the move toward a Ubiquitous Network Society. In Taiwan, three implementation phases of the Mechanism Plan or Development Program have been completed, and information security management system has become increasingly robust. Personal information security awareness has also been raised. However, it is critically important to bring together resources and capabilities from industry, government, academic and research sectors to enable the network society to grow in a healthy fashion. The Program has adopted the vision of "Building a secure information security environment and becoming a quality network society" and aims to gradually promote and implement a high-quality network community under the guidance of forward-looking policies and with joint efforts from both the public and private sectors, as well as with the support of Taiwan's combined resources and strengths (see Figure 8).

Figure 8. Vision and strategic objectives

II STRATEGIC GOALS

In order to enhance the international competitiveness in the IT industry, Taiwan is actively involved in the research, development and implementation of information technology. The key initiative of the government's i-Taiwan 12 Projects is "Intelligent Taiwan", the purpose of which is to give all citizens regardless of background access to e-services that are economical, convenient, safe and personalized via a variety of channels. The plan also calls for the construction of high-quality e-services that promote a safe, healthy, convenient and cultured society so that the vision of an "Information Services Island" can be realized. With the promotion of information technology and widespread availability of IT services, Taiwan is now facing the same information security risks and threats that confront other countries highly dependent on information technology infrastructures. As information security incidents become more prevalent, information security issues are of critical importance to the national and economic security. In order to fully implement the Ubiquitous Network Society vision, the following four strategic goals have been proposed:

l Goal 1: Enhance national information security policies and establish a secure information environment.

The rapid development of the Internet has led to a broad range of information security threats, including in the political, economic, social, cultural, technological and military spheres. In Taiwan, the government is now focused on the following areas: establishing a secure and trusted information security environment; protecting individuals, businesses and government agencies from information security threats; safeguarding critical infrastructures; enhancing citizens' confidence; and ensuring economic and national security. In the complex Internet environment, since information and communication security is an all-encompassing endeavor, it is necessary to develop strategies based on factors of legal compliance, external competitive environment changes, asset risk assessment principles, asset value and related information services. Only when Taiwan's information security policy is in a state of continuous improvement, with considerable investment of resources and self-reliance in strengthening of information and communication security protection capabilities, can information security threats be effectively neutralized.

l Goal 2: Improving information security protection management and sharing intelligence.

In order to create a trusted information and communication security environment as well as to safeguard data, equipment and network systems and to protect citizens' rights, the government has implemented a dedicated Government-Information Security Management System (G-ISMS). This system offers assurance on the confidentiality, integrity and availability of information systems of government agencies, as well as creating a government-wide joint-defense mechanism to reduce risks associated with information security incidents to an acceptable level. In addition, the scope of information security surveillance has been expanded by an enhanced Government-Security Operation Center (G-SOC) with integrated second-line monitoring and intelligence gathering and sharing functions, as well as cloud-based information security services. In addition, an automated incident notification system has been implemented through the Government-Information Sharing and

Analysis Center (G-ISAC) platform.

l Goal 3: Building a firm foundation for information security technology capabilities and integrating practical technological applications.

Strengthening collaboration with industry, academic and research sectors on information security research and developing the next generation of comprehensive information security technology solutions are the government's objectives. This includes core technology areas such as information security vulnerability detection, penetration testing, intrusion threats, web application security, firewall applications and incident reporting management. At the same time, with respect to Internet applications, the government aims to conduct research on emerging information security applications and technical specifications; become self-reliant on key technologies associated with cloud computing, virtualization and mobile information security protection; improve Big Data computational capabilities in integrated analysis of information security threats; and carry out practical application of emerging information security technologies.

l Goal 4: Expanding information security talent cultivation and increasing international information security exchanges.

This goal includes expanding cooperation in talent cultivation and expertise in information security research; formulating plans and support packages to attract talent and skills training; developing information security professional competency and associated certification mechanisms; learning from other countries' experiences in personnel training; implementing a specialized learning environment for personnel training and drills; establishing an international cooperation and exchange platform; participating in international information security organizations events; maintaining memberships such as the Asia Pacific Computer Emergency Response Team (APCERT), Anti-Phishing Working Group (APWG), Association of anti-Virus Asia Researchers (AVAR) and Forum of Incident Response and Security Teams (FIRST); keeping abreast of the latest international development trends; and expanding collaboration programs with the following information security

organizations via the G-ISAC platform: Japan Computer Emergency Response Team / Coordination Center (JPCERT/CC), Malaysian Computer Emergency Response Team (MyCERT) and Korea Computer Emergency Response Team / Coordination Center (KrCERT/CC).

III DEVELOPMENT ROADMAP FOR INFORMATION SECURITY STRATEGIES

The Program forms the basis from which Taiwan's information security defense will be implemented over the next four years (from 2013 to 2016), and it will be a value-added hub that serves the government, industry and the general public. Through a macroscopic analysis of information security technology trends, the Program carries out overall planning on information security, and with the investment and implementation of information security protection resources, the competitiveness of the information security industry can be enhanced, which will be a driving force for Taiwan's information security defense and industrial innovation. In the Program each goal has several corresponding implementation strategies, and each implementation strategy corresponds to a number of action plans (see Figure 9).

Figure 9. Implementation strategies and action plans

By promoting information security configurations in information security infrastructures, enhancing second-line monitoring services and intelligence gathering for information security protection management, strengthening information security contingency functions and recovery capabilities and creating a Security Project Management Office (SPMO) mechanism, the Program aims to achieve the following four strategic objectives: (1) Enhancing national information security policies and establishing a secure information environment, (2) Improving information security protection management and sharing diverse intelligence on information security, (3) Building a firm foundation for information security technology capabilities and integrating practical technological applications and (4) Expanding information security talent cultivation and increasing international information security exchanges.

In addition, the essence of the Program may be considered from the three aspects of: demand side, supply side and infrastructure (refer to Figure 10 for more detailed information).

Figure 10. Development roadmap

"Demand side" reflects the endeavors of three principal entities, the government, CIs and enterprises, in achieving the objectives of

enhancing overall response and handling capabilities, providing safe and reliable information security services and raising competitiveness of the information security industry, by implementing the following measures: enhancing information security contingency, processing and recovery capability; promoting information security management systems and audits in government agencies; enhancing information security protection technology and software security management; and training information security professionals and fostering international exchange and cooperation.

With respect to raising competitiveness to improve the country's information security industry, it is also necessary to have the support of the "supply side." By supporting the development environment for the information security services industry, including technology, professional talent and skills as well as joint agreements, the Security Project Management Office (SPMO) mechanism can be utilized to drive service innovation and to increase value-added services of the industry.

Infrastructure involves aspects such as creating comprehensive information security regulations and legislation, strengthening nationwide information security awareness, enhancing government's information security defense, and implementing mobile and cloud-based information security environments, which require the design of corresponding action plans to achieve the goal of "becoming a Ubiquitous Network Society."

CHAPTER 5 IMPORTANT IMPLEMENTATION STRATEGIES AND ACTION PLANS

In order that information security tasks can be carried out smoothly, in the Program a total of 20 implementation strategies and 52 action plans have been designed to address the four strategic goals (refer to Table 2). The demarcation of responsibilities is based on the nature of the action plans, which are assigned to the appropriate ministries or councils of the Executive Yuan and various government agencies.

Table 2 Major implementation strategies and action plans (by specialization/responsibility)

Objectives	Implementation strategies	Action plans	Responsible unit(s)	Co-organizer(s)
Objective 1:	1.1.Developing information	1.1.1. Develop information	Office of Information and	Research, Development and

Enhancing national information security policies and establishing a secure information security environment.	security-related criteria	security policies	Communication Security	Evaluation Commission
		1.1.2.Upgrade information security specifications, guidelines, standards and manuals	Office of Information and Communication Security, Ministry of Economic Affairs	Research, Development and Evaluation Commission
	1.2.Improving information security management regulations	1.2.1.Deliberation on information security management-related regulations	Office of Information and Communication Security	Ministry of Justice, other competent authorities
		1.2.2. Promote personal information security protection mechanisms	Office of Information and Communication Security, Ministry of Economic Affairs	Office of Information Services, Executive Yuan; Ministry of Justice; various agencies
	1.3.Promoting functional information security organizations	1.3.1. Promote reasonable information security human resources and budget	Office of Information and Communication Security	Research, Development and Evaluation Commission, Directorate-General of Personnel Administration, Directorate General of Budget, Accounting and Statistics, various agencies
		1.3.2. Create a Security Project Management	Office of Information and Communication	Office of Science and Technology

Objectives	Implementation strategies	Action plans	Responsible unit(s)	Co-organizer(s)
		Office (SPMO) mechanism	Security	
		1.3.3. Promote transformation of the Security Technology Center into an administrative institution	Office of Information and Communication Security	Directorate-General of Personnel Administration
	1.4.Constructing information security key indicators	1.4.1. Develop overall information security protection indicators	Office of Information and Communication Security	National Security Council, National Security Bureau, Ministry of National Defense
		1.4.2. Research information security warning levels and indicators	Office of Information and Communication Security	National Security Council, National Security Bureau, Ministry of National Defense
	1.5.Raising capacity of the information security industry	1.5.1. Foster the growth of value-added services in information security	Ministry of Economic Affairs, National Communications Commission	Office of Science and Technology
		1.5.2. Promote an information security jump-start program for key industries	Ministry of Economic Affairs	
Objective 2: Achieving comprehensive information security	2.1. Continuing to promote information security governance and its classification	2.1.1. Promote the establishment of an information security governance framework	Office of Information and Communication Security, various agencies	

protection management and sharing of related intelligence.	and categorization			
		2.1.2. Implement classification and categorization as well as protection regulations for information systems	Office of Information and Communication Security, other competent authorities	
	2.2.Improving the information security defense network	2.2.1. Strengthen the depth of information security protection	Office of Information and Communication Security, various agencies	National Security Bureau
		2.2.2. Expand joint information security defense domestically and internationally	Office of Information and Communication Security	Ministry of Foreign Affairs, Ministry of National Defense, various agencies
		2.2.3. Strengthen information security emergency response, handling and recovery capabilities	Office of Information and Communication Security, various agencies	
		2.2.4. Establish information security baseline protection for critical information infrastructures	Office of Information and Communication Security	Office of Homeland Security, various agencies
		2.2.5. Enhance Internet content safety management mechanisms	National Communications Commission	Ministry of the Interior, Ministry of Education, Ministry of Economic Affairs, Ministry of Culture , Ministry of Health and Welfare, Office

				of Information and Communication Security
		2.2.6. Implement information security offensive/defensive drills	Office of Information and Communication Security	Office of Homeland Security
	2.3.Implementing information security	2.3.1. Promote government information security management systems	Office of Information and Communication Security	Various agencies

Objectives	Implementation strategies	Action plans	Responsible unit(s)	Co-organizer(s)
	management and audit systems	2.3.2. Promote secure information security infrastructure configuration	Office of Information and Communication Security	Various agencies
		2.3.3. Implement information security audits	Various agencies, Office of Information and Communication Security	National Security Bureau; Office of Information Services, Executive Yuan
		2.3.4. Implement information security analysis operations	Office of Information and Communication Security, various agencies	
	2.4 Obtaining complete information security threat scenarios	2.4.1. Strengthen second-line monitoring mechanisms	Office of Information and Communication Security	Various agencies
		2.4.2. Develop Big Data analysis capabilities	Office of Information and Communication Security	
	2.5.Gathering and sharing	2.5.1. Enhance information	Office of Information and	Various agencies

	intelligence	sharing and analysis	Communication Security	
		2.5.2. Enhance intelligence gathering on information security threats	Office of Information and Communication Security	Various agencies
		2.5.3. Gather and disseminate essential information security intelligence	Office of Information and Communication Security	Various agencies
Objective 3: Building a firm foundation for information security technology capabilities and integrating practical technological applications.	3.1.Mastering self-reliant information security defense technology	3.1.1. Develop research capabilities in information security protection technology	National Science Council, Ministry of Economic Affairs, Ministry of National Defense	Office of Information and Communication Security
		3.1.2. Promote integrated information security protection technology applications	Ministry of Economic Affairs, Office of Information and Communication Security	National Security Bureau
	3.2.Enhancing cybercrime investigation capabilities	3.2.1. Strengthen cybercrime investigation technology applications	Ministry of the Interior, Ministry of Justice	Office of Information and Communication Security
		3.2.2. Construct an integrated cybercrime investigation "knowledge base"	Ministry of the Interior, Ministry of Justice	Office of Information and Communication Security

Objectives	Implementation strategies	Action plans	Responsible unit(s)	Co-organizer(s)
	3.3.Developing preservation and identification capabilities in digital forensic evidence	3.3.1. Improve procedures for preservation of digital forensic evidence	Ministry of Justice, Ministry of the Interior	Office of Information and Communication Security
		3.3.2. Develop a verification system for digital forensics laboratories	Ministry of Justice, Ministry of the Interior	Office of Information and Communication Security
	3.4. Enhancing software security management	3.4.1. Create national software asset control mechanisms	Office of Information and Communication Security	Various agencies
		3.4.2. Promote the Security Software Development Life Cycle (SSDLC)	Office of Information and Communication Security	Office of Science and Technology, various agencies
	3.5. Developing government mobile security mechanisms	3.5.1. Develop government security detection mechanisms for mobile apps	Office of Information and Communication Security	Research, Development and Evaluation Commission
		3.5.2. Plan government mobile security and protection mechanisms	Office of Information and Communication Security	Research, Development and Evaluation Commission
		3.5.3. Upgrade security measures for government wireless networks	Office of Information and Communication Security	Research, Development and Evaluation Commission
Objective 4: Expanding information security talent	4.1. Boosting information security awareness nationwide	4.1.1. Organize information security promotional activities	Ministry of Education, Office of Information and Communication	Various agencies

cultivation and improving international information security exchanges.			Security	
		4.1.2. Promote nationwide information security awareness and personal information protection	Office of Information and Communication Security	Various agencies
	4.2. Developing professional talent in information security	4.2.1. Develop information security seed instructors and professional talent	Office of Information and Communication Security, Ministry of Education, Ministry of the Interior, Ministry of Justice	
		4.2.2.Promote information security professional training and certification mechanisms	Office of Information and Communication Security	Ministry of Education
	4.3. Developing diverse learning channels for information security	4.3.1. Incorporate information security into curricula or programs at all educational levels	Ministry of Education	Office of Information and Communication Security
		4.3.2.Plan diverse learning channels for information security	Ministry of Education, Office of Information and Communication Security	
	4.4. Promoting information security competency training and	4.4.1.Plan and determine information security knowledge and	Office of Information and Communication Security	

Objectives	Implementation strategies	Action plans	Responsible unit(s)	Co-organizer(s)
	assessment for government employees	skills required for each job function		
		4.4.2.Establish standards for developing and assessing job competency training courses	Office of Information and Communication Security	
		4.4.3.Develop digital and physical course materials for information security competency	Office of Information and Communication Security	
		4.4.4.Establish an information security competency evaluation system	Office of Information and Communication Security	
	4.5. Enhancing domestic and	4.5.1.Participate in conferences and events organized by domestic	Office of Information and Communication	Ministry of Foreign Affairs
	international exchanges and cooperation in information security	and international information security organizations	Security	
		4.5.2.Participate in international events related to cybercrime investigation and prevention	Ministry of Justice, Ministry of the Interior	Office of Information and Communication Security
		4.5.3.Boost international publication of academic information security research	National Science Council	Office of Information and Communication Security, Ministry of Education

CHAPTER 6 PROMOTION ORGANIZATION, RESOURCE REQUIREMENTS AND PROGRAM MANAGEMENT

I ORGANIZATION RESPONSIBLE FOR PROGRAM PROMOTION

Pursuant to the Guidelines for Establishing the National Information and Communication Security Taskforce of the Executive Yuan, the Office of Information and Communication Security of the Executive Yuan is charged with the responsibility of overall planning and advancement of information security-related policies, and will therefore be responsible for the general planning and promotion of the Program.

II PLANNING AND EXECUTION

With respect to key implementing specifications and performance indicators of the action plans described in the Program, an annual plan containing detailed execution and planning will be developed by each responsible agency based on the review procedures and regulations of the government's administrative plan.

III BUDGET SOURCE AND IMPLEMENTATION

Budget sources for annual plans proposed by the responsible authorities are determined and allocated by the corresponding agencies or obtained through relevant administrative procedures. Execution of annual plans should be reviewed each year, and necessary amendments should be carried out in coordination with budget reviews and comprehensive evaluations.

IV EVALUATION OF RELEVANT ACTION PLANS

Key implementation specifications and performance indicators of the Program are under the evaluation of the Office of Information and Communication Security, Executive Yuan, in accordance with established supervisory mechanisms.

V APPROVAL AND AMENDMENT OF THE PROGRAM

A The Program shall become effective upon approval of the Executive Yuan; the same shall apply to all amendments.

B The Program should undergo comprehensive review and revision prior to completion of its 4-year implementation period in order to determine future versions of the Program (i.e. for the following 4-year period). If necessary an annual rolling review of the Program and related promotional plans may also be conducted.

IMPORTANT LAWS AND REGULATIONS

ELECTRONIC SIGNATURES ACT

COMPUTER-PROCESSED PERSONAL DATA PROTECTION LAW

CHAPTER I GENERAL PROVISIONS

Article 1 This Law is enacted to govern the processing of personal data by computers so as to prevent infringement upon personal rights, and to facilitate the proper utilization of personal data.

Article 2 The protection of personal data shall be governed by the provisions of this Law, or governed by other laws if so provided in such other laws.

Article 3 The terms used herein denote the following meanings:1.Personal data: the name, date of birth, I.D. Card number, characteristic, fingerprints, marital, family, educational, occupational, and health status, medical history, financial conditions, social activities of a natural person and other data which can serve to identify said specific person;2.Personal data file: gathering of personal data through storage at magnetic storage or at other similar media for certain specific purpose;3.Computer processing: to use computers or automatic machinery to key in, store, compile, correct, search, delete, output, or transmit data or process otherwise;4.Collection: to collect personal data for the establishment of personal data file;5.Utilization: refers to use of personal data file by government agency or non-government agency kept by it for internal use or for use by a third party other than the principal;6.Government agency: refers to a government agency at the central government or local government level which is empowered to exercise sovereign power;7.Non-government agency: refers to the following enterprises or groups or individuals other than those mentioned above:(1)credit search businesses and groups or individuals whose major line of business is to collect or process personal data by computers;(2)hospitals, schools, telecommunication, financial, securities, insurance, and mass communications industries; and(3)other businesses, groups or individuals designated by the Ministry of Justice in conjunction with the government authority in charge of such industry at the central government level.8.Principal: the individual to which the personal data belongs; and9.Specific purpose: refers to those purposes prescribed by the Ministry of Justice in conjunction with the government authority in charge of the industry at the central government level.

Article 4 The following rights exercisable by the principal with regard to his personal data shall not be waived in advance nor limited by specific agreement:1.any inquiry and request for review of the personal data thereof;2.any request to make copies of the personal data thereof;3.any request to supplement or correct the personal data thereto;4.any request to discontinue processing of personal data by computers or utilization of personal data thereof; and5.any request for deletion of personal data therefrom.

Article 5 Where a group or an individual is designated by a government agency or non-government agency to process data, the group or individual so designated to process data shall be considered part of the staff of said designating agency within the meaning of this Law.

Article 6 The collection or utilization of personal data shall respect the rights and interests of the principal and such personal data shall be handled in accordance with the principles of honesty and credibility so as not to exceed the scope of the specific purpose.

CHAPTER II DATA PROCESSING BY THE GOVERNMENT AGENCY

Article 7 The government agency shall not collect or process personal data unless it has a certain specific purpose which complies with at least one of the followings:1.it is within the scope of job functions provided by laws and regulations;2.a written consent has been obtained from the principal; and3.there is no possibility that it shall infringe upon the rights and interests of the principal.

Article 8 The government agency shall utilize the personal data in accordance with the scope of its job functions provided by laws and regulations, and in compliance with the specific purpose of collection, provided, however, that it may utilize the personal data other than for the specific purpose upon occurrence of any of the following conditions:1.such utilization is provided for in the laws and regulations;2.such utilization is justifiable and for internal purpose only;3.such utilization shall safeguard the national security;4.such utilization shall improve public interests;5.such utilization shall eliminate any emergency danger which could endanger the principal's life, body, freedom or property;6.such utilization shall prevent the rights and interests of another from being seriously damaged, and there is a need to utilize the same;7.such utilization shall serve academic study purposes and the material interests of the principal will not be adversely affected;8.such utilization shall benefit the rights and interests of the principal; and9.such utilization has the written consent of the principal.

Article 9 The international transmission and utilization of personal data by the government agency shall be handled in accordance with relevant laws and regulations.

Article 10 A government agency which keeps personal data file shall announce the following in a government gazette or by other proper means; the above provisions apply to any amendment thereof:1.name of personal data file;2.name of the government agency keeping the personal data file;3.name of the government agency utilizing the personal data file;4.basis on which the personal data file is kept and the specific purpose for keeping the file;5.classification of personal data;6.scope of personal data;7.means of collecting personal data;8.places where personal data are normally transmitted and recipient of said data; and9.the direct recipient of personal data transmitted through international channel; and10. name and address of government agency accepting applications for inquiries making, correction or review. The classification of personal date referred to in Item 5 above shall be prescribed by the Ministry of Justice with the government authority in charge of the industry at the central government level.

Article 11 The provisions of the preceding article have no application to utilization of the following personal data file:1.where national security, foreign affairs and military secrets, overall economic interests or other major national interests are involved;2.where cases are being reviewed by the grand justice of the Judicial Yuan, or cases are being reviewed by the Government Official Disciplinary Committee, and matters under investigation, trial, judgment, enforcement or handling of non-litigious matters by court;3.where matters relevant to precautionary measures against criminal offenses, criminal investigation, enforcement, correction or protective measures or rehabilitation affairs are involved;4.where matters relevant to administrative punishment and compulsory enforcement thereof are involved;5.where matters relevant to administration of entry/exit of the country, security check or investigation and verification of refugees are involved;6.where matters relevant to collection of taxes and dues are involved;7.where matters relevant to personnel, job duties, salary payment, sanitation, welfare or other relevant issues of a government agency are involved;8.where the personal data file is used for computer processing for experimental purpose;9.where deletion will be made prior to announcement in the government gazette;10. where the name, address, exchange of money and articles of the principal is recorded for the purpose of official contacts;11. where a personal data file is specifically produced by the government official for performance of duties for internal use in said government agency; and12. where laws and regulations specify otherwise.

Article 12 With regard to the personal data files kept by the government agency, the said government agency shall, at the request of the principal, reply to his inquiry, provide files for his review, or make copies of the files for him, provided, however, that the above provisions do not apply to any of the following:1.where the file shall not be made public pursuant to the provisions of the preceding article;2.where the performance of official duties may be interfered with; and3.where the material interests of a third party may be adversely affected.

Article 13 The government agency shall maintain the accuracy of personal data, and shall make corrections or supplements thereto in accordance with its duty or at the request of the principal.In the event there is a dispute about the accuracy of personal data, the government agency shall, pursuant to its duty or at the request of the principal, discontinue the computer processing or utilization thereof, provided, however, that the above provisions do not apply to a situation where the processing or utilization is necessary for performance of an official duty, and the dispute is specifically identified or a written consent is obtained from the principal.In the event the specific purpose for processing the personal data no longer exists or the period for processing has expired, the government agency shall, pursuant to its duty or at the request of the principal, delete or discontinue the processing or utilization of said personal data, provided, however, that the above provisions do not apply to a situation where the processing or utilization thereof is necessary for performance of an official duty, or the use purpose is changed pursuant to the provisions of this Law or a written consent is obtained from the principal.

Article 14 The government agency shall maintain a book to record all the particulars required to be made public pursuant to the provisions of Paragraph 1 of Article 10 hereinabove for review.

Article 15 Where a request is made by the principal to the government agency pursuant to the provisions of this Law, it shall be handled within thirty days. Where said request is not handled within the aforesaid time period, a written notice stating the reason said request was not handled shall be sent to the principal.

Article 16 The government agency may charge a fee to those who make an inquiry or request to review, or make a copy of the personal data.The amount of the fee shall be prescribed by the said government agency.

Article 17 The government agency which keeps personal data files shall, pursuant to relevant laws and regulations, appoint a full time employee to handle matters relevant to the security and maintenance of said files to prevent personal data from being stolen, altered without authorization, damaged, lost or disclosed.

CHAPTER III DATA PROCESSING BY NON-GOVERNMENT AGENCY

Article 18 A non-government agency shall not collect or process by computer any personal data unless it has some specific purpose and it complies with any of the followings:1.where a written consent is obtained from the principal;2.where an agreement or similar contractual relationship is entered into with the principal whereby the rights and interests of the principal shall not be infringed upon;3.where the information is already known to the public and no material adverse effect will be caused to the interests of the principal;4.where there is a need for academic study, and no material adverse effect will be caused to the interests of the principal; and5.the provisions of Article 3, Item 7 Subitem 2 of this Law and other laws and regulations otherwise specify.

Article 19 Any non-government agency which is not registered with the government authority in charge of the industry and does not have a license issued thereto pursuant to the provisions of this Law shall not collect, process by computer, make international transmission or utilize personal data.Credit search industry and groups or individuals whose major line of business is to collect or process by computer personal data shall obtain a special permit from and register with the government authority in charge of the industry for issuance of a license.The registration procedures, qualifications required for applying issuance of a special permit and handling fee referred to in the two preceding paragraphs shall be prescribed by the government authority in charge of the industry at the central government level.

Article 20 Those applying for registration referred to in the preceding article shall submit an application stating thereon the followings:1.name, domicile and residential address of the applicant; if the applicant is a juristic person or a group of non juristic persons, the name, address of the head office and branch office(s), and the name, domicile and residential address of the statutory representative or administrator;2.name of personal data file;3.the specific purpose for keeping the personal data file;4.classification of personal data;5.scope of personal data;6.period for keeping the personal data file;7.method used for collecting personal data;8.scope of utilization of personal data file;9.the recipient who directly receives personal data through international transmission;10. name of the person responsible for maintaining personal data file; and11. security and maintenance plan for personal data file.In the event there is any change to the entries of registration, an application for amendment registration shall be filed within 15 days after said change. In the event of termination of business operations, an application for terminating business operations shall be filed within one month after the cause of business termination occurs.Those applying for termination of business operations shall report their method of handling personal data to the government authority in charge of the industry for approval.The specific purpose referred to in Item 3 of Paragraph 1 and the classification referred to in Item 4 above shall be prescribed by the Ministry of Justice in conjunction with the government authority in charge of the industry at the central government level.

Article 21 After applications for registration filed pursuant to the provisions of the preceding Article are approved, the non-government agency shall list all the particulars referred to in Items 1 to 10 of Paragraph 1 of the preceding Article in the government gazette or by public notice in a local newspaper.

Article 22 The non-government agency shall maintain a book to record all the particulars referred to in Items 1 to 10 of Paragraph 1 of Article 20 for review.

Article 23 The non-government agency shall utilize the personal data within the scope of the specific purpose, provided, however, that it may utilize the personal data otherwise upon occurrence of any of the following:1.such utilization shall improve public interests;2.such utilization shall protect the life, body, freedom or property of the principal from imminent danger;3.such utilization shall prevent the rights and interests of another person from sustaining material adverse effect; and4.such utilization has the written consent of the principal.

Article 24 Where the international transmission or utilization of personal data by a non-government agency meets any one of the following criteria, the government agency in charge of the industry may limit the transmission and utilization thereof:1.where major national interests are involved;2.where national treaty or agreement specifies otherwise;3.where the nation receiving personal data lacks laws which fairly protect the rights and interests of the principal thereby causing injury to the principal; and4.where international transmission and utilization of personal data are made through a circuitous means in order to evade the provisions of this Law.

Article 25 Where the government authority in charge of the industry deems it necessary, it may send officials with identification certificates to any non-government agency which is subject to its jurisdiction and granting of a special permit or approval of registration and order such non-government agency to present relevant information with regard to matters provided by this Law or to take other necessary measures to comply with this Law, or to enter the premises of the non-government agency to conduct an investigation. In the event the investigations show the relevant information is in violation of the provisions of this Law, it may be confiscated.With regard to the above order, investigation, or confiscation by the government authorities, the non-government agency shall not evade, obstruct or refuse.

Article 26 The provisions of Articles 12, 13, 15, 16 Paragraph 1 and 17 shall be applied mutatis mutandis to all non-government agencies.The criteria for the charging of a fee by a non-government agency pursuant to the provisions of Paragraph 1 of Article 16 hereinabove shall be prescribed by the government authority in charge of the industry at the central government level.

CHAPTER IV DAMAGES AND OTHER REMEDY

Article 27 A government agency which infringes upon the rights and interests of the principal and violates any provision of this Law shall be liable for the damages arising therefrom, provided, however, that the above provisions do not apply to damages arising from natural disaster, incident or other force majeure.With regard to damages caused to non-property, the injured party may also request proper monetary compensation. With regard to damages of reputation, the injured party may also request the rehabilitation of his reputation.The total amount of compensation for the damages referred to in the two preceding paragraphs shall not be less than NT$20,000 but not more than NT$100,000 for each case of damages per person, provided, however, that the above provisions do not apply to the situation where the injured party can prove that the damages sustained by it are more than the aforesaid prescribed amount.With regard to damages caused to the principal by the same cause and fact, the total amount of compensation shall not be more than NT$20 million.The right of claim referred to in the second Paragraph above shall not be transferred or inherited, provided, however, that these provisions do not apply to the situation where the monetary compensation is undertaken in an agreement or is claimed in a legal action.

Article 28 A non-government agency which infringes upon the rights and interests of a principal as a result of its violation of this Law shall be liable for the damages arising therefrom, provided, however, that these provisions do not apply to the situation where the non-government agency can prove that the damages are not caused by its willful conduct or negligence.The provisions of Paragraphs 2 to 5 of the preceding Article are applicable to claims for damages made in accordance with the provisions of the preceding Paragraph.

Article 29 The right to claim damages is subject to a statute of limitation of two years calculated from the time the claimant has knowledge of the damages and the identity of the party liable for the damage arising therefrom or five years calculated from the date the damaged actually occurs.

Article 30 With regard to compensation for damages, apart from complying with the provisions of this Law, the government agency shall comply with the provisions of the State Compensation Law, while the non-government agency shall comply with the provisions of the Civil Code.

Article 31 Where a principal exercises his right prescribed in Article 4 hereinabove against a government agency, but the government agency refuses or fails to handle his case within the time period specified in Article 15 hereinabove, the principal may, within twenty days after refusal or upon expiry of the specified time period, file a written application with the supervising government agency requesting proper handling.The supervising government agency shall, within two months after accepting said application, notify the principal in writing of the results of his application.

Article 32 Where a principal exercises his right prescribed in Article 4 hereinabove against a non-government agency, but the non-government agency refuses to handle his case, the principal may, within twenty days after refusal or upon expiry of the specified time period, file a written application with the government authority in charge of the industry requesting proper handling of his case.The said government authority in charge of the industry shall, within two months after accepting said application, notify the principal of the results of his application. If the application is considered reasonable, the government authority in charge of the industry shall order the non-government agency to make corrections within the specified time period.

CHAPTER V PENALTIES

Article 33 A person who intends to make profits for himself by violating the provisions of Articles 7, 8, 18, 19 Paragraphs 1 & 2, and 23 hereinabove or the injunction order make in accordance with Article 24 hereinabove and cause injury to another shall be punished with an imprisonment of less than two years, detention or, in lieu thereof or in additional thereto, a criminal fine of less than NT$40,000.

Article 34 A person who intends to make unlawful gains for himself or for a third party or intends to infringe upon the interests of another by illegally outputting, interfering, changing, deleting personal data file or by other illegal means to impede the accuracy of personal data file thus causing damages to another shall be punished with an imprisonment for less than three years, or detention, or a fine of less than NT$50,000.

Article 35 A government official who takes advantage of his position, or opportunity or means available to him to commit the offenses prescribed in the two preceding articles shall be subject to punishments half as severe as those enumerated above.

Article 36 The offenses referred to in this Chapter may be instituted only upon complaint.

Article 37 In the event a more severe punishment is provided for in other laws with respect to the offenses outlined in this Chapter, the more severe punishment shall apply.

Article 38 Upon occurrence of any of the following, the government authority in charge of the industry shall impose an administrative fine of not less than NT$20,000 but not more than NT$100,000 on the responsible person, and order the said responsible person to take corrective measures within a specified time period. In the event the responsible person fails to take corrective measures within the specified time period after having been ordered to do so, the government authority in charge of the industry may continue to impose a fine each time a violation of any of the following occurs:1.a violation of the provisions of Article 18 hereinabove;2.a violation of the provisions of Article 19 Paragraph 1 or Paragraph 2 hereinabove;3.a violation of the provisions of Article 23 hereinabove; and4.a violation of the injunction order imposed in accordance with the provisions of Article 24 hereinabove.In the event the degree of violations referred to in Item 1, 3 or 4 above is serious, an order to revoke the special permit or registration granted in accordance with this Law may be issued.

Article 39 Upon occurrence of any of the following, the government authority in charge of the industry may order the responsible person to take corrective measures within a specified time period. If corrective measures are not taken within the specified time period, an administrative fine of not less than NT$10,000 but not more than NT$50,000 may be imposed upon the responsible person each time a violation of any of the following occurs:1. A violation of the provisions of Article 20 Paragraph 2 hereinabove;2. A failure to place an announcement in the local newspaper which would cause a violation of the provisions of Article 21 hereinabove;3. A violation of the provisions of Article 22 hereinabove;4. A violation of the provisions of Article 12, 13, 15 and 17 in accordance with the provisions of Article 26 Paragraph 1 hereinabove; and5. A violation of the criteria for fee charge provided for under Article 26 Paragraph 2 hereinabove.In case the degree of violations referred to in Items 1, 2, 3, or 4 of the preceding Paragraph is serious, an order to revoke the special permit or registration granted in accordance with this Law may be issued.

Article 40 Upon occurrence of any of the following, the government authority in charge of the industry may impose an administrative fine of not less than NT$10,000 but not more than NT$50,000 on the responsible person each time a violation of any of the following occurs:1.a failure to handle personal data pursuant to the means approved by the government authority in charge of the industry in accordance with Article 20 Paragraph 3 hereinabove;2.a violation of the provisions of Article 25 Paragraph 2 hereinabove; and3.a failure to comply with an order to take corrective measures issued in accordance with Article 32 Paragraph 2 hereinabove.In the case the degree of violation referred to in Item 2 or 3 of the preceding Paragraph is serious, an order to revoke the special permit or registration granted in accordance with this Law may be issued.

Article 41 Failure to pay administrative fines imposed according to this Law shall cause the case to be referred to court for compulsory execution if fines are still not paid within the specified time period even upon due notice.

CHAPTER VI SUPPLEMENTARY PROVISIONS

Article 42 The Ministry of Justice shall be responsible for coordinating and contacting matters relevant to the enforcement of this Law. Rules governing said coordination and contact shall be prescribed by the Ministry of Justice.With regard to matters which are prescribed to be handled by the government authority in charge of the industry, if there is no such government authority in charge of the industry to handled the same, they shall be handled by the Ministry of Justice.The administration governing the collection, computer processing, utilization of personal data, and registration, public announcement or other matters by non-government agency may be handled by public interests group designated by the Ministry of Justice or the government authority in charge of the industry when deemed necessary.

Article 43 Those who are already engaged in the collection or computer processing of personal data before promulgation and enforcement of this Law and are required to process registration or special permit pursuant to the provisions of this Law shall process the same within one year after enforcement of this Law.Enterprises, groups or individuals designated by the Ministry of Justice in conjunction with the government authority in charge of the industry pursuant to the provisions of Article 3 Item 7 Sub-item 3 shall process registration or special permit within six months after designation.Those who fail to process registration prescribed in the two preceding paragraphs or those whose applications are disapproved shall be considered as un-registered or without a special permit and shall be punished accordingly.

Article 44 The enforcement rules of this Law shall be prescribed by the Ministry of Justice.

Article 45 This Law shall become effective upon promulgation.

TELECOMMUNICATIONS ACT

CHAPTER I GENERAL PROVISIONS

Article 1 This Act is enacted to ensure the sound development of telecommunications, promote the public welfare, safeguard the security of communications and protect the rights and interests of users. Matters not provided herein shall be subject to the provisions of other applicable laws.

Article 2 For the purpose of this Act, the terms adopted herein are defined as follows:1. "Telecommunications" means convey, transmission or reception of signs, signals, writing, pictures, sounds or messages of any other nature in a wire or wireless manner through the use of optical, electromagnetic systems, or other scientific products;2. "Telecommunications facilities" means the machinery, apparatus, lines and other related equipment used for telecommunications;3. "Conduit Infrastructure" means the ducts, man holes, hand holes, towers, poles, main distribution frame, telecommunication equipment room and other auxiliary or related facilities required for installation of telecommunications lines, lead-in lines, telecommunication subscribers lines, and various transmission lines and circuits, whether over-pass, underground or submerged, necessary for establishment of a telecommunications network;4. "Telecommunications service" means communication services provided via telecommunications facilities;5. "Telecommunications enterprise" means an enterprise operating telecommunications services for public use;6. "Dedicated telecommunications" means the telecommunications established by public or private institutions, organizations, or nationals for their exclusive use; and7. "Government telecommunications" means the telecommunications established by a government agency for its exclusive use.8. "Communication record" means all information generated by a telecommunications system concerning use of a telecommunications service, including calling and called party's telecommunication numbers, communication dates, beginning and ending times of communications. Such records shall be provided to the extent that the technology of the telecommunications equipment and system allows. Telecommunication numbers are defined in this paragraph as telephone numbers or user identification codes.

Article 3 The competent authority for telecommunications enterprises shall be the Ministry of Transportation and Communications (hereinafter referred to as the "MOTC").The MOTC, for the purpose of supervising and guiding telecommunications enterprises, and regulating telecommunications, shall establish a Directorate General of Telecommunications (hereinafter referred to as the "DGT"). The organization of the DGT shall be governed by a separate law.In order to enhance public welfare, the aforementioned DGT shall devise an integrated telecommunications development plan, supervise telecommunications enterprises, and promote the development of an information society.

Article 4 No assets or facilities of a telecommunications enterprise shall be inspected, expropriated or seized unless the law provides otherwise.

Article 5 Local governments as well as military, military police, and police authorities, including the officers thereof, shall be responsible for safeguarding telecommunications facilities. If a telecommunications enterprise is in danger of being infringed upon, the above authorities and the officers thereof shall take prompt preventive or recovery measures upon the request of the enterprise or its employees.

Article 6 Communications processed through telecommunications enterprises or dedicated telecommunications shall not be accessed or taped without authorization, nor shall the privacy thereof be violated through other illegal means.A telecommunications enterprise shall implement appropriate and necessary measures to safeguard the confidentiality of its processed communications.

Article 7 A telecommunications enterprise or its employees, including the retired, shall hold the existence and contents of communications in strict confidence.The preceding paragraph is not applicable to inquiries conducted in accordance with law. The DGT shall promulgate rules governing operational procedures for telecommunications enterprises to handle inquiries for communications records and users' data by relevant institutions.Each telecommunications enterprise shall supply the relevant communications records to any subscriber who requests his own communications records, after paying necessary charges, to the extent that the technology of the telecommunications equipment and system allows. The above is not constrained by Paragraph 1. The DGT shall promulgate governing operational regulations for subscribers of the telecommunications enterprise who wish to request copies of their own communications records.

Article 8 A telecommunications user shall be held responsible for the contents of its telecommunications, and any consequent effect and/or influence.A telecommunications enterprise may terminate the use of telecommunications by a user, whose business is providing telecommunications contents to the detriment of public order and good morals.In case of any unsightly advertisement set up, posted or painted at will, which contains, for the purposes of advertising and propaganda, one or the other's telephone number or any other identification signs or numbers of telecommunications services, the competent authority governing such advertisement may inform the telecommunications enterprise to terminate the provision of the telecommunications service indicated in that advertisement.

Article 9 For a telecommunications enterprise, the use of telecommunications by a person without legal capacity or with limited legal capacity shall be deemed as an act performed by a person with legal capacity. Other acts resulting from use of telecommunications shall not be so construed.

Article 10 For the purpose of promoting the development of telecommunications enterprises, the competent authority may, in consultation with the Ministry of Education, establish telecommunications schools, or additional relevant departments and/ or graduate schools, in senior high or vocational schools, colleges and universities so as to develop telecommunications specialists; and may request a telecommunications enterprise to allocate a proportionate amount of its turnover for research and development.

CHAPTER II OPERATION OF TELECOMMUNICATIONS ENTERPRISES

Article 11 Telecommunications enterprises are classified into Type I telecommunications enterprises and Type II telecommunications enterprises.A Type I telecommunications enterprise means an enterprise that installs telecommunications line facilities and equipment in order to provide telecommunications services.The aforementioned telecommunications line facilities and equipment refer to network transmission facilities connecting the sending and receiving terminals, the switching facilities installed to be integrated with the network transmission facilities, and the auxiliary facilities of both.A Type II telecommunications enterprise means a telecommunications enterprise other than Type I telecommunications enterprises.

Article 12 A Type I telecommunications enterprise may not operate without franchise and license issued by the MOTC.A Type I telecommunications enterprise shall be a company limited by shares incorporated pursuant to the Company Law.The chairman of the Board, of a Type I telecommunications enterprise shall be a nationals of the Republic of China. The total direct shareholding by foreigners may not exceed forty-nine percent, and the sum of direct and indirect shareholding by foreigners may not exceed sixty percent.The percentage of indirect shareholding by foreigners mentioned in the preceding paragraph shall be calculated by multiplying the percentage of shareholding by domestic juristic persons in the Type I telecommunication enterprise by the percentage of shareholding or capital paid by foreigners in the said domestic juristic persons.The percentage of shareholding by foreigners in Chunghwa Telecom Co., Ltd. shall be separately prescribed by the MOTC, and the provision in paragraph three shall not be applied hereto.The operating items and scope, the timetable for deregulation, and the number of operators to be allowed for Type I telecommunications enterprises shall be announced by the Executive Yuan.With respect to granting franchise to Type I telecommunications enterprises' service provisions, the MOTC may adopt a system of evaluation and examination, open tender or any other appropriate method, in consideration of the objectives of liberalization policy, conditions of the telecommunications market, consumers' rights, and other needs of public interests.In the process of privatization of Chunghwa Telecom Co., Ltd., the authority-in-charge for the enterprise may order the said company to issue special shares, which are to be subscribed at a face value thereof by the authority-in-charge, who is entitled to exercise, within three years after the date of issuance, the rights prescribed in paragraph 9 of this Article and the rights of being guaranteed directors and supervisors.If Chunghwa Telecom Co., Ltd. intends to engage in any of the following acts, it shall beforehand obtain the consent from the shareholders of special shares:1. change of the name of the company;2. change of the company's operating business; or3. assignment of the whole or the main part of the business or properties.Any act violating the aforementioned provisions shall be invalid.The special shares issued according to paragraph 8 of this Article may not be assigned. But upon expiration of the period prescribed in paragraph 8, the special shares shall be nullified by the said enterprise after being purchased back at face value.

Article 13 An applicant for operation of Type I telecommunications enterprise shall apply with the MOTC for establishment of its operation by submission of an application, business proposal and other specified documents.The aforementioned business proposal shall specify the following:1. operating items.2. service areas.3. mode of communication.4. general description of telecommunications facilities.5. financial structure.6. technical capability and development plan.7. tariff schedule and formula.8. personnel structure.9. scheduled date of operation.If the mode of communication under subparagraph 3 of the preceding paragraph is wireless communication, a detailed plan of radio spectrum allocation shall be included.If the documentation submitted by the applicant under paragraph 1 of this Article is incomplete, or if the information contained therein is inadequate, the MOTC shall notify the applicant to make up the documentation or information as required at a prescribed time frame. If the required documentation is not provided within the prescribed time frame, or the documentation remains incomplete after the required documentation is made up, the application shall be rejected.

Article 14 Once an application for the operation of a Type I telecommunications enterprise has been reviewed and approved or awarded the bid, the MOTC shall issue an establishment permit for the establishment to such an enterprise.The MOTC may order the applicant to pay a performance bond as required before issuing the establishment permit. For those applicants who fail to establish operations as required by regulations or fail to complete the operation establishments in accordance with the approved plan, the MOTC will not refund the performance bond or part thereof, and may annul the establishment permit as well.An applicant who has obtained a establishment permit in accordance with paragraph 1 of this Article shall complete the establishment of its operation in the designated region within the prescribed time frame, and proceed with company registration as required by law. If the applicant is unable to complete incorporation and company registration within the prescribed time frame, it may file with the MOTC a petition for extension of the said time frame, together with reasons, before the expiry thereof.An applicant, who has completed the aforementioned establishment in accordance with the provisions of preceding paragraph, may file with the MOTC an application for technical inspection of the said establishment. After passing the inspection, the applicant will be granted a franchise license for Type I telecommunications enterprise.A Type I telecommunications enterprise shall start its operations within 6 months from the date the license is issued; otherwise, the license shall be annulled.The MOTC shall prescribe, for the Type I telecommunications enterprise, the rules governing the operating items, service areas, technical specifications and inspection items, terms and conditions for granting a franchise, requirements and procedures, the term of validity of a franchise, establishment of the enterprise, method of payment and conditions of refund of a performance bond, and the matters in relation to the supervising and managing the said enterprise, and other compulsory rules.The enactment of rules within the permitted scope of business referred to in the preceding paragraph shall comply with International Telecommunications Union standards and adhere to the principle of technological neutrality, not compel Type I telecommunication enterprises to use a particular technology, and maintain the same degree of regulation on the provision of the same services.

Article 15 Without prior approval from the MOTC, a Type I telecommunications enterprise may not:1. suspend or terminate operations in whole or in part;2. transfer the whole or substantial parts of the enterprise or its assets; or3. engage in interlocking investment or merger with any other Type I telecommunications enterprise.

Article 16 Request for network interconnection between or among Type I telecommunications enterprises shall not be rejected, unless the law specifies otherwise.The arrangement of network interconnection mentioned in the preceding paragraph shall follow the principles of transparency, reasonableness, non-discrimination, network unbundling and cost-based pricing. The DGT shall designate the telecommunications enterprises to which the said principles shall apply.Among Type I telecommunications enterprises, an agreement shall be reached within three months from the date one party requested for network interconnection. If the agreement can not be reached within three months, the DGT shall arbitrate the matter upon receipt of request therefor or by its official authority.Among Type I telecommunications enterprises, if the agreement cannot be reached within three months from the date of one party's request for amendment or renewal of a network interconnection agreement, the DGT may arbitrate the matter upon receipt of request therefor.In the event Type I telecommunication enterprises do not carry out network interconnection as agreed which failure is within the scope of those mandatory terms required by law to be included in interconnection agreements, the DGT may arbitrate the matter upon the receipt of request therefor.One who does not agree with DGT's arbitration described in the preceding three paragraph may request for relief in accordance with the administrative procedure.Type I telecommunications enterprises shall not reject the request for network interconnection by Type II telecommunication enterprises without due cause, unless the law specifies otherwise. The preceding paragraph 3 and 6 shall apply, mutatis mutandis, to the agreement of network interconnection.The Type II enterprises to which the preceding paragraph shall apply shall be announced by the DGT.The DGT shall enact governing rules with respect to network interconnection, tariff calculation, negotiation, mandatory terms within interconnection agreements, arbitration procedures , and matters requiring compliance related thereto, between or among Type I telecommunications enterprises and other telecommunications enterprises.The DGT may disclose a part or the whole of the interconnection agreement between or among Type I telecommunications enterprises which are Dominant Market Players and other telecommunications enterprises. Upon request, the DGT may elect not to disclose such portions of the agreement related to patent or other intellectual property rights.This Article shall apply to applicants who have obtained an Establishment Approval in accordance with paragraph 1 of Article 14.

Article 17 A Type II telecommunications enterprise shall apply to the DGT for an operation license, and may only commence its operation when the enterprise completes its company or business registration in accordance with the laws and receives the operation license.The MOTC shall enact governing rules on business items, technical specifications and inspection items of Type II telecommunications enterprise; the licensing method, conditions and procedures; the term of validity of a franchise license, supervision and administration of business operation, and other compulsory matters.

Article 18 A Type II telecommunications enterprise shall apply to DGT for an operation license by submitting an application, a business proposal and other specified documentation.The application under the preceding paragraph shall specify the following:1. applicant's name and domicile; or, in case of a juristic person, name of the representative and the principal place of business.2. operating items.3. service areas .4. mode of communications.5. general description of telecommunications facilities.If the documentation required in the application as specified under the preceding paragraph is incomplete, or the contents thereof are inadequate, DGT shall notify the applicant to make up the documentation or contents within a prescribed time period. Either if the required documentation is not submitted within the prescribed time frame, or if the information furnished remains inadequate after the required documentation is made up, the application shall not be accepted.

Article 19 Type I telecommunications enterprise shall, in accordance with their operating items, establish separate accounting systems to calculate profits and losses and may not employ cross-subsidy to hinder fair competition. The same applies to Type I telecommunications enterprises that also operates a Type II telecommunication enterprise or any other non-telecommunication business.The MOTC shall establish for Type I Telecommunication enterprises the accounting separation system, accounting method, procedures, and principles, guidelines for accounting supervision and administration and other compulsory accounting criteria.

Article 20 To protect the basic telecommunications rights and interests of R.O.C. nationals, The MOTC may designate, based on different areas and service items, a Type I telecommunications enterprise to provide universal telecommunications services.The term "universal telecommunications services" (hereinafter as "universal service(s)", stipulated in the preceding paragraph, means the necessary telecommunications services of certain quality that may be fairly enjoyed by all nationals at a reasonable price. A fund dedicated to the universal services shall be established for achieving the goal of universal services.The losses and necessary management expenses arising from the universal services shall be shared and paid out to the said fund by the telecommunications enterprises publicly designated by the MOTC.The MOTC shall enact regulations governing the identification of scope and service areas and selection of providers of the universal services, and the matters with respect to the accounting and allocation of losses incurred therefor.The telecommunications universal services fund shall not be construed as a "fund" described in the Budget Act.

Article 20- 1 Telecommunication numbers including numbering codes, subscriber numbers and identification codes used by telecommunication networks shall be planned and administered by the DGT. The telecommunication network numbering plan shall be announced by the DGT.The telecommunication numbers referred to in the preceding paragraph shall not be used or altered without the approval of the DGT or of an institution authorized by the DGT.The DGT may adjust or retrieve the assigned telecommunication numbers for the purpose of maintaining the reasonable and effective use thereof, and may collect telecommunication number usage fees. The criteria of telecommunication numbers usage fees shall be enacted by the DGT.For the purpose of protecting consumer rights and promoting effective competition in the telecommunications market, Type I telecommunication enterprises shall provide number portability service and equal access service. The applicable regulatory rules for such services related to scope, manner of provision, implementation timetable, and other compulsory rules shall be enacted by the DGT.The number portability service referred to in the preceding paragraph means the service which enables subscribers to retain their existing telephone numbers when switching from their original Type I enterprise to another Type I enterprise engaging in the same business; equal access service means the service provided by a Type I enterprise which allows its subscribers to select the long distance and international network service of other telecommunication enterprises.The DGT shall enact the administrative rules relating to the matters referred to in paragraphs 1 to 3 regarding allocation, adjustment and retrieval of telecommunication numbers, the qualifications of a delegatee institution and conditions for such delegation of authority and the authority which may be delegated to it, and other compulsory matters.The DGT shall supervise and provide guidance for matters related to the administration of registration of Internet Addresses and Internet Domain Names and shall promulgate rules related thereto.The administrative work referred to in the preceding paragraph shall only be performed by non-profit legal entity.

Article 21 A telecommunications enterprise shall provide services in a fair and non-discriminatory manner unless otherwise provided for herein.

Article 22 A telecommunications enterprise shall not refuse reception and transmission of telecommunication signals unless otherwise stipulated by law. However, it may refuse or discontinue the transmission of telecommunication signals whose contents appear to endanger national security or public order.

Article 23 The telecommunications enterprise shall not be held liable to its user for damages arising out of error, delays, interruption, suspension or failure in transmissions due to a failure or breakdown of telecommunication line facilities and equipment. However, the service fees shall be deducted accordingly.

Article 24 In the event of any breakdown of telecommunications line facilities and equipment as a result of any disaster or other major incidents, a telecommunications enterprise may, after making a public announcement, suspend its communications services either in whole or in part.

Article 25 A telecommunications enterprise shall give priority to the handling of the following:1. communications to prevent disasters, provide relief or maintain order in the event , or the likely occurrence of a natural disaster, accident or any other emergency;2. emergency communications for traffic safety, as it relates to distress signals from land, sea, or air transportation vehicles and aerial weather reports; or3. other emergency communications necessary for the protection of national security or public interests.

Article 26 The tariff regulation of Type I telecommunications enterprises shall adopt the price cap method.The aforementioned method means the percentage of adjustment of controlled tariffs of the regulated telecommunications enterprises shall not exceed the annual increase rate of consumers' price index of Taiwan area announced by the Directorate General of Budget, Accounting and Statistics of the Executive Yuan, minus index.The MOTC shall enact administrative rules governing the tariffs of Type I telecommunications enterprise including administration and examination of tariffs, initial offer of each tariff, the entities to which the price adjustment cap shall be applied, the services to which the tariffs shall be applied, tariff items, the adjustment coefficient and other compulsory rules.The determination of tariffs of Type I telecommunications enterprise shall not involve cross subsidy to hinder fair competition. The same is applicable to a Type I telecommunications enterprises that also operates a Type II telecommunications enterprises or other non-telecommunications business.The tariffs for a Type II telecommunications enterprise shall be determined by the enterprise itself.

Article 26- 1 A Dominant Market Player (DMP) of Type I telecommunications enterprises shall not engage in the following conducts:1. to obstruct, directly or indirectly, the request of interconnection of networks proposed by other Type I telecommunications enterprises with its proprietary techniques;2. to refuse to release to other Type I telecommunications enterprises the calculation methods of its interconnection fees and other relevant materials;3. to improperly determine, maintain, or change its tariffs or methods of offering telecommunications services;4. to reject the request of leasing network component by other Type I telecommunications enterprises without due cause;5. to reject the request of leasing circuits by other telecommunications enterprises or users without due cause;6. to reject the request of negotiation or testing by other telecommunications enterprises or users without due cause;7. to reject the request of co-location negotiation by other telecommunications enterprises without due cause;8. to discriminate against other telecommunications enterprises or users without due cause; or9. to abuse its DMP status, or to engage in other unfair competition acts.The aforementioned DMP shall be identified by the DGT.

Article 27 A Type I telecommunications enterprise shall establish its business rules in connection with the terms for provision of services and submit the same to the MOTC through the DGT for approval prior to announcement and implementation. The same shall apply for amendments to the rules.A Type II telecommunications enterprise shall establish its business rules in connection with the terms for provision of services and submit the same to the DGT for record prior to implementation. The same shall apply for amendments to the regulations.

Article 28 The business rules stipulated in the preceding article shall establish fair and reasonable service conditions, and be placed at every operation places and websites of the telecommunications enterprise. The DGT shall order changes of the business rules within a prescribed time frame if it encroaches upon consumers' rights and benefits, and appears patently unfair.If the operation of a telecommunications enterprise fails to ensure the secrecy of communications, or violate the provision of Article 21, DGT may order the enterprise to make improvements within a prescribed time frame.

Article 29 Except for indoor relocation, the function, purpose or installation site of telecommunications lines facilities and equipment leased to users by a telecommunications enterprise shall not be altered by users or others without authorization.

Article 30 MOTC shall establish the Chunghwa Telecom Co., Ltd. to operate telecommunications services. The establishment and management of the said state-run company shall be stipulated by law separately.

CHAPTER III TELECOMMUNICATIONS CONSTRUCTION AND MANAGEMENT

Section 1 Acquisition and Use of Land

Article 31 When a Type I telecommunications enterprise engages in the construction of infrastructure for the lines and pipes of its fixed networks, it may request co-location for its lines and pipes with the facilities at the bottleneck of telecommunications networks with the owners of such facilities for a charge.With respect to the request of using the infrastructure described in the preceding paragraph, the party being so requested shall not reject such request without due cause.

Article 32 Type I telecommunications enterprises or government agencies which establish dedicated telecommunications facilities may use public and private land and buildings for establishment of conduit infrastructure and terminal equipment. Governmental authorities shall not reject a request to use public land or buildings without due cause. If any such use of land or buildings causes material damage, appropriate compensation shall be made. The location and manner of use shall be the least harmful to governmental entities and owners, occupants or users of such land or buildings.Type I telecommunications enterprises or government agencies which establish dedicated telecommunications facilities may use rivers, embankments, roads, public forest or other public-use land and public buildings for establishment of radio stations; provided that such establishment was necessary and proper, does not impair the original effective uses of such land or buildings, and prior approval from the authorities concerned has been requested. The authorities concerned shall not reject such request without due cause.Construction or restoration by Type I telecommunications enterprises or government agencies which establish dedicated telecommunications facilities shall comply with the regulations enacted by authorities concerned.Public land and buildings shall be provided on a priority basis when constructing conduit infrastructure, terminal equipment and radio stations as referred to in the preceding paragraphs 1 and 2 unless it is impossible not to use private land or buildings for construction of the facilities or such construction on/in public land or buildings would be difficult.In the event that the private building to be used in accordance with paragraph 1 is an apartment building, the approval of the apartment building management committee shall be obtained. Provided that there is no management committee, the permission of each owner shall be obtained and Article 8, paragraph 1 of the Statute for Management of Apartment Buildings shall not apply to such approval.The central and local government authorities shall assist Type I telecommunications enterprises in constructing conduit infrastructure.Regarding the new construction of conduit infrastructure and terminal equipment, Type I telecommunications enterprises shall jointly establish a Conduit Infrastructure Deployment Negotiating Group which shall negotiate matters related to the planning, application, construction and facilities-sharing of conduit infrastructure. If necessary, the MOTC may mediate the aforementioned matters.

Article 33 If the local urban development plan or rural development plan fails to allocate land for public telecommunications facilities necessary to establish switching offices in particular locations or the land reserved for public telecommunications facilities by the local urban development plan or rural development plan is not sufficient for use, Type I telecommunications enterprises or government agencies which establish dedicated telecommunications facilities, may select an appropriate location based on community development and population distribution, and apply to the MOTC for approval of the selected location, and further apply to the local construction authority for permission to proceed with construction which construction shall not be subject to urban zoning regulations or regulations on the use of non-urban land.To accommodate the needs of radio communications construction, a Type I telecommunications enterprise or a government agency which establish dedicated telecommunications facilities may, with payment of compensation, erect radio stations on private buildings, provided that such use shall not affect the safety of the building concerned.In the event that the building to be used in accordance with the preceding paragraph is an apartment building, the approval of the apartment building management committee shall be obtained; provided that if there is no management committee, the permission of each owner shall be obtained. Article 8, paragraph 1 of the Statute for Management of Apartment Buildings shall not apply to such approval.

Article 34 To ensure free transmission of radio waves from the antenna of major radio facilities such as satellite communications and microwave communications, the MOTC may, in consultation with the Ministry of the Interior, select a method or designate a certain area which will cause the least damages, and then, following approval from the Executive Yuan, issue a public notice prohibiting or restricting any construction that may jeopardize free transmission of radio waves in such an area.The MOTC shall, in consultation with relevant authorities, impose measures to regulate and/or restrict power transmissions and distribution systems that induce voltage harmful to telecommunications facilities.

Article 35 On-duty personnel of a Type I telecommunications enterprise or government telecommunications may, upon presentation of proper identification, be given priority access in the event of any holdups or slowdowns at checkpoints and customs stations.

Article 36 In order to survey, install or maintain lines, employees of a Type I telecommunications enterprise or government telecommunications may pass through agricultural or residential land except those that are fenced or have enclosing walls which obstruct free access. If any buildings or vegetation are damaged as a result of such passage, the Type I telecommunications enterprise or the agency establishing government telecommunications shall verify the damage and tender appropriate compensation. Disagreements shall be conciliated by the local government.

Article 37 A Type I telecommunications enterprise or an agency establishing government telecommunications may, after notifying the property owner, cut down, trim or transplant plants that impede or are likely to impede the survey, installation or maintenance of lines. In cases of emergencies, prior notification is not required.The above trees or plants shall be cut, trimmed or transplanted in a manner that results in the least damage. In the event of any damage, the enterprise or agency responsible shall verify the damage and tender appropriate compensation. Disagreements shall be conciliated by local government.

Article 38 When constructing a building, the builder shall install indoor and outdoor telecommunications equipment according to the regulations and shall allocate a telecommunications room and other spaces for the installation of telecommunications equipment. But buildings announced by the DGT are not subject to this restriction.The aforementioned telecommunications equipment includes entrance conduit, main distribution box, customer-premises distribution block, distribution box, telecommunications cable and other equipment that a user must install within the demarcation point of responsibility in accordance to user's needs of telecommunications service.In the event that an existing building lacks sufficient telecommunications facilities or space for the installation of telecommunications equipment that results in the failure of the said building to comply with the telecommunications service requirements, the owner of the building shall consult with a local network operator that provides telecommunications service and make improvements accordingly.The telecommunications equipment and space installed for the use of the said building, in accordance with the requirements set forth in first and the aforesaid paragraphs, shall be connected to and used by the local network operators at no charge subject to user's needs of telecommunications service in the said building.A local network operator before using the telecommunications equipment installed in the telecommunications room of the building must obtain prior consent of the owner of the building to provide telecommunications service for outside users of the building. The local network operator shall negotiate with the owner for an appropriate compensation.Regulations governing the indoor and outdoor telecommunications equipment and spaces that must be installed within a building, its installation and use, the determination of the demarcation point of responsibility, defined range of buildings within a community, and other related matters shall be made by the MOTC in consultation with the Ministry of Interior. The installation of the indoor and outdoor telecommunications equipment of the building shall comply with the technical specifications as announced by the DGT.The blueprint of the design for the telecommunications equipment of a building and related space for its installation shall be examined by the DGT before applying for the commencement of the construction. The DGT shall inspect the said equipment and space after completion of the building.The DGT may engage institutions with telecommunications expertise to conduct examination of design for the installation and its space of telecommunications equipment in a building and inspection of its completion as stipulated in the above paragraph.Rules governing the qualifications of the institutions with telecommunications expertise as stipulated in the above paragraph, the delegated authority, cancellation or termination of the engagement, and supervision related to the engagement shall be made by the DGT.

Article 38- 1 Facilities of public fixed telecommunications outside the demarcation point of responsibility of users building installed and maintained by the local network operators who provide telecommunication services. However, connection of the network infrastructure between buildings of a community must be installed by the building constructor or the owner and maintained by the owner.The telecommunications equipment set up in accordance with the aforesaid article must be installed by the building constructor or the owner and maintained by the owner.The agreements prepared by local network operators or any third person delegated by the building constructor or by the owner to install or maintain the telecommunications equipment of users building or any persons responsible for the payment of installation, maintenance and usage shall not violate the following regulations:1. Said persons shall not prevent the users from choosing another operator to provide telecommunications service.2. Said persons shall not prevent another telecommunications service operator from competing for business opportunities.Any agreement that violates the aforementioned regulations shall be deemed invalid. Telecommunication equipment installed by an invalid agreement shall not be removed or its use prohibited without the authorization of the building constructor or the owner.

Section 2 Maintenance and Management of Telecommunications Facilities.

Article 39 Telecommunications facilities installed by telecommunications enterprises shall conform to the technical specifications provided by the DGT.The following matters shall be taken into consideration in the enactment of aforementioned technical specifications:1. the provision of full-scale telecommunications services shall not be made difficult by the damage or malfunction of telecommunications facilities;2. the maintenance of an appropriate quality of telecommunications services; e.g. upon request by a subscriber renting a dedicated fixed data line, a record-keeping system tracking quality of service shall be established, for such subscribers to access the recorded data pertaining to quality of service;3. the interconnecting telecommunications facilities of users or telecommunications enterprises shall not be damaged; nor shall the functioning of such facilities be impeded;4. a clear identification of responsibilities among telecommunications facilities which are interconnected .

Article 40 If the telecommunications facilities installed by a telecommunications enterprise fails to conform to the technical specifications prescribed in the first paragraph of the preceding article, the DGT may order the enterprise to either make improvements within a prescribed time period or limit its use of such facilities.

Article 41 A Type I telecommunications enterprise shall employ qualified senior telecommunications engineers to be in charge of and supervise the constructions, maintenance and utilization of telecommunications facilities. Depending on the deployment of its telecommunications facilities, a Type II telecommunications enterprise shall employ such personnel in accordance with relevant rules.

Article 42 The telecommunications terminal equipment for connection to the telecommunications machinery and line facilities of a Type I telecommunications enterprise shall conform to technical specifications, and be certified and approved before import and sale. The technical specifications shall be prescribed and announced by the DGT.The DGT shall enact regulations regarding the compliance approval mode and procedure of the telecommunications terminal equipment, the issuance, renewal, replacement and termination of the certificate of approval, and the embossment, marking and use of Approval Label, as well as the regulations with respect to the supervision and administration of compliance approval.The technical specifications mentioned in the first paragraph must ensure the following items:1. the connection shall not damage telecommunications machinery and line facilities of Type I telecommunications enterprise, or cause a malfunction of the said facilities;2. no nuisance shall be caused to other users of the telecommunication machinery and line facilities of a Type I telecommunications enterprise;3. the demarcation of responsibility between the telecommunications machinery and line facilities of a Type I telecommunications enterprise and the terminal equipment connected by users shall be clearly stipulated;4. ensure electromagnetic compatibility to harmonize and make effective use of the radio spectrum shall be ensured;5. ensure electrical safely to prevent harm to network operator personnel or users.

Article 43 Telecommunications equipment that connects to Type I telecommunications enterprises shall be constructed and maintained by the telecommunications engineering enterprises. However, all telecommunications equipment within the demarcation point of responsibility of the building may be constructed and maintained by electrical apparatus enterprises.The equipment in the preceding paragraph is categorized by the competent authority as basic equipment and is not subject to limits.Telecommunications engineering enterprises shall register to the competent authority, and join the relevant telecommunications engineering industry association within one month of the commencement of operations. The relevant telecommunications engineering industry association is obliged to accept the enterprise as a member.The enterprises which engaged in the construction of relevant telecommunications equipment mentioned in the first paragraph shall dispose qualified telecommunications engineers.Governing regulations with respect to the registry, revocation or annulment of telecommunications engineering enterprises shall be enacted by the competent authority.Qualifications and regulations of senior telecommunications engineers under Article 41, and telecommunications engineers under paragraph 4 shall be prescribed by the competent authority.

Article 44 The DGT or the certification bodies commissioned by the DGT shall be responsible for compliance approval of telecommunications terminal equipment.Rules governing the qualifications, the scope and limitations of delegated power, cancellation or termination of the commission, and supervision related to the commission of the aforementioned certification bodies shall be enacted by the DGT.

Article 45 Request for relocation of lines shall be made in writing with reasons to a Type I telecommunications enterprise or an agency establishing government telecommunications. Lines will be relocated after acceptance of said requests.Compensation shall be made in the event of damages to telecommunications facilities arising from repairs or construction of buildings, roads, irrigation ditches, or the laying of underground pipes, cables or other projects.The MOTC shall determine the criteria and procedure for requesting relocation of lines as mentioned in paragraph 1, the calculation and sharing of the relocation fee, the responsibility of persons who have caused any of the aforementioned damages to telecommunications equipment and the standard calculation for compensation.The aforementioned criteria for responsibility and methods of damage compensation shall not affect the injured party's right to claims by litigation.

CHAPTER IV REGULATION FOR TELECOMMUNICATIONS

Article 46 A station may not be established without prior approval from the MOTC, and shall be put into operation only after passing the inspection and a license issued, unless waived by the announcement of the MOTC.The aforementioned station, means a unit comprised of telecommunications facilities and operating personnel, which uses wire or wireless methods to receive or transmit radio frequency signals.Regulations governing establishment permit procedure, set-up and inspection of stations, issuance, renewal and replacement of certification, termination of permit, administration of the use and establishment, qualifications of engineers, assessment system and other related matters shall be made by the MOTC.The establishment and use of such stations shall comply with the technical specifications of the equipment enacted and announced by the DGT.R.O.C. nationals may not establish or use radio broadcast stations or television broadcast stations on ships, aircraft, or other objects floating on water or in the air, which are outside R.O.C. territory, to transmit radio frequency signals to interfere with legal use of radio waves.

Article 47 Dedicated telecommunications shall not be set up and operated without approval and license from the MOTC.Dedicated telecommunications shall not be connected to public communication systems or used for purposes other than those contemplated in its establishment, unless approved by the MOTC for such connections.The applicable regulations with respect to establishment, use of dedicated telecommunications and its connection to public communication systems shall be enacted by the MOTC.Foreigner applying to establish dedicated telecommunications shall obtain special approval on a case-by-case basis from the MOTC.A special approval on a case-by-case basis by the MOTC is required before the establishment and utilization of telecommunications network for the purpose of academics, education, or dedicated experiment of research and development of networks. Such applicable regulations governing the establishment and utilization of the aforementioned networks shall be enacted by the DGT.

Article 48 The MOTC shall regulate radio frequency, power, mode of transmission, radio station identification signals and call signs, and other radio wave related matters. Permission from the MOTC must be obtained for operation or alteration of radio wave related matters. The MOTC shall enact regulations governing the planning and allocation of radio frequency, application procedures, principles of assignment, termination of approval, use administration of radio frequency, handling of interference the standard definition of interference and regulations related to the supervision of radio waves.In order to effectively utilize the resources of radio waves, MOTC shall mandate the term of utilization of frequency, and establish a fee schedule to collect usage fees from radio frequency users.For overall development of telecommunications and information, the MOTC shall conduct periodic reviews to ensure the harmony and effectiveness of the common usage of frequencies. If necessary, the MOTC may adjust frequencies in use or request facilities upgrade by enterprises or users. Such adjustments or requests shall not be refused, nor shall compensation be demanded. However, appropriate compensation shall be paid to an amateur radio user for an actual loss incurred as a result of an adjustment in frequency or upgrade in facilities, which are made in accordance with instructions from the MOTC. The MOTC shall consult with the Ministry of National Defense to adjust military communications.Regulations governing radiation emitted from industrial, scientific, medical or other electrical machinery or equipment shall be enacted by the MOTC, in consultation with competent authorities in charge of the relevant industries.The stipulation of auction or open tendering of Article 94 of the Budget Law is not applicable to the following allocations of frequencies:1. the radio frequencies for the military, police, navigational, ships, amateur radio, government telecommunications, industrial, scientific, medical, low power radio frequency devices, academic experiment, emergency save and rescue, and other benevolent or public uses;2. the radio frequencies for mobile telecommunications networks, satellite telecommunications networks, radio broadcast stations or TV stations whose operation are based on the utilization of specific radio frequencies, which shall be designated at the time of issuance of operation permit or franchise license, or networks thereof could not function; and any radio frequency increased for further improvement of quality of local telecommunications; or3. the radio frequencies, which could be used repeatedly under certain conditions of use, for wireless local loop of fixed networks, satellite links or wireless microwaves links.

Article 49 To ensure national security and maintain the orderly sequence of radio waves, permission to manufacture, import, install or possess controlled telecommunications radio frequency devices shall be obtained from the MOTC; the model numbers and quantities of such devices manufactured or imported shall be reported to the MOTC for further reference.Regulations governing the operation permit of manufacture or import of controlled telecommunications radio frequency devices, the issuance, renewal, replacement and termination of operation license, administration of manufacture, import, installation and possession of the said devices, and other related matters shall be enacted by the MOTC.No controlled telecommunications radio frequency device shall be manufactured, imported, sold or publicly displayed unless it has received type approval and recognition of inspections. However, the manufacture of such devices in connection with academic studies, technological research and developments or experiments, as well as uses exclusively for exportation, re-importation after exportation and other uses permitted by the MOTC of such devices are exempted.The items of controlled telecommunications radio frequency devices mentioned in the first paragraph shall be announced by the MOTC.

Article 50 Technical specifications for controlled telecommunications radio frequency devices shall be mandated and announced by the DGT. In the event that national standards are already in place, said standards shall prevail.Regulations governing the compliance approval mode and procedure of the devices mentioned in the preceding paragraph, the issuance, renewal, replacement and termination of inspection or compliance approval or certificate of approval, the affixing, embossment and use of the inspection Approval Label, as well as regulations related to the supervision and administration of inspection shall be enacted by the DGT.The DGT or the certification bodies engaged by the DGT shall conduct the compliance approval on of the controlled telecommunications radio frequency devices. Rules governing the qualifications of the said certification bodies, the delegated power, cancellation or termination of the engagement, and supervision related to the engagement shall be enacted by the DGT.The inspection and technical specifications as prescribed in Article 42 shall apply to controlled telecommunications radio frequency devices that are used in telecommunications terminal equipment.

Article 51 Any amateur radio operator shall obtain a license from the MOTC prior to initiating operations. The MOTC shall enact regulations with respect to the class of amateur radio operators, qualifying examination, issuance, renewal, replacement, termination and administration of licenses, and other related matters.

Article 52 If necessary, the DGT may order a telecommunications enterprise or dedicated telecommunications user to submit reports relating to the following:1. business.2. finance.3. telecommunications facilities.

Article 53 Distress calls or communications from ships and aircrafts shall receive priority handling, prompt response and immediate action regardless of from where such signals and communications are sent.

Article 54 Except for distress communications, radio station of ships or aircrafts entering the territorial waters or airs of the R.O.C. shall not communicate with radio stations not designated by the MOTC.

Article 55 The DGT may dispatch personnel or cooperate with the police, with search warrants and evidentiary documents, to enter the establishments that harbor violations of this Act to conduct inspections or extract relevant information. The owner, responsible person, resident, custodian, user or the capable representative of the establishments shall not evade, obstruct or refuse such endeavors. For violations of Article 56 to Article 60, any search and detainment shall conform to relevant regulations of the Criminal Procedural Act.For the purpose of monitoring telecommunications activities, and to supervise or to regulate telecommunications enterprises, the DGT may request telecommunication enterprises, users of dedicated telecommunications or installers and users of radio stations to provide relevant materials, or to express their opinions by such parties hereof.

CHAPTER V PENALTIES

Article 56 Unauthorized access or use of another person's telecommunications facilities to communicate either through wire-based, wireless or other electromagnetic means, for personal gains or benefits of a third party, shall result in imprisonment of not more than five years, with a possible fine of not more than NT$1,500,000.Manufacturing, altering or importing telecommunications equipment for unauthorized access or use of another person's telecommunications facilities, either for personal gains or benefits of a third party, shall result in imprisonment of one to seven years, with a possible fine of not more than NT$3,000,000. The same penalties shall also be applicable to sale, transfer, rental or lending of telecommunications equipment for such purposes.Possession of telecommunications equipment for perpetrating a crime by oneself or a third party shall result in imprisonment of not more than three years, with a possible fine of not more than NT$500,000.Inchoate violators of the first and second paragraphs shall be penalized too.

Article 56- 1 Violators of Paragraph 1 of Article 6 regarding infringement on others' secrecy of communications shall be penalized with imprisonment of not more than five years, with a possible fine of not more than NT$1,500,000.The legal representative or service personnel of a telecommunication enterprise who takes advantage of opportunity of his business to commit the aforementioned crimes shall be penalized with imprisonment of six months to five years, with a possible fine of not more than NT$2,000,000.The inchoate violators of the first two paragraphs shall be penalized.The violator of the first paragraph shall be subject to prosecution instituted only upon complaints.

Article 57 An operator of a Type I telecommunications enterprise who violates paragraph 1 of Article 12 shall be subject to an imprisonment penalty of not more than three years, detention, and/or a fine of not more than NT$10,000,000.

Article 58 Anyone who sets up or uses a radio broadcast station or TV station to send radio frequency signals in violation of paragraph 5 of Article 46, that results in disturbing legal utilization of radio waves shall be penalized with imprisonment of not more than two years, detention, and/or a fine of not more than NT$600,000.Anyone who arbitrarily uses or alters radio frequency in violation of paragraph 1 of Article 48 without authorization shall be penalized with detention, and/or a fine of not more than NT$200,000.Anyone who has committed the aforementioned offence, thereby disturbing legal utilization of radio waves, shall be penalized with imprisonment of not more than two years, detention, and/or a fine of not more than NT$600,000.

Article 59 Representatives, agents or employees of a juristic person who commits any of the offenses under Articles 56 through 58 shall be penalized. In addition, the juristic person shall be fined according to the provision(s) violated.

Article 60 Violators of Articles 56 through 58 shall have their telecommunications equipment confiscated regardless of whether these are owned by the offender or not.

Article 61 A telecommunications enterprise that fails to contribute to the universal services fund as stipulated in paragraph 3 of Article 20, shall be fined three to five times of the required contribution amount, and served notice to contribute within a prescribed time period. Failure to make the contribution within the prescribed time frame shall, in MOTC's discretion, result in annulment of franchise or permission.A telecommunications enterprise that fails to pay its franchise fee or permission fee shall be fined additionally one percent of such fee as default penalty for every two days of late payment. After thirty days of default, the telecommunications enterprise shall be notified to pay up such fee within a prescribed time period. Any further overdue thereafter may result in annulment of franchise or permission.A radio frequency user who fails to pay its usage fee shall be fined additionally one percent of such fee as default penalty for every two days of late payment. After thirty days of default, the telecommunications enterprise shall be notified to pay up such fee within a prescribed time period. Any further overdue thereafter may result in annulment of usage of that radio frequency.Any failure to pay up as stipulated in the preceding three paragraphs the contribution to the universal service fund, franchise fee, permission fee, frequency usage fee and default penalty after receipt of notification to make payment within a prescribed time period shall be referred to the Court for compulsory execution.

Article 61- 1 Violators of paragraph 2 of Article 20.1 regarding usage or alteration of the telecommunication number without authorization, or violation of regulations enacted by the DGT in accordance with paragraph 6 of Article 20.1, shall result in a fine of NT$100,000 to NT$3,000,000, together with a notice to comply within a prescribed time frame. Failure to comply within the prescribed time frame may result in consecutive fines until full compliance, or partial or full suspension of the violator's operations, or annulment of its franchise or permission.A telecommunication enterprise or other telecommunication number user who fails to pay the number usage fee shall be fined additionally one percent of such fee as default penalty for every two days of late payment. After thirty days of default, the telecommunications enterprise or user shall be notified to pay up such fee within a prescribed time period. Any continued failure to pay thereafter may result in regular suspension or annulment of the permission for use.Failure by a Type I enterprise to provide the service of number portability or equal access stipulated in paragraph 4 of Article 20.1, or violateion by it of regulations enacted by the DGT in accordance with paragraph 4 of Article 20.1, shall result in a fine of NT$300,000 to NT$3,000,000, together with a notice to comply within a prescribed time frame. Failure to comply within the prescribed time frame may result in consecutive fines until full compliance, or partial or full suspension of the violator's operations, or annulment of its franchise.Violation of regulations enacted by the DGT in accordance with paragraph 7 of Article 20.1 shall result in a fine of NT$300,000 to NT$3,000,000 together with a notice to comply within a prescribed time frame. Failure to comply within the prescribed time frame may result in consecutive fines until full compliance, or partial or full suspension of the violator's operations.If the telecommunication fees and default penalty stipulated in paragraph 2 are not paid within the prescribed time frame as notified, the case shall be referred to the courts for compulsory execution.

Article 62 A Type I telecommunications enterprise that violates paragraph 3 of Article 12, or fails to comply with paragraph 6 of Article 12 as stipulated by the MOTC, shall be fined NT$500,000 to NT$2,500,000 if it failed to comply after a notice to comply within a prescribed period of time. If such telecommunication enterprise still failed to comply after further notification to request such compliance therewith within a prescribed period of time, its franchise approval shall be annulled.

Article 62- 1 If a Type I telecommunication enterprise had committed any of the following acts, it shall be penalized with a fine of NT$300,000 to NT$5,000,000, together with a notice to comply within a prescribed time frame. Failure to comply within the prescribed time frame may result in consecutive fines until full compliance, or partial or full suspension of its operations, or annulment of its franchise:1. violation of paragraph 1 of Article 19;2. violation of principles set forth by the MOTC in accordance with provision of paragraph 2 of Article 19;3. failure to provide universal services as instructed by the MOTC in violation of paragraph 1 of Article 20;4. violation of regulations set forth by the MOTC in accordance with provision of paragraph 3 of Article 26;5. violation of paragraph 4 of Article 26;6. violation of paragraph 1 of Article 26.1;7. violation of paragraph 2 of Article 31 to reject the request of sharing infrastructure for lines and pipes without appropriate reasons; or8. evading, obstructing or rejecting inspections by the DGT, refusing to provide materials, or refusing to show up to present opinions to the same agency as mandated in Article 55.In the event of commission of any of the following acts, the violator shall be penalized with a fine of NT$300,000 to NT$1,500,000, together with a notice to comply within a prescribed time frame. Failure to comply within the prescribed time frame may result in consecutive fines until full compliance, or partial or full suspension of the violator's operations, or annulment of its franchise or permission: 1. A Type I telecommunication enterprise rejects interconnection with another telecommunication enterprise in violation of paragraph 1 and 7 of Article 16;2. Violation of paragraph 3, 4, 5, or 7 of Article 16 by failing to comply with an arbitral decision of the DGT within 2 months from the date of notice of the decision;3. Violation of regulations enacted by the DGT in accordance with paragraph 9 of Article 16.

Article 63 Violation of regulations enacted by the MOTC in accordance with paragraph 6 of Article 14 shall result in a fine of NT$300,000 to NT$3,000,000, together with a notice to comply within a prescribed time frame. Failure to comply within the prescribed time frame may result in consecutive fines until full compliance, or annulment of its franchise .

Article 64 Violation of paragraph 1 of Article 17 to operate a Type II telecommunications enterprise shall result in a fine of NT$200,000 to NT$1,000,000, and, in DGT's discretion confiscation of the telecommunications equipment thereof.Violation of the regulations enacted by the MOTC in accordance with paragraph 2 of Article 17 shall result in a fine of NT$200,000 to NT$1,000,000, together with a notice to comply within a prescribed time frame. Failure to comply within a prescribed time period shall, in MOTC's discretion, result in annulment of its permission.

Article 65 A fine of not less than NT$100,000 and not more than NT$500,000 shall be imposed under any of the following circumstances:1. suspension or termination of business operations, transfer of the enterprise or its assets, interlocking investments or mergers consummated without prior approval in violation of Article 15;2. failure to acquire approval for its business rules, or failure to comply with the approved business rules in violation of paragraph 1 of Article 27;3. violation of paragraph 1 of Article 46 or the regulations enacted by the MOTC pursuant to paragraph 3 of Article 46;4. violation of paragraph 1, paragraph 2 of Article 47 or the regulations enacted by the MOTC pursuant to paragraph 3 of Article 47;5. violation of paragraph 4 of Article 47 by a foreigner who sets up dedicated telecommunications without seeking special approval on a case-by-case basis;6. unauthorized establishment of telecommunications networks in violation of paragraph 5 of Article 47, or violation of regulations enacted by the DGT pursuant to paragraph 5 of Article 47;7. violation of paragraph 1 of Article 48 or regulations enacted by the MOTC pursuant to paragraphs 1 of Article 48;8. unauthorized manufacture or importation of controlled telecommunications radio frequency devices, or failure to report the model numbers and amount of such controlled devices thereof to the MOTC for reference in violation of paragraph 1 of Article 49;9. violation of regulations enacted by the MOTC pursuant to paragraph 2 of Article 49; or10. unauthorized manufacture, importation, sale, or public display of controlled telecommunications radio frequency devices without type approval or inspection in violation of paragraph 3 of Article 49.Violations of subparagraph 3 to 10 of the preceding paragraph may additionally result in confiscation of devices in part or in whole, and annulment of franchise, permission, grant or license issued thereto.The confiscation of devices pursuant to the stipulation of the preceding paragraph shall be imposed to the property of anybody.Consecutive penalties until full compliance may be applicable to violations of subparagraph 1, 2, 6 or 8 of paragraph 1.

Article 66 A fine of not less than NT$60,000 and not more than NT$300,000 shall be imposed under any of the following circumstances:1. a telecommunications enterprise in violation of instructions issued by the DGT pursuant to Article 28 or Article 40;2. a telecommunications enterprise in violation of Article 41; or3. violations of the regulations for type approval and inspection enacted by the DGT pursuant to paragraph

2 of Article 50.Consecutive penalties until full compliance may be applicable to violations of subparagraph 1 or 2 of the preceding paragraph.

Article 67 A fine of not less than NT$30,000 and not more than NT$300,000 shall be imposed under any of the following circumstances.1. Failure to file operational rules for records in violation of paragraph 2 of Article 272. Failure to place operational rules at the place of its business and on its websites by a telecommunications enterprise in violation of paragraph 1 of Article 283. Importation or sale of uninspected telecommunications terminal equipment in violation of paragraph 1 of Article 424. Failure to join the relevant association in violation of paragraph 3 of Article 43; or operations of relevant telecommunications construction projects without disposing the qualified telecommunications engineers in violation of paragraph 4 of Article 435. Violation of regulations enacted by the competent authority pursuant to paragraph 4 of Article 486. Violation of the instructions issued by the competent authority pursuant to Article 527. Evasion, obstruction or rejection by a party other than a Type I telecommunications enterprise to comply with the inspections conducted by the competent authority pursuant to the provision of Article 55, or such failure of the same party thereof to provide relevant information, or to present opinions as requested.Confiscation of equipment may be imposed for violations of subparagraph 3 of the preceding paragraph. Suspension of operations shall be imposed for violations of subparagraph 4.Unauthorized installation or possession of controlled telecommunications radio frequency devices in violation of paragraph 1 of Article 49 shall be penalized with a fine of not less than NT$10,000 and not more than NT$50,000, as well as the possible confiscation of its equipment.Confiscation of equipment or devices pursuant to two preceding two paragraphs shall be imposed to the property of anybody.Consecutive penalties until full compliance may be imposed for violations of subparagraph 1, 2, 4 to 7 of paragraph 1.

Article 67- 1 Any local network operator or other third person who violates paragraph 3 or 4 of Article 38.1 will be notified and required to make corrections within a given period. In the event that the violation continues to exist at the expiry of the given period, the said person shall be penalized with a fine no more than NT$300,000 and no less than NT$30,000 and may be penalized repeatedly until improvement is made.Any violations of the regulations enacted by the DGT in accordance with paragraph 2 of Article 42 with respect to the renewal or replacement of certification approval, the affixing, marking and use of Approval Label, and the supervision and administration of inspection will be penalized with a fine no more than NT$300,000 and no less than NT$30,000.Anyone who, in violation of Article 51, arbitrarily initiates radio operations without obtaining an amateur radio operator license from the MOTC, or violates regulations enacted by the MOTC in accordance with Article 51 with respect to the administration of amateur radio operators, and other compulsory rules, shall be penalized with a fine no more than NT$50,000 and no less than NT$10,000.

Article 68 The MOTC may mandate the DGT in charge of imposition of fines, confiscation, annulment of franchise, grant or licenses, notification of removal or compliance within a prescribed period time as provided for therein. However, the DGT shall be responsible for the imposition of penalties stipulated under Article 61.1, paragraph 2 of Article 62, subparagraph 8 of paragraph 1 and paragraph 2 of Article

62.1, Article 64, subparagraph 6 and 10 of paragraph 1 of Article 65, Article 66, subparagraph 1, 3, 5 and 6 of paragraph 1 and paragraph 2 of Article 67, and annulment of permission of Type II telecommunications enterprises.Those whose certificate has been annulled in accordance with this Act shall, upon receipt of notice, return the certificate to the DGT within the prescribed time period; in the event of failure to make such return by the prescribed deadline, an announcement of cancellation shall be made.If a fine is imposed pursuant to this Act is not paid within a prescribed time frame as notified, the case shall be referred to the courts for compulsory execution.If a violation punishable pursuant to this Act carries a more severe punishment under the stipulations of another law, the other law shall be applied accordingly.

CHAPTER VI SUPPLEMENTARY PROVISIONS

Article 69 Military communications shall not be subject to this Act, except Article 31 to 37, Article 45, paragraph 2 of Article 47, paragraphs 1 and 3 of Article 48, and Article 53.

Article 70 With respect to processing of applications for franchise approvals, permissions, examinations, type approvals, inspections, registries and issuance of licenses pursuant to this Act, an applicant shall be charged a franchise fee, permission fee, examination fee, type approval fee, inspection fee, registry fee and license fee according to the fee schedule established by the competent authority.

Article 71 For matters not provided herein, the MOTC may adopt and implement the criteria, recommendations, regulations or procedures set forth under relevant international telecommunications conventions and the riders thereof.

Article 72 This Act shall come into effect as of the date of promulgation.

REGULATIONS FOR THE LICENSE RENEWAL OF SATELLITE BROADCASTING AND FOREIGN SATELLITE BROADCASTING BUSINESSES

Announced Date 2016-07-06

Promulgated in accordance with the Order Tung-Chuan-Nei-Rong No. 10548018400 issued by National Communications Commission on July 7, 2016

Article 1 These Regulations are hereby enacted pursuant to Paragraph 3, Article 18 of the Satellite Broadcasting Act (hereinafter referred to as "the Act").

Article 2 A branch company or an agent of a satellite broadcasting business or foreign satellite broadcasting business shall, within six months prior to the expiration of its license, submit an application and operations plans for license-renewal to competent authorities, adhering to the following stipulations and methods.

Article 3 A direct satellite broadcasting service operator (hereinafter referred to as "service operator") that applies for license renewal shall submit the application (Attached Form 1-1), complete with an Operations Plan and Status Report covering the fourth year of the licensed period to six months prior to license expiry, as well as an Operations Plan for the forthcoming six years of operations, and shall state the following matters separately:

1. The Operations Plan and Status Report from the fourth year of the licensed period to six months prior to the license expiry:

(1) Market positioning and status of the channel's implementation;

(2) Status of the implementation of internal control mechanism and self-disciplinary organization;

(3) Financial planning and fee standards;

(4) Company organization and status of the implementation of personnel training;

(5) Status of the implementation of customer service and complaint procedures.

2. The Operations Plan for the forthcoming six years of operations:

(1) The name, nationality, frequency, and transponder of the satellite, and the coverage area of the satellite signals; and the number of satellite channels;

(2) Financial structure and personnel organization;

(3) Channel or program planning;

(4) Internal control mechanism;

(5) Methods of operation and plan for technological development;

(6) Fee standards and calculation method; and

(7) Other items, as specified by the regulatory agency.

The aforementioned Operations Plan and Status Report and Operations Plan shall be completed as per the specified items in Attached Form 4-1, Attached Form 3, and shall also include the Operations Plan Summary Form (Attached Form 2-1), along with a table of comparison on dissimilarity between the application and the previous license renewal's operations plan, and any other document or substantive data the competent authorities specify.

Article 4 A foreign direct satellite broadcasting service operator (hereinafter referred to as "foreign service operator") that applies for license renewal shall submit the application (Attached Form 1-2), complete with an Operations Plan and Status Report

from the fourth year of the licensed period to six months prior to the license expiry, as well as an Operations Plan for the forthcoming six years of operations, and shall state the following matters separately:

1. The Operations Plan and Status Report from the fourth year of the licensed period to six months prior to the license expiry:

(1) Market positioning and the status of the channel's implementation;

(2) Status of the implementation of the internal control mechanism and self-disciplinary organization;

(3) Financial planning and fee standards;

(4) Company organization and status of the implementation of personnel training;

(5) Status of the implementation of customer service and complaint procedures.

2. The Operations Plan for the forthcoming six years of operations:

(1) The name, nationality, frequency, and transponder of the satellite, and the coverage area of the satellite signals; and the number of satellite channels;

(2) Channel or program planning;

(3) Fee standards and calculation method; and

(4) Other items, as specified by the regulatory agency.

The aforementioned Operations Plan and Status Report and Operations Plan shall be completed as per the specified items in Attached Form 4-1 and Attached Form 3, and shall also include the Operations Plan Summary Form (Attached From 2-1), complete with a table

of comparison on the dissimilarity between the previous application or the operations plan of the previous license renewal, and other documents and supporting documentation, as specified by the regulatory agency.

Article 5 A Satellite broadcasting program supplier (hereinafter referred to as "program supplier") that applies for license renewal shall submit the application (Attached Form 1-3), complete with an Operations Plan and Status Report from the fourth year of the licensed period to the six months prior to the license expiry, as well as an Operations Plan for the following six years of operations, and shall state the following matters separately:

1. The Operations Plan and Status Report from the fourth year of the licensed period to six months prior to the license expiry:

(1) Status of channel philosophy and the program or content arrangement;

(2) Status of the implementation of the internal control mechanism and self-disciplinary organization;

(3) Financial status;

(4) Status of the implementation of customer service and complaint procedures;

(5) Other items, as specified by the regulatory agency.

2. The Operations Plan for the forthcoming six years of operations:

(1) The number of operating channels, channel name, and method of transmitting signals;

(2) Program planning;

(3) Proposals for broadcasting domestically produced programs and programs that promote local culture;

(4) Internal control mechanism and program editorial system;

(5) Fee standards and calculation method; and

(6) Other items, as specified by the regulatory agency.

In the case where the application is for a channel in the general channel category, the aforementioned Operations Plan and Status Report and the Operations Plan shall be completed as per the specified detailed items in the Attached Form 4-2, Attached Form 3,

and shall also include the Operations Plan Summary Form (Attached Form 2-2), along with a table of comparison on dissimilarity between the application or the operations plan of the previous license renewal, and any other document or substantive data the competent authorities specify.

In the case where the application is for a channel in the shopping channel category, the Operations Plan and Status Report and the Operations Plan, as stated in Paragraph 1, shall be completed as per the specified detailed items in Attached Form 4-3 and Attached

Form 3, and shall also include the Operations Plan Summary Form (Attached Form 2-3), along with a table of comparison on dissimilarity between the application and the operations plan of the previous license renewal, and any other document or substantive data the competent authorities specify.

Article 6 A foreign satellite broadcasting program supplier (hereinafter referred to as "foreign program supplier") that applies for license renewal shall submit the application (Attached Form 1-4), complete with an Operations Plan and Status Report from the

fourth year of the licensed period to the six months prior to the license expiry, as well as an Operations Plan for the forthcoming six years of operations, and shall state the following matters separately:

1. The Operations Plan and Status Report from the fourth year of the licensed period to six months prior to the license expiry:

(1) Status of channel philosophy and the program or content arrangement;

(2) Status of the implementation of the internal control mechanism and self-disciplinary organization;

(3) Financial status;

(4) Status of the implementation of customer service and complaint procedures;

(5) Other items, as specified by the regulatory agency.

2. The Operations Plan for the forthcoming six years of operations:

(1) The name, nationality, frequency, and transponder of the satellite, and the coverage area of the satellite signals; and the number of satellite channels;

(2) Program planning;

(3) Internal control mechanism and program editing review system;

(4) Fee standards and calculation method; and

(5) Other items, as specified by the regulatory agency.

In the case where the application is for a channel in the general channel category, the aforementioned Operations Plan and Status Report and the Operations Plan shall be completed as per the specified items in the Attached Form 4-2, Attached Form 3, and shall also include the Operations Plan Summary Form (Attached Form 2-2), along with a table of comparison on dissimilarity between the application and the operations plan of the previous license renewal, and any other document or substantive data the competent authorities specify.

In the case where the application is for a channel in the shopping channel category, the Operations Plan and Status Report and the Operations Plan, as stated in Paragraph 1, shall be completed as per the specified items in Attached Form 4-3 and Attached Form

3, and shall also include the Operations Plan Summary Form (Attached Form 2-3), along with a table of comparison on the dissimilarity between the application and the operations plan of the previous license renewal, and any other document or substantive data the competent authorities specify.

Article 7 The regulatory agency shall hold advisory meetings to examine the cases of license establishment and renewal applications and provide advisory opinions to satellite broadcasting businesses, foreign satellite broadcasting businesses, and other type channel and program supply businesses.

Article 8 Should the application for license renewal, Operations Plan and Status Report and the Operations Plan of a satellite broadcasting business or foreign satellite broadcasting business be deemed incomplete, the applicant shall be required to submit retroactive

correction within a specified period; when failing to re-submit the application correction within the specified period or when the retroactive correction should be deemed incomplete, the application shall be rejected.

Article 9 A satellite broadcasting business that applies for license renewal and falls under one of the following circumstances may not submit retroactive correction, and the application shall be denied citing reasons for the denial:

1. In violation of Paragraph 3, Article 4 of the Act, stipulating circumstances where foreign nationals directly hold shares of the satellite broadcasting business shares in excess of fifty percent of outstanding total shares the said enterprise has issued;

2. In violation of provisions of Article 5 of the Act, stipulating circumstances of personnel from government, political parties, or related businesses, and foundations investing or taking office.

Article10 Except for the circumstances aforementioned in the preceding two articles, where the application for license renewal for service operators and foreign service operators shall be rejected, applications shall be examined according to the following items and assessment standards:

1. The Operations Plan and Status Report from the fourth year of the licensed period to six months prior to the license expiry – 40 points

(1) Market positioning and the status of the channel's implementation;

(2) Status of the implementation of the internal control mechanism and self-disciplinary organization;

(3) Financial status and fee standards;

(4) Company organization and status of the implementation of personnel training;

(5) Status of the implementation of customer service and complaint procedures.

2. The Operations Plan for the forthcoming six years of operations – 60 points:

(1) Market positioning and channel planning;

(2) Internal control mechanism;

(3) Financial planning and fee standards;

(4) Company organization and personnel training;

(5) Customer service and complaint procedures.

Applicants with the foresaid grading totaling to less than 60 points shall be deemed as unsatisfactory, and shall not be issued with a permit.

The review criteria set forth under Subparagraph 1 Paragraph 1 may commensurate to the review criteria defined by the satellite broadcasting business and foreign satellite broadcasting business's evaluation review measures; the grading criteria for various

review items as set forth under Subparagraph 2 Paragraph 1 may commensurate to stipulations set forth under the examination regulations on the establishment application of satellite broadcasting businesses and foreign satellite broadcasting businesses Paragraph

1, Article 12.

In the case where an application violates stipulations of Subparagraphs 3 or 4, Paragraph 1,

Article 10, Article 4, Article 12 or Article 19 first section of the Act, the application shall be denied, citing reasons for the denial.

Article 11 Except for the circumstances aforementioned in Articles 8 or 9, where the application for license renewal for program suppliers and foreign program suppliers of the channel category of general channel shall be denied, applications shall be examined according to the following items and assessment standards:

1. The Operations Plan and Status Report from the fourth year of the licensed period to six months prior to the license expiry – 40 points

(1) The status of channel philosophy and the program or content arrangement;

(2) Status of the implementation of the internal control mechanism and self-disciplinary organization;

(3) Financial status;

(4) Status of the implementation of customer service and complaint procedures;

(5) Other items, as specified by the regulatory agency.

2. The Operations Plan for the forthcoming six years of operations – 60 points:

(1) Market positioning and channel planning;

(2) Internal control mechanism and control review system;

(3) Financial planning and fee standards;

(4) Company organization and personnel training;

(5) Customer service and complaint procedures.

Applicants with the foresaid grading totaling to less than 60 points shall be deemed as unsatisfactory, and shall not be issued with a permit.

The review criteria set forth under Subparagraph 1 Paragraph 1 may commensurate to the review criteria defined by the satellite broadcasting business and foreign satellite broadcasting business's evaluation review measures; the grading criteria for various

review items as set forth under Subparagraph 2 Paragraph 1 may commensurate to stipulations set forth under the examination regulations on the establishment application of satellite broadcasting businesses and foreign satellite broadcasting businesses Paragraph

1, Article 13.

In the case where an application violates provisions as stipulated in Subparagraphs 3 or 4, Paragraph 1, Article 10, Article 4, Article 12 or first section of Article 19 of the Act, the application shall be denied, citing reasons for the denial.

Article 12 Except for circumstances as specified in Article 8 or Article 9 in which the applicant shall be denied, applications for license renewal of a program supplier and foreign program that falls under shopping channels applications shall be examined according to the following items and assessment standards:

1. The Operations Plan and Status Report from the fourth year of the licensed period to six months prior to the license expiry – 40 points

(1) The status of channel philosophy and the program or content arrangement;

(2) Status of the implementation of the internal control mechanism and self-disciplinary organization;

(3) Financial status;

(4) Status of the implementation of customer service and complaint procedures ;

(5) Other items, as specified by the regulatory agency.

2. The Operations Plan for the forthcoming six years of operations – 60 points:

(1) Channel positioning and content planning;

(2) Internal control mechanism and content editorial system;

(3) Financial planning and fee standards;

(4) Company organization and personnel training;

(5) Customer service and complaint procedures.

Applicants with the foresaid grading totaling to less than 60 points shall be deemed as unsatisfactory, and shall not be issued with a permit.

The review criteria set forth under Subparagraph 1 Paragraph 1 may commensurate to the review criteria defined by the satellite broadcasting business and foreign satellite broadcasting business's evaluation review measures; the grading criteria for various

review items as set forth under Subparagraph 2 Paragraph 1 may commensurate to stipulations set forth under the examination regulations on the establishment application of satellite broadcasting businesses and foreign satellite broadcasting businesses Paragraph

1 Article14.

If an application violates provisions as stipulated in Subparagraphs 3 or 4, Paragraph 1, Article 10, Article 4, Article 12 or the first section of Article 19 of the Act, the application shall be denied, citing reasons for the denial.

Article 13 The satellite broadcasting business and foreign satellite broadcasting business' s license renewal application shall heed to each channel as an application unit, with the license also to be approved and issued separately.

An application shall be determined within six months from the case receiving date.

If an application case cannot be processed and concluded within the foresaid period, the competent authorities may extend the review period up to the date the license validation period expires.

Article 14 The provisions of the Regulations on satellite broadcasting program supplier shall apply mutatis mutandis to the approval procedures, examination items, assessment standards, and other matters that shall be complied of other type channel and program supply business, unless otherwise provided by law.

Article 15 The applicants shall remit payment of examination fees and license fees to the regulatory agency according to relevant provisions.

Article 16 These Regulations shall take effect from the date of promulgation

STATUTE FOR INVESTMENT BY OVERSEAS CHINESE

(Amended on November 19, 1997)

Article 1 Matters relating to the encouragement, protection, and administration of domestic investments by overseas Chinese shall be governed by this Statute.

Article 2 The term "Competent Authority" as used in this Statute shall mean the Ministry of Economic Affairs.

The Competent Authority may delegate its subordinate or commission other institutions or organizations to administer the investments set forth in this Statute.

Article 3 Overseas Chinese making investments in the Republic of China (ROC) in accordance with this Statute are hereinafter referred to as investors or the investor.

Article 4 Investments as referred to in this Statute shall be as follows:

1. Holding shares issued by an ROC company, or contributing to the capital of an ROC company;

2. Establishing a proprietary business or a partnership in the territory of the Republic of China; and

3. Providing loan(s) to the invested business referred to in the preceding two Paragraphs for a period exceeding one (1) year.

Article 5 If the investor holds, in an aggregate, more than one third (1/3) of the total shares issued by an enterprise in which he/she invests, or if an investor contributes, in an aggregate, more than one third (1/3) of the total capital amount of an enterprise in which he/she invests, the reinvestment to be made by the invested enterprise shall be subject to the Competent Authority's approval.

Article 6 Investments as referred to in this Statute consist of the following kinds:

1. Cash;

2. Machinery and equipment or raw materials for own use;

3. Patent right, trademark right, copyright, technical know-how or other intellectual property right; and

4. Other property in which an investor may invest under the Competent Authority's approval.

Article 7 The investor is prohibited from investing in the following industries:

第一條 Those which may negatively affect national security, public order, good customs and practices, or national health; and

二、 Those which are prohibited by the law.

The investor, who applies to invest in an industry in which investment is restricted by law or by an order given under the applicable law, shall obtain anapproval thereof or a consent thereto from the competent authority in charge of the industry in question.

The industries prohibited under Paragraph 1 above or restricted under Paragraph 2 above shall be prescribed and reviewed on a regular basis by the Executive Yuan.

Article 8 The investor who makes an investment in accordance with this Statute is required to submit an investment application, together with his/her investment plans and relevant documents, to the Competent Authority for approval. The same shall apply if and when his/her investment plan changes.

The investment application form shall be prescribed by the Competent Authority.

The Competent Authority shall make its decision on an investment application within one (1) month after the completion of the application procedures by the applicant, or if the application is also subject to the approval of the competent authority in charge of the relevant end enterprise, within two (2) months thereafter.

Regulations governing investors' investments in securities shall be stipulated by the Executive Yuan.

Article 9 The investor shall have his/her approved capital contribution remitted in full into the Republic of China within the prescribed time limit, and shall submit a report on the receipt of the contribution amount to the Competent Authority for examination.

If, after being granted an approval to make an investment under this Statute, the investor fails to implement his/her investment, in whole or in part, within the prescribed time limit, the approval of his/her unimplemented investment shall be revoked upon expiration of the prescribed time limit. However, for good cause shown, the investor may, prior to the expiration, apply to the Competent Authority for an extension of the prescribed time limit.

After implementing his/her investment, the investor shall request the Competent Authority to verify the total amount of his/her investment. The rules of the verification shall be prescribed by the Competent Authority.

Article 10 In case the investor intends to transfer his/her investment already implemented by him/her to an industry other than those prohibited from investment under Paragraph 1 of Article 7 hereof, he/she shall apply to the Competent Authority for cancellation of his/her original investment and for approval of his/her new investment.

In case the investor intends to assign his/her investment, the assignor and the assignee shall jointly apply to the Competent Authority for approval of the assignment.

Article 11 An investor shall be entitled to exchange settlement under this Statute. This entitlement is not transferable, except to the legitimate heir of the assignee of his/her investment, or to other authorized foreign nationals or overseas Chinese to whom he/she has assigned his/her investment.

Article 12 The investor may apply for exchange settlement against the interests accrued on his/her annual income, or against the profit surplus distributed to him/her from his/her investment. When the investor is approved to transfer his/her shares, to withdraw or decrease his/her investment, he/she may apply for exchange settlement, in a lump sum, against the total amount of his/her investment as approved. The foregoing clause is also applicable to the capital gain realized from the investor's investment.

The investor's application for exchange settlement against the payment of the principal and interest of his/her loan investment shall be governed by the agreed terms and conditions approved by the Competent Authority.

Article 13 In case the government expropriates or acquires an invested enterprise for national defense reasons, the investor thereof whose investment is less than 45% of the total capital amount of the invested enterprise shall be entitled to a reasonable compensation.

The compensation under the preceding Paragraph shall be permitted for exchange settlement.

Article 14 In case the investor's investment accounts for 45% or more of the total capital amount of the enterprise in which he invests, the invested enterprise shall not be subject to requisition or expropriation as long as the said capital contribution rate of the investor remains unchanged for a period of twenty (20) years after the commencement of business of the invested enterprise.

If the investor's investment is made in conjunction with a foreign national who makes the investment under the Statute for Investment by Foreign Nationals, and if their aggregate amount of investment accounts for 45% or more of the total capital amount of the invested enterprise, the provisions referred to in the preceding Paragraph shall, mutatis mutandis, apply thereto.

Article 15 The preferential measures regarding the imposition of inheritance tax on the amount of the investor's investment as approved by the Competent Authority after the investor's implementation of his/her investment shall be prescribed by the Executive Yuan.

Article 16 Where an invested enterprise is organized as a company under the Company Law, the investor thereof may be exempt from the restrictions on his/her domicile in the Republic of China and on the amount of investment under Articles 98-1, 108-2, 128-1, 208-5, and 216-1 of the same Law.

The provisions of Article 156-4 of the Company Law requiring issuance of stock certificates to the public, and the provisions of Article 267 of the same Law requiring setting aside a certain percentage of new shares (issued as a result of capital increase by cash) to be purchased by the employees of the invested enterprise shall not apply to an investor's investment if such investment accounts for 45% or more of the total capital of the enterprise in which he/she invests.

If the investor's investment is made in conjunction with a foreign national who makes the investment under the Statute for Investment by Foreign Nationals, and if their aggregate investment amount accounts for 45% or more of the total capital amount of the invested enterprise, the provisions referred to in the preceding Paragraph shall, mutatis mutandis, apply thereto.

Article 17 Except as otherwise provided for in other laws, the enterprise in which the investor has invested hereunder shall be accorded the same rights and obligations to which an enterprise operated by local Chinese nationalsis entitled.

Article 18 The provisions of this Statute shall apply to overseas Chinese who make investments in Taiwan, and to their enterprises established in Taiwan prior to the enforcement of this Statute in accordance with the Regulation for the Encouragement of Investment in Productive Enterprises by Overseas Chinese and Chinese Residents in Hong Kong and Macao, the Regulations Governing the Importation of Commodities with Self-provided Foreign Exchange by Overseas Chinese for the Purpose of Making Investment in Productive Enterprises, and the Regulations Governing Overseas Chinese Investment.

Article 19 Unless otherwise provided for in this Statute, if the investor violates the provisions of this Statute, or fails to perform any matters approved by the Competent Authority, the Competent Authority may deal with the situation in the following manner:

1. Revoke the investor's right of exchange settlement against his/her income of the profit from his/her investment and the interest accrued thereon in a prescribed period of time; and

2. Revoke the approval for the investor's investment and his/her rights under this Statute.

Article 20 An overseas Chinese who fails to make an investment in accordance with this Statute prior to the amendment to this Statute may, within one (1) year from the enforcement of this amended Statute, apply to the Competent Authority for registration for the application of this amended Statute to his/her prior investment.

The procedure of registration referred to in the preceding Paragraph shall be prescribed by the Competent Authority.

Article 21 This Statute shall become effective as of its date of promulgation.

STATUTE FOR INVESTMENT BY FOREIGN NATIONALS

(Amended on November 19, 1997)

Article 1 Matters relating to domestic investment by foreign nationals, and the protection, restrictions, and administration of such investments shall be governed by this Statute.

Article 2 The term "Competent Authority" as used in this Statute shall mean the Ministry of Economic Affairs.

The Competent Authority may delegate its subordinate or may commission other institutions or organizations to administer the investments set forth in this Statute.

Article 3 Foreign national as referred to in this Statute shall include foreign juridical persons.

The nationality of a foreign juridical person shall be determined by the law under which the foreign juridical person is incorporated.

Foreign nationals making investments within the territory of the Republic of China ("ROC") under this Statute are hereinafter referred to as "investors" or the "investor."

Article 4 Investments as referred to in this Statute shall be as follows:

1. Holding shares issued by an ROC company, or contributing to the capital of an ROC company;

2. Establishing a branch office, a proprietary business or a partnership in the territory of the Republic of China; and

3. Providing loan(s) to the invested business referred to in the preceding two Paragraphs for a period exceeding one (1) year.

Article 5 If the investor holds, in an aggregate, more than one third (1/3) of the total shares issued by an enterprise in which he/she invests, or if an investor contributes, in an aggregate, more than one third (1/3) of the total capital amount of an enterprise in which he/she invests, the reinvestment to be made by the invested enterprise shall be subject to the Competent Authority's approval.

Article 6 Investments made under in this Statute consist of the following kinds:

1. Cash;

2. Machinery and equipment or raw materials for own use;

3. Patent right, trademark right, copyright, technical know-how or other intellectual property right; and

4. Other property in which the investor may invest under the Competent Authority's approval.

Article 7 The investor is prohibited from investing in the following industries:

1. Those which may negatively affect national security, public order, good customs and practices, or national health; and

2. Those which are prohibited by the law.

The investor, who applies to invest in an industry in which investment is restricted by law or by an order given under the applicable law, shall obtain an approval thereof or a consent thereto from the competent authority in charge of the industry in question.

The industries prohibited under Paragraph 1 above or restricted under Paragraph 2 above shall be prescribed and reviewed on a regular basis by the Executive Yuan.

Article 8 The investor who makes an investment in accordance with this Statute is required to submit an investment application, together with his/her investment plans and relevant documents, to the Competent Authority for approval. The same shall apply if and when his/her investment plan changes.

The investment application form shall be prescribed by the Competent Authority.

The Competent Authority shall make its decision on an investment application within one (1) month after the completion of the application procedures by the applicant, or if the application is also subject to the approval of the competent authority in charge of the relevant end enterprise, within two (2) months thereafter.

Regulations governing investors' investments in securities shall be stipulated by the Executive Yuan.

Article 9 The investor shall have his/her approved capital contribution remitted in full into the Republic of China within the prescribed time limit, and shall submit a report on the receipt of the contribution amount to the Competent Authority for examination.

If, after being granted an approval to make an investment under this Statute, the investor fails to implement his/her investment, in whole or in part, within the prescribed time limit, the approval of his/her unimplemented investment shall be revoked upon expiration of the prescribed time limit. However, for good cause shown, the investor may, prior to the expiration, apply to the Competent Authority for an extension of the prescibed time limit.

After implementing his/her investment, the investor shall request the Competent Authority to verify the total amount of his/her investment. The rules of the verification shall be prescribed by the Competent Authority.

Article 10 In case the investor intends to transfer his/her investment already implemented by him/her to an industry other than those probibited from investment under Paragraph 1 of Article 7 hereof, he/she shall apply to the Competent Authority for cancellationof his/her original investment and for approval of his/her new investment.

In case the investor intends to assign his/her investment, the assignor and the assignee shall jointly apply to the Competent Authority for approval of the assignment.

Article 11 An investor shall be entitled to exchange settlement under this Statute. This entitlement is not transferable, except to the legitimate heir of the assignee of his/her investment, or to other authorized foreign nationals or overseas Chinese to whom he/she has assigned his/her investment.

Article 12 The investor may apply for exchange settlement against the interests accrued on his/her annual income, or against the profit surplus distributed to him/her from his/her investment.

When the investor is approved to transfer his/her shares, to withdraw or decrease his/her investment, he/she may apply for exchange settlement, in a lump sum, against the total amount of his/her investment as approved. The foregoing clause is also applicable to the capital gain realized from the investor's investment.

The investor's application for exchange settlement against the payment of the principal and interest of his/her loan investment shall be governed by the agreed terms and conditions approved by the Competent Authority.

Article 13 In case the government expropriates or acquires an invested enterprise for national defense reasons, the investor thereof whose investment is less than 45%of the total capital amount of the invested enterprise shall be entitled to a reasonable compensation.

The compensation under the preceding Paragraph shall be perrnitted for exchange settlement.

Article 14 In case the investor's investment accounts for 45%or more of the total capital amount of the enterprise in which he invests, the invested enterprise shall not be subject to requisition or expropriation as long as the said capital contribution rate of the investor remains unchanged for a period of twenty (20) years after the commencement of business of the invested enterprise.

If the investor's investrnent is made in conjunction with an overseas Chinese who makes the investment under the Statute for Investment by Overseas Chinese, and if their aggregate amount of investment accounts for 45%or more of the total capital amount of the invested enterprise, the provisions referred to in the preceding Paragraph shall, mutatis mutandis, apply thereto.

Article 15 Where an invested enterprise is organized as a company under the Company Law, the investor thereof may be exempt from the restrictions on his/her domicile in the Republic of China, Chinese nationality, and the amount of investment under Articles 98-1, 108-2, 128-1, 208-5, and 216-1 of the same Law.

The provisions of Article 156-4 of the Company Law requiring issuance of stock certificates to the public, and the provisions of Article 267 of the same Law requiring setting aside a certain percentage of new shares (issued as a result of capital increase by cash) to be purchased by the employees of the invested enterprise shall not apply to an investor's investment if such investment accounts for 45%or more of the total capital of the enterprise in which he/she invests.

If the investor's investment is made in conjunction with an overseas Chinese who makes the investment under the Statute for Investment by Overseas Chinese, and if their aggregate amount of investment accounts for 45%or more of the total capital amount of

the invested enterprise, the provisions referred to in the preceding Paragraph shall, mutatis mutandis, apply thereto.

Article 16 After special approval by the Executive Yuan, the investor or the enterprise in which he/she invests shall not be subject to the following restrictions:

1. Article 5-1, proviso of Article 5-3, Article 8-1 regarding Chinese nationals, and Sub-paragraph 2 of Article 43 of the Mining Law;

2. Sub-paragraph 7 of Article 17 of the Land Law;

3. Item 1, 2, 3 and 4 of Sub-paragraph 3, and Sub-paragraph 4 of Article 2 of the Maritime Law; provided, however, that inland and coastal navigation enterprises or those which are not in the form of jointly invested enterprises shall remain subject to the foregoing restrictions; and

4. Items 1, 2, 3, 4 and 5 of Sub-paragraph 3 of Paragraph I of Article 10, and Paragraph I of Article 45 of the Civil Aviation Law.

Article 17 Except as otherwise provided for in other laws, the enterprise in which the investor has invested hereunder shall be accorded the same rights and obligations to which an enterprise operated by local Chinese nationals is entitled.

Article 18 Unless otherwise provided for in this Statute, if the investor violates the provisions of this Statute, or fails to perform any matters approved by the Competent Authority, the Competent Authority may deal with the situation in the following manner:

1. Revoke the investor's right of exchange settlement against his/her income of the profit from his/her investment, and the interest accrued thereon in a prescribed period of time; and

2. Revoke the approval for the investor's investment and his/her rights under this Statute.

Article 19 A foreign national, who fails to make an investment in accordance with this Statute prior to the amendment to this Statute may, within one (1) year from the enforcement of this amended Statute, apply to the Competent Authority for registration for the application of this amended statute to his/her prior investment.

The procedure of registration referred to in the preceding Paragraph shall be prescribed by the Competent Authority.

Article 20 This Statute shall become effective as of its date of promulgation.

PRACTICAL INFORMATION FOR CONDUCTING BUSINESS IN TAIWAN[5]

INVESTMENT AND BUSINESS CLIMATE - STRATEGIC INFORMATION AND CONTACTS FOR STARTING BUSINESS

Contact for More Information

-Michael Pignatello
-Deputy Chief, Economic Section, American Institute in Taiwan
-No. 7, Lane 134, Sec. 3, Xinyi Road, Taipei 110659 Taiwan
-+886-2-2162-2000
-pignatellomx@state.gov

Strategically located between Northeast and Southeast Asia, Taiwan is an important hub for regional and global trade and investment, especially in the high-technology industry. Indicative of its developed and open investment environment, Taiwan ranks in the upper 15th percentile of major global indices measuring ease of doing business, economic freedom, and competitiveness. To promote Taiwan's regional economic integration and as part of seeking participation in multilateral free trade arrangements, regulatory agencies have initiated reforms across many sectors of the economy, including enhancements to protection of intellectual property rights and other investment-related regulations.

As a relatively open and liberal economy, Taiwan benefits from substantial foreign direct investment, with a total cumulative stock of USD 137 billion in approved investment as of December 2015. Taiwan's GDP growth slowed to 0.65 percent in 2015, largely as a result of declining exports due to slow regional and global economic growth. Taiwan attracts a wide range of U.S. investors, including in high-tech, traditional manufacturing, and services. The United States is Taiwan's largest single source of foreign investment, with the stock of committed U.S. foreign direct investment reaching USD 17.1 billion in 2014. U.S. private commercial services exports to Taiwan totaled over USD 12.8 billion in 2014.

Structural impediments in Taiwan's investment environment include stalled progress on the privatization of Taiwan's state-owned enterprises (SOEs), which exert influence in the utilities, aerospace, energy, postal, transportation, financial, and real estate sectors. Foreign ownership limits remain in place for wireless and fixed-line telecommunications, television broadcast, and transportation. Restrictions on investments from mainland China in some sectors have been relaxed as cross-Strait ties have improved. The Taiwan Central Bank retains a currency convertibility policy in which it reserves the right to require large transactions that could impact the foreign exchange market to be scheduled over several days. Foreign private equity firms have noted a lack of transparency and predictability in the investment approvals process.

[5] This section base in part on materials of the US Department of Commerce

Aiming to promote Taiwan as a regional financial hub, Taiwan's Financial Supervisory Commission (FSC) adopted a series of liberalization measures in 2014, including liberalization of financial firms' overseas investments and expansion of overseas business units. Amendments passed by the Legislative Yuan in June 2015 to investment-related statutes clarified review criteria for mergers and acquisitions. Other regulatory revisions and amendments to existing statutes proposed in 2015 aim to clarify review criteria for foreign investment in Taiwan, but these were not implemented or passed by the legislature.

Table 1

Measure	Year	Index or Rank	Website Address
TI Corruption Perceptions index	2015	30 of 167	http://www.transparency.org/cpi2015#results-table
World Bank's Doing Business Report "Ease of Doing Business"	2015	11 of 189	doingbusiness.org/rankings
Global Innovation Index	N/A	N/A	https://www.globalinnovationindex.org/content/page/data-analysis/ Taiwan data are not provided
U.S. FDI in partner country ($M USD, stock positions)	2015	23,631	Taiwan Ministry of Economic Affairs http://www.moeaic.gov.tw/system_external/ctlr?PRO=DownloadFile&t=4&id=807
World Bank GNI per capita	N/A	N/A	N/A

1. OPENNESS TO, AND RESTRICTIONS UPON, FOREIGN INVESTMENT

Attitude toward Foreign Direct Investment

Promoting inward FDI has been an important policy goal for the Taiwan authorities because of Taiwan's self-imposed public debt ceiling that limits public spending and Taiwan's low levels of domestic private investment, which on average grew only 2.8 percent per year over the last five years. Taiwan has pursued various measures to attract FDI from both foreign companies and Taiwan firms operating overseas. A network of science and industrial parks, export processing zones, and free trade zones aims to expand trade and investment opportunities by granting tax incentives, tariff exemptions, low-interest loans, and other favorable terms.

Taiwan maintains a negative list of industries closed to foreign investment for reasons the authorities assert relate to national security and environmental protection, including public utilities, power distribution, natural gas, postal service, telecommunications, mass media, and air and sea transportation. These sectors constitute less than one percent of the production value of Taiwan's manufacturing sector and less than five percent of the services sector. Railway transport, freight transport by small trucks, pesticide manufactures, real estate development, brokerage, leasing, and trading are open to foreign investment. The negative list of industries is available at http://www.moeaic.gov.tw/system_external/ctlr?PRO=LawsLoad&lang=1&id=32.

At the end of 2015, accumulated FDI stock in Taiwan totaled approximately USD 137 billion, according to Taiwan's Ministry of Economic Affairs (MOEA) foreign investment approval data. However, discrepancies exist between Taiwan official data and the 2015 World Investment Report of the United Nations Conference of Trade and Development (UNCTAD), which calculated Taiwan's net FDI stock at a much lower USD 68 billion as of 2014. The Taiwan authorities assert that the difference was due to UNCTAD's deduction of outward remittances of profits by foreign investors, in addition to foreign investors' ability to easily obtain low-cost financing directly from within Taiwan.

Other Investment Policy Reviews

Taiwan has been a member of the WTO since 2002. In September 2014, the WTO conducted the third review of the trade policies and practices of Taiwan. Related reports and documents are available at: https://www.wto.org/english/tratop_e/tpr_e/tp402_e.htm

The OECD and UNCTAD have not conducted investment policy reviews of Taiwan.

Laws/Regulations on Foreign Direct Investment

Regulations governing FDI principally derive from the *Statute for Investment by Foreign Nationals* and the *Statue for Investment by Overseas Chinese*. These two laws permit foreign investors to transact either in foreign currency or the New Taiwan Dollar (NTD). The laws specify that foreign-invested enterprises must receive the same regulatory treatment accorded local firms. Foreign companies may invest in state-owned firms undergoing privatization and are eligible to participate in publicly financed research and development programs.

Amendments the Legislative Yuan passed in June 2015 to investment-related statutes clarified investment review criteria for mergers and acquisition transactions. Other amendments were proposed in 2015 but were not passed, including one that would replace a pre-investment approval requirement with a post-investment reporting system for investments under a USD 1 million threshold. Ex ante approval would still be required for investments in restricted industries and those exceeding the threshold. In 2015, Taiwan authorities ceased consideration of a private equity investment's impact on capital markets and resulting thin capitalization as review criteria. Other criteria remain listed on the Ministry of Economic Affairs (MOEA) Investment Commission's Frequently

Asked Questions website (located in Chinese only
at http://www.moeaic.gov.tw/system_external/ctlr?PRO=FAQLoad&id=464).

In recent years, the Taiwan authorities revised rules to improve the business climate for startups. With the goal of developing Taiwan into a startup hub in Asia, Taiwan launched an entrepreneur visa program allowing young foreign entrepreneurs to remain in Taiwan if they raise minimum funding of NTD 2 million (USD 66,000). Taiwan has initiated rules to enable intellectual property (IP) rights holders to use IP as collateral in obtaining bank loans, and this and other rules would apply to foreign investors.

Please refer to the "Doing Business" section of the MOEA's Invest in Taiwan Center website, which provides useful information for foreign investors:

http://investtaiwan.nat.gov.tw/eng/show.jsp?LV=1&ID=18&MID=3

The Investment Commission website lists the rules, regulations, and required forms for seeking foreign investment approval: http://www.moeaic.gov.tw/

Business Registration

The MOEA operates a business registration website that describes the
process: https://onestop.nat.gov.tw/oss/web/Show/engWorkFlow.do

Approval from the Investment Commission is required before proceeding with business registration. After receiving an approval letter from the Investment Commission, an investor can apply for capital verification and may then file an application for a corporate name and proceed with business registration. The new company must register with the Bureau of Labor Insurance and the Bureau of National Health Insurance before it can start recruiting and hiring employees.

The MOEA Department of Investment Services' (DOIS) Invest in Taiwan Center serves as Taiwan's investment promotion agency and provides streamlined procedures for foreign investors. DOIS services are available to all foreign investors.

For the manufacturing, construction, and mining industries, the MOEA defines small and medium-sized enterprises (SMEs) as companies with less than NTD 80 million (USD 2.5 million) of paid-in capital and fewer than 200 employees. For all other industries, SMEs are defined as having less than NTD 100 million (USD 3.1 million) of paid-in capital and fewer than 100 employees. Taiwan runs a Small and Medium Enterprise Credit Guarantee Fund to help SMEs obtain financing from local banks. Foreign firms may pay a fee to obtain a guarantee from the Fund. Taiwan's National Development Fund has set aside NTD 10 billion (USD 330 million) to invest in SMEs.

Industrial Promotion

MOEA's Invest in Taiwan Center website provides information about government programs to attract foreign investment. The *Statute for Industrial Innovation*provides the legal basis for offering tax credits for companies' research and development (R&D) expenditures. MOEA also runs several research and development subsidy programs. MOEA's current target industries for investment are offshore wind energy, logistics, electric passenger and cargo vehicles, information services, mobile broadband services, digital content, semiconductor equipment, biotechnology, and electronic materials.

Limits on Foreign Control and Right to Private Ownership and Establishment

Foreign entities are entitled to establish and own business enterprises and engage in all forms of remunerative activity as local firms unless otherwise specified in relevant regulations. Taiwan sets foreign ownership limits in certain industries, such as a 60 percent limit on direct foreign ownership of wireless and fixed line telecommunications firms, and a 49 percent limit on direct foreign investment in that sector. State-owned Chunghwa Telecom Co., which controls 97 percent of the fixed line telecom market, maintains a 55 percent limit on indirect foreign investment and a 49 percent limit on direct foreign investment. There is a 20 percent limit on foreign direct investment in cable television broadcasting services, but foreign ownership of up to 60 percent is allowed through indirect investment via a Taiwan entity. In addition, there is a foreign ownership limit of 49.99 percent for satellite television broadcasting services and piped distribution of natural gas, and a 49 percent limit for high-speed rail services. The foreign ownership cap on airport ground services firms, air-catering companies, aviation transportation businesses (airlines), and general aviation businesses (commercial helicopters and business jet planes) is less than 50 percent, with a separate limit of 25 percent for any single foreign investor. For Taiwan-flagged merchant ships, foreign investment is limited to 50 percent for Taiwan shipping companies operating international routes.

Since 2009, Taiwan has gradually been relaxing restrictions on investments from the People's Republic of China (PRC) in some sectors as cross-Strait relations have improved. Taiwan has opened more than two-thirds of its aggregate industrial categories to PRC investors, with 97 percent of manufacturing sub-sectors and 51 percent of construction and services sub-sectors open to PRC capital. PRC investors, however, continue to be prohibited from serving as a Taiwan company's Chief Executive Officer, although a PRC board member may retain management control rights of a Taiwan company. In June 2013, Taiwan and the PRC signed the cross-Strait Agreement on Trade in Services under the Economic Cooperation Framework Agreement (ECFA), but legislative review of the services agreement has stalled due to public opposition in Taiwan. As of early 2016, regulators were assessing whether to relax rules regarding PRC investment in portions of Taiwan's integrated circuits sector, and separately the Legislative Yuan was reviewing legislation that would create an oversight mechanism for cross-Strait agreements.

Privatization Program

There are currently no privatization program is in progress. Taiwan's most recent privatization, of the Aerospace Industrial Development Corporation (AIDC) in 2014, included institution of a foreign ownership ceiling of 10 percent due to the sensitive nature of the defense sector.

Screening of FDI

The Investment Commission screens applications for FDI, mergers, and acquisitions. Taiwan authorities claim that 95 percent of investments not subject to the negative list and with capital less than NTD 500 million (USD 18 million) obtain approval at the Investment Commission staff-level between two and four days. Investments between NTD 500 million and NTD 1.5 billion (USD 50 million) in capital take three to five days to screen and the approval authority rests with the Investment Commission's Executive Secretary. For investment in restricted industries, in cases where the investment amount or capital increase exceeds NTD 1.5 billion (USD 50 million), or for mergers, acquisitions, and spin-offs, screening takes 10 to 20 days and includes review by relevant supervisory ministries and final approval from the Investment Commission's Executive Secretary. Screening for foreign investments involving cross-border mergers and acquisitions or other special situations takes 20-30 days, as these transactions require interagency review and deliberation at the Investment Commission's monthly meeting.

The screening process has provided Taiwan's regulatory agencies opportunities to attach conditions to investments in order to mitigate concerns about ownership, structure, or other factors. Screening also may include an assessment of the impact of proposed investments on a sector's competitive landscape and protection of the rights of local shareholders and employees. Screening is also used to detect investments with unclear funding sources, including PRC-source capital. To ensure monitoring of PRC-source investment in line with Taiwan law and public sentiment, Taiwan's National Security Bureau has participated in every investment review meeting since April 2014 regardless of the size of the investment.

Foreign investors must submit an application form containing the funding plan, business operation plan, entity registration, and documents certifying the inward remittance of investment funds. Applicants and their agents must provide a signed declaration certifying that any PRC investors in a proposed transaction do not hold more than a 30 percent ownership stake and do not retain managerial control of the company. When an investment fails review, an investor may re-apply when the reason for the denial no longer exists. Foreign investors may also petition the regulatory agency that denied approval, or may appeal to the Administrative Court.

U.S. investors have expressed concerns about a lack of transparency, consistency, and predictability in the investment review process, particularly with regard to transactions involving private equity investment. Current guidelines on foreign investment state that private equity investors seeking to acquire companies in "important industries" must provide, for example, a detailed description of the investor's long term operational commitment and the investment's impact on sector competition. Investors have experienced lengthy review periods for private equity transactions.

Competition Law

Taiwan's Fair Trade Act was enacted in 1992. Taiwan's Fair Trade Commission examines business practices that might impede fair competition.

2. CONVERSION AND TRANSFER POLICIES

Foreign Exchange

There are few restrictions in place in Taiwan on converting or transferring direct investment funds. Foreign investors with approved investments can readily obtain foreign exchange from designated banks. The remittance of capital invested in Taiwan must be reported in advance to the Investment Commission, but the Commission's approval is not required. Declared earnings, capital gains, dividends, royalties, management fees, and other returns on investment may be repatriated at any time.

For large transactions requiring the exchange of NTD into foreign currency that could potentially disrupt Taiwan's foreign exchange market, the Taiwan Central Bank may require the transaction to be scheduled over several days. There is no written guideline on the size of such transactions, but according to law firms servicing foreign investors amounts in excess of USD 100 million may be affected. Capital movements arising from trade in merchandise and services, as well as from debt servicing, are not restricted. No prior approval is required for movement of foreign currency funds not involving conversion between NTD and foreign currency. The exchange rate is based on the market rate offered by each bank. The NTD fluctuates under a managed float system.

Remittance Policies

There are no restrictions on remittances deriving from approved direct investment and portfolio investment. No prior approval is required if the cumulative amount of inward or outward remittances does not exceed the annual limit of USD 5 million for an individual or USD 50 million for a corporate entity. There is no legal parallel currency market in Taiwan.

Taiwan is not a member of Financial Action Task Force (FATF) but is a member of the Asia-Pacific Group on Money Laundering, a FATF-style regional body. In January 2016, a new draft *Terrorist Financing Prevention Act* was forwarded to the Legislative Yuan for review.

3. EXPROPRIATION AND COMPENSATION

According to Taiwan law, the authorities may expropriate property whenever such a course is determined to be necessary for the public interest, such as for national defense, public works, and urban renewal projects. The U.S. government is not aware of any previous or recent cases of nationalization or expropriation of foreign-invested assets in Taiwan. There are no reports of indirect expropriation or any official actions tantamount to expropriation. Under Taiwan law, no venture with 45 percent or more foreign investment may be nationalized, as long as the 45 percent capital contribution ratio remains unchanged for a period of 20 years after the establishment of the foreign business. Taiwan law requires fair compensation be paid within a reasonable period when the authorities expropriate constitutionally-protected private property for public use.

4. DISPUTE SETTLEMENT

Legal System, Specialized Courts, Judicial Independence, Judgments of Foreign Courts

Taiwan has a codified system of law. In addition to the specialized courts, Taiwan has a three-tiered court system composed of the District Courts, the High Courts, and the Supreme Court. The *Compulsory Enforcement Act* provides a legal basis for enforcing the ownership of property. Taiwan does not have discrete commercial or contract laws. A variety of different laws regulate businesses and specific industries, such as the *Company Law*, *Commercial Registration Law,Business Registration Law*, and *Commercial Accounting Law*. Taiwan's Civil Code provides the basis for enforcing contracts.

Taiwan's court system is generally viewed as independent and free from overt interference by other branches of government. The U.S. Department of State's 2015 Human Rights Report stated that although Taiwan authorities made efforts to eliminate corruption and diminish political influence in the judiciary, some residual problems remained. Judicial reform advocates pressed for greater public accountability, reforms of the personnel system, and other procedural reforms. Some political commentators and academics publicly questioned the impartiality of judges and prosecutors involved in high-profile and politically sensitive cases.

Taiwan established its Intellectual Property Court in July 2008, in response to the need for a more centralized and professional litigation system for disputes relating to intellectual property rights. There are also specialized divisions in the District Courts and High Courts to deal with labor disputes. Foreign courts' judgments are final and binding, and enforced on a reciprocal basis.

Bankruptcy

Taiwan has a bankruptcy law that guarantees creditors the right to share the assets of a bankrupt debtor on a proportional basis. Secured interests in property are recognized and enforced through a registration system. Bankruptcy is not criminalized in Taiwan. Corporate bankruptcy was generally governed by the*Company Act* and the *Bankruptcy Act*. In 2014, there were 132 rulings on bankruptcy petitions.

Investment Disputes

Foreign investment disputes with the Taiwan authorities are rare. Taiwan resolves disputes according to its domestic laws and based on national treatment or investment guarantee agreements.

International Arbitration

Taiwan is not a signatory of any international investment treaties, but it has entered into bilateral investment treaties with countries including Singapore, Thailand, Malaysia, and India. Taiwan does not have an investment treaty with the United States. Taiwan's bilateral investment treaties serve to promote and protect foreign investments.

A court order on recognition and enforcement must be obtained before a foreign arbitral award can be enforced in Taiwan. Any foreign arbitral award may be enforceable in Taiwan, provided that it meets the requirements of Taiwan's *Arbitration Act*. In November 2015, the Legislative Yuan amended the *Arbitration Act*to stipulate that a foreign arbitral award, after an application for recognition has been granted by a court, shall be binding on the parties and have the same force as a final judgment of a court, and is enforceable. Taiwan referred to the UNCITRAL model law when the *Arbitration Act* was revised in 1998.

Parties to a dispute may pursue mediation by a court, a mediation committee of a town or city, and/or the Public Procurement Commission. Mediation is generally non-binding unless parties agree otherwise. Civil mediation approved by a court has the same power as a binding ruling under civil litigation.

Arbitration associations in Taiwan include the Chinese Arbitration Association, Taiwan Construction Arbitration Association, Labor Dispute Arbitration Association, and the Chinese Construction Industry Arbitration Association in Taiwan.

ICSID Convention and New York Convention

In part due to its unique political status, Taiwan is not a member of the International Centre for the Settlement of Investment Disputes (ICSID Conventions), and is not a signatory to the 1958 New York Convention on the Recognition and Enforcement of Foreign Arbitral Awards.

Duration of Dispute Resolution – Local Courts

There is no time limit for court rulings on disputes.

5. PERFORMANCE REQUIREMENTS AND INVESTMENT INCENTIVES

WTO/TRIMS

Taiwan has not notified the WTO of any measures that are inconsistent with the Trade Related Investment Measures (TRIMs) obligations. Taiwan does not require foreign firms to transfer technology, locate in specified areas, or hire a minimum number of local employees as a prerequisite to investment.

Investment Incentives

Taiwan has instituted investment incentives as stipulated in the *Statute for Industrial Innovation* and the *Act for the Establishment and Management of Free Trade Zones*. Domestic and foreign investors can receive tax incentives for investing in free trade zones, in public construction, and in biotechnology/pharmaceuticals. Investment support from the central authorities may be available for priority projects. Industrial zones, export processing zones, science parks, and local governments offer various types of subsidies, financing, and tax deductions. For a detailed list of investment incentives programs, please refer to the Invest-in-Taiwan website at: http://investtaiwan.nat.gov.tw/eng/show.jsp?ID=10&MID=3

Research and Development

Investors may receive low-interest loans or subsidies for participating in industrial R&D and industry revitalization programs. Research and development tax credits, equivalent to 15 percent of total R&D expenditures, are available only to companies who file corporate income taxes in Taiwan. Government procurement tenders are open to the public, including foreign firms. Under the *Government Procurement Act*, government procurement includes construction work, purchase or lease of property, and retention or employment of services.

Performance Requirements

Taiwan does not mandate any performance requirements.

Data Storage

Taiwan does not have forced localization policies related to data storage.

6. PROTECTION OF PROPERTY RIGHTS

Real Property

Interests in property are enforced in Taiwan. Taiwan maintains a reliable recording system for mortgages and liens. Taiwan law protects the land use rights of indigenous peoples. Taiwan's *Land Act* stipulated that forests, fisheries, hunting grounds, salt fields, mineral deposits, sources of water, and lands lying within fortified and military areas and those adjacent to the national frontiers may not be transferred or leased to foreigners. As in other investment categories, Taiwan has specific regulations governing property acquisition by PRC investors.

Intellectual Property Rights

Taiwan is not a member of the World Intellectual Property Organization (WIPO) but adheres to key international agreements such as the Berne Convention and the Agreement on Trade-related Aspects of Intellectual Property Rights (TRIPS). Reflecting progress in Taiwan's IPR legal regime and enforcement, the Office of the U.S. Trade Representative (USTR) removed Taiwan from the Special 301 Watch List in 2009. The United States continues to monitor a number of IPR issues in Taiwan, including online piracy of copyrighted materials, illegal textbook copying on university campuses, end-user piracy of software, satellite signal theft, corporate trade secret theft, and weak pharmaceutical patent protections. The importation and transshipment of counterfeit products, mainly from mainland China, is also a problem. The United States is actively working with the Taiwan authorities to address these issues.

Taiwan authorities have announced their intent to revise IP-related laws to meet criteria stipulated in the Trans-Pacific Partnership text, such as extending copyright protection from life plus 50 years to life plus 70 years, adopting a patent linkage system, extending market protection on biologics, and imposing criminal liability on persons importing counterfeit products. Amendments to the *Pharmaceutical Affairs Act* in 2015 increased penalties for the production, distribution, and sale of counterfeit medicines. The law authorizes pharmaceutical regulatory data protection for five years, the same period as in the United States, for chemical compound drugs. Amendments extending regulatory data protection to new indications were submitted to the Executive Yuan in December 2015 and are currently pending submission to the legislature.

Taiwan's Intellectual Property Police reported that the value of trademark and copyright seizures in 2015 totaled NTD 14.4 billion (USD 432 million). Taiwan Customs reported that the number of cases involving seizures of imported counterfeit branded goods increased by 34 percent from 149 cases in 2014 to 199 cases in 2015. Customs officials attribute the rise in seizures to increased detection of small parcel air freight shipments of counterfeit goods purchased from mainland Chinese e-commerce sites.

A trademark or patent applicant must file an application with Taiwan's Intellectual Property Office (TIPO). TIPO normally renders a decision within six months after it receives all supporting documents. If the application is approved, the mark/patent will be published and registered after the applicant pays registration fees within two months upon receiving the approval notice. Taiwan's patent application review period was expected to shorten from an average of 41 months in 2013 to less than 22 months in 2016, following the implementation of Patent Prosecution Highway (PPH) agreements with the United States, Japan, Spain, and the Republic of Korea in 2011, 2012, 2013, and 2015 respectively.

Taiwan has no patent linkage system, and there have been several cases of approvals and reimbursements for generic drugs despite of the existence of valid patents. As of April 2016, Taiwan was conducting final public hearings on *Pharmaceutical Affairs Act* amendments that would establish a patent linkage system, prior to their submission for Executive Yuan and legislative approval.

Patent holders may request the Taiwan Customs authorities suspend clearance and detain goods suspected of infringing their patent rights. An affected rights holder must submit a written statement detailing the infringement allegation and a security deposit equivalent to the import value. If final judgment confirms that the detained goods have infringed the patentee's rights, the owner of the detained goods will be responsible for all relevant expenses incurred.

Resources for Rights Holders

Contact at AIT:
-Kris Kvols
-Economic Officer
-+886-2-2162-2000
-kvolsdk@state.gov
American Chamber of Commerce in Taipei (http://amcham.com.tw/)

7. TRANSPARENCY OF THE REGULATORY SYSTEM

Taiwan has transparent policies and effective laws that foster competition and establish clear rules. Accounting, legal, and regulatory procedures are mostly transparent and consistent with international standards. All publicly listed companies were required to prepare financial reports using International Financial Reporting Standards (IFRS) as of 2013. Unlisted public companies, credit cooperatives, credit card companies, and insurance intermediaries were required to prepare financial reports using IFRS starting in 2015.

In November 2015, the Executive Yuan extended the public comment period for the amendment, promulgation, and abolishment of legislation from seven days to no less than 14 days, a step toward greater regulatory transparency. To help foreign investors obtain updated information regarding regulatory changes, the Executive Yuan Gazette in September 2015 launched an online platform and email subscription service to release draft bills and regulations for public comment. In February 2016, the Gazette dedicated a section to providing information concerning technical barriers to trade (TBT) and sanitary and phytosanitary measures (SPS), which require a public comment period of at least 60 days under WTO rules. Taiwan's National Development Council (NDC) operates the Regulatory Reform Platform (http://law.ndc.gov.tw) with the goal of enhancing policy communication with the general public. Through the platform, the public can submit comments on specific legislation, offer policy suggestions, and obtain information on newly promulgated or amended regulations.

8. EFFICIENT CAPITAL MARKETS AND PORTFOLIO INVESTMENT

Taiwan authorities welcome foreign portfolio investment in the Taiwan Stock Exchange (TWSE), with foreign investment now accounting for 37 percent of TWSE capitalization. In recent years, in addition to the offshore banking units that have been in operation since 1983, Taiwan launched offshore securities and offshore insurance units, aiming to attract a broader investor base. The Financial Supervisory Commission (FSC) has switched to a negative list approach toward local banks' overseas business not involving the conversion of the NTD.

Taiwan's capital market is mature and active. As of the end of 2015, there were 874 companies listed on the TWSE, with total market trading volume of USD 703 billion (including transactions of stocks, Taiwan Depository Receipts, exchange traded funds, and warrants). Foreign portfolio investors are not subject to a foreign ownership ceiling except in certain restricted companies, and are not subject to any ceiling on portfolio investment. Payments and transfers resulting from international trade activities are fully liberalized in Taiwan. A wide range of credit instruments, all allocated on market terms, are available to both domestic- and foreign-invested firms.

Money and Banking System, Hostile Takeovers

Taiwan's banking sector is healthy and banks are tightly regulated. The sector's non-performing loan (NPL) ratio has remained below one percent since 2010, with a sector average of 0.23 in December 2015. Capital-adequacy ratios (CAR) are generally high, and several of Taiwan's leading commercial lenders are government-controlled, enjoying implicit state guarantees. The sector as a whole had a CAR of 12.67 percent as of September 2015, far above the Basel III regulatory minimum of 10.5 percent required by 2019. Taiwan banks' liquidity coverage ratio, which was required by Basel III to reach 100 percent by 2019, already averages about 119 percent. Taiwan's banking system is mostly deposit-funded and has little exposure to global financial wholesale markets. Regulators have encouraged local banks to expand to overseas markets, especially to Southeast Asia, and to minimize exposure to mainland China. Taiwan Central Bank statistics show that Taiwan banks' exposure to mainland China on an ultimate risk basis declined for five consecutive quarters to USD 65 billion in 2015, after peaking at USD 94 billion in the third quarter of 2014. Taiwan's largest banks in term of assets are the state-owned Bank of Taiwan, which has USD 157 billion in assets, followed by the state-controlled Mega Bank, with USD 100 billion in assets.

The Taiwan Central Bank operates as an independent agency under the Executive Yuan free from political interference. The Central Bank's mandates are to maintain financial stability, develop Taiwan's banking business, guard the stability of the New Taiwan Dollar's external and internal value, and promote economic growth within the scope of the three aforementioned goals.

To promote the asset management business in Taiwan, starting May 2015 foreigners holding a valid visa entering Taiwan have been allowed to open an NTD account with local banks, replacing the previous dual-identification (passport and resident card) requirements.

Mergers and acquisitions are governed by a variety of laws and regulations (see Section 1). Hostile takeovers are rare in Taiwan.

9. COMPETITION FROM STATE-OWNED ENTERPRISES

Taiwan launched privatization programs in 1989 transforming many state-owned enterprises (SOEs) into private industries. In March 2016, the Executive Yuan instructed the NDC to compile a consolidated list of all SOEs in Taiwan managed by different ministries, but the list had not been published as of April 2016. As of December 2015, the authorities owned 19 SOEs, including official agencies such as the Taiwan Central Bank. Some existing SOEs are large in scale and exert significant influence in their industries, especially monopolies such as Taiwan Power Co. (Taipower) and Taiwan Water Co. MOEA plans to amend the*Electricity Industry Act* to liberalize the power generation and distribution businesses. Other SOEs such as the CPC Corporation (petroleum) and Taiwan Tobacco and Liquor Co. remained industry giants after their sectors were opened to competition. CPC controls over 70 percent of Taiwan's gasoline retail market. In August 2014, the Aerospace Industrial Development Corp. (AIDC) was successfully privatized through a public listing in the TWSE. MOEA holds a 45.7 percent stake in AIDC and intends to lower its stake to 34 percent by 2017.

The Taiwan authorities retain control over some SOEs that were privatized, including through managing appointments to boards of directors. These enterprises include Chunghwa Telecom, China Steel, Taiwan Fertilizer Co., Taiwan Salt, China Shipbuilding Co., Yang Ming Marine Transportation Co., as well as eight public banks. Taking the banking sector as an example, as of 2015, Taiwan's four largest banks were either wholly owned or controlled by the authorities and accounted for 30 percent of Taiwan domestic banks' total assets.

In 2014, the 19 SOEs contributed NTD 210 billion (USD 7 billion) to Taiwan's treasury, with the Taiwan Central Bank contributing NTD 180 billion (USD 6 billion) of that total. The number of employees working in SOEs was 118,000 in 2014 after several years of gradual decline. R&D spending among SOEs in 2014 totaled NTD 5.7 billion (USD 190 million), concentrated in oil field exploration, drilling technology, and development of alternative energy.

Taiwan acceded to the WTO's Agreement on Government Procurement (GPA) in 2009. Taiwan's central and local government entities, as well as SOEs, are now all covered by the GPA. Except for the state monopolies, SOEs compete directly with private companies. SOEs' purchases of goods or services are regulated by the *Government Procurement Act* and are open to private and foreign companies via public tender. Private companies in Taiwan have the same access to financing as SOEs. Taiwan banks are generally willing to extend loans to enterprises meeting credit requirements. SOEs are subject to the same tax obligations as private enterprises and are regulated by the *Fair Trade Act* as private enterprises. The Legislative Yuan reviews SOEs' budget each year.

OECD Guidelines on Corporate Governance of SOEs

Taiwan has not adopted the OECD Guidelines on Corporate Governance for SOEs. In Taiwan, SOEs are defined as public enterprises in which the government owns more than 50 percent of the shares. Public enterprises with less than a 50 percent government stake are not subject to Legislative Yuan supervision but the authorities may retain managerial control through senior management appointments, which may change with each administration. Each SOE operates under the authority of the supervising ministry, and government-appointed directors should hold more than one-fifth of an SOE's board seats. The Executive Yuan, the Ministry of Finance, and MOEA have criteria in place for selecting individuals for senior management positions. Each SOE has a board of directors, and some SOEs have independent directors sitting on the board.

Sovereign Wealth Funds

Taiwan does not have a sovereign wealth fund. Members of the incoming administration that will take office in May 2016 have publicly stated they may consider setting up a quasi-sovereign wealth fund to promote economic development.

10. RESPONSIBLE BUSINESS CONDUCT

The Taiwan public has high expectations for and is sensitive to responsible business conduct (RBC), in part due to concerns about such issues as food safety and environmental pollution. The Taiwan authorities actively promote responsible business conduct. MOEA and the FSC have issued guidelines on ethical standards and internal control mechanisms to urge businesses to take responsibility for the impact of their activities on the environment, consumers, employees, and communities. MOEA maintains an online newsletter to publicize best practices and raise awareness of about latest RBC-related developments in Taiwan and abroad.

Companies with more than NTD 10 billion (USD 330 million) in capital and firms with direct impact on consumers such as food processing, restaurants, chemicals, and financial services were mandated to prepare annual social responsibility reports as of 2015. According to the TWSE, 77 percent of Taiwan's top 100 companies have published social responsibility reports, and 30 percent (or 255) of all total listed companies have issued reports. In August 2014, the TWSE launched the Taiwan Top Salary 100 Index, a government effort to promote corporate social responsibility and expand the use of profit-sharing for the benefit of employees.

In response to a series of food safety and environmental protection scandals in recent years, the authorities have imposed stricter monetary penalties on violators and launched a registration platform for food industry suppliers to track food ingredients used in the industry's production chain. Taiwan authorities encourage Taiwan firms to adhere to the OECD Due Diligence Guidance for Responsible Supply Chains of Minerals from Conflict-Afflicted and High-Risk Areas. Taiwan does not participate in the Extractive Industries Transparency Initiative.

11. POLITICAL VIOLENCE

Taiwan is a relatively young and vibrant multi-party democracy. The January 2016 presidential and legislative elections were peaceful and orderly, as was the transition of power between administrations. There are no recent examples of politically motivated damage to foreign investment.

12. CORRUPTION

Taiwan has implemented laws, regulations, and penalties to combat corruption, including in public procurement. The *Corruption Punishment Statute and Criminal Code* contain specific penalties for corrupt activities, including maximum jail sentences of life in prison and a maximum fine of up to NTD 100 million (USD 3.3 million). Laws provide for increased penalties for public officials who fail to explain the origins of suspicious assets or property. The U.S. government is not aware of cases where bribes have been solicited for foreign investment approval.

UN Anticorruption Convention, OECD Convention on Combatting Bribery

Taiwan is not a party to the OECD Convention on Combatting Bribery.

Resources to Report Corruption

-Agency Against Corruption (AAC), Ministry of Justice
- Overall Planning Division
- No. 318, 2nd floor, Song-jiang Road, Taipei
- aac2043@mail.moj.gov.tw

Transparency International Chinese Taipei http://www.tict.org.tw/front/bin/home.phtml

13. BILATERAL INVESTMENT AGREEMENTS

Bilateral Taxation Treaties

Taiwan does not have a bilateral taxation treaty with the United States. Taiwan has 29 bilateral tax agreements entered into force (available athttp://investtaiwan.nat.gov.tw/cht/show.jsp?ID=58) and has concluded similar agreements with Japan and Canada that are pending approval by those governments.

Taiwan has concluded economic cooperation (free trade) agreements with El Salvador, Guatemala, Honduras, Nicaragua, Panama, Singapore, and New Zealand, and has concluded 29 bilateral investment or related agreements (available at http://www.dois.moea.gov.tw/asp/relation1_1_3.asp).

Under the Taiwan Relations Act, the terms of the 1948 Friendship, Commerce, and Navigation Treaty between the Republic of China and the United States remain in force. U.S. investors are guaranteed national treatment and are provided a number of protections, including protection against expropriation. Representatives of the United States and Taiwan signed a Trade and Investment Framework Agreement (TIFA) in 1994 to serve as the basis for consultation on trade and investment issues. TIFA discussions were suspended in 2007 in response to Taiwan policies affecting U.S. beef imports, but resumed in 2013.

14. OPIC AND OTHER INVESTMENT INSURANCE PROGRAMS

Taiwan and the United States have an Overseas Private Investment Corporation (OPIC) agreement. The agreement, signed in 1952, is called the Agreement Dealing with Guaranty of American Investment of Private Capital in Taiwan. There are no active OPIC projects in Taiwan.

15. LABOR

Taiwan's unemployment rate declined to 3.78 percent in 2015 from 3.96 percent in the previous year. The unemployment rate for people aged between 15 and 24 years was 15.4 percent in 2015. Taiwan's labor force is decreasing as the society ages, with residents over 65 years of age expected to account for 20 percent of the total population by 2025. In the industrial sector, the number of blue-collar foreign workers increased from 331,585 in 2014 to 363,584 in 2015. Industry groups claim that a lack of blue-collar workers is one of the major issues facing manufacturers operating in Taiwan and have urged the authorities to increase the ceiling on foreign workers. Skilled white-collar labor, especially in the information technology sector, remains a strength of Taiwan's talent pool. However, Taiwan's low wage growth compared with neighboring economies poses a challenge for talent recruitment and retention. The authorities sponsor training and certificate programs for college graduates to increase the talent pool for the manufacturing industry.

Private companies are not subject to rules requiring the hiring of nationals. Local workers have expressed concern about displacement by lower-cost foreign workers. Employers may institute unpaid leave with employees' consent but must notify the labor authorities and continue to make health insurance, labor insurance, and pension contributions. Taiwan provides unemployment relief based on the *Employment Insurance Law*, vocational training allowances for jobless persons, and employment subsidies to encourage hiring.

Labor flexibility is the main reason Taiwan firms hire temporary workers. Financial and logistics industries hire temporary workers for entry-level administrative positions such as customer services representatives, administrative clerks, security guards, and janitors. SOEs also hire contract workers. Companies in specific hardship (labor-intensive) industries are entitled to a higher foreign labor quota. The authorities are considering relaxing rules for the hiring of foreign white-collar professionals in designated foreign trade zones.

Labor unions have become more active in Taiwan over the past decade, and the *Collective Agreement Act* outlines the negotiation mechanism for collective bargaining in order to protect labor's interests in the negotiations. If a proposal is refused, a union may submit an application for arbitration to the Committee for Dispute Resolution for Unfair Labor Practices under the Ministry of Labor Affairs (MOL). Taiwan has labor dispute resolution mechanisms in operation at all levels of labor, and the authorities accept about 20,000 cases per year. Starting in 2011, an arbitration mechanism was introduced to preempt disputes through a professional and neutral mediation system, which resolves about 60 percent of all cases.

Labor relations in Taiwan are generally harmonious. Although Taiwan is not a member of the International Labor Organization (ILO), it adheres to ILO conventions on the protection of workers' rights. Taiwan law, including related regulations and statutory instruments, protects the right to join independent unions, conduct legal strikes, and bargain collectively. Taiwan's labor authorities have sought to increase the frequency and coverage of labor inspections. MOL has proposed a law that would allow temporary workers to receive the same pay as full-time employees in equal positions.

Link to the U.S. Department of State Human Rights Report on Taiwan: http://www.state.gov/j/drl/rls/hrrpt/humanrightsreport/index.htm#wrapper

16. FOREIGN TRADE ZONES/FREE PORTS/TRADE FACILITATION

The first free trade/free port zone began operation in 2004 at Keelung, Taiwan's northern port. Another four were established in 2005 at Taoyuan International Airport and the international harbors in Kaohsiung, Taichung, and Taipei. In May 2010 and August 2013, the Executive Yuan approved free trade zones at Suao and Anping ports, respectively, bringing total free trade zones in Taiwan to seven. Taiwan authorities have relaxed restrictions on the movement of merchandise, capital, and personnel into and out of these zones. As part of a broader restructuring and to increase the competitiveness of Taiwan's ports, the Ministry of Transportation and Communication established the Taiwan International Ports Corp. (TIPC) in 2012 to manage commercial activities of Taiwan's ports and free trade zones. TIPC facilitates cooperation with foreign shipping operations and related businesses.

Taiwan seeks to promote the unique advantages its ports offer as hubs for the Asian regional market. In June 2013, the London Metal Exchange (LME) board approved Kaohsiung Port as an LME delivery port of primary aluminum, aluminum alloy, copper, lead, nickel, tin, and zinc.

17. FOREIGN DIRECT INVESTMENT AND FOREIGN PORTFOLIO INVESTMENT STATISTICS

Table 2: Key Macroeconomic Data, U.S. FDI in Host Country/Economy

		Host Country Statistical source*	USG or international statistical source	USG or International Source of Data: BEA; IMF; Eurostat; UNCTAD, Other	
Economic Data	Year	Amount	Year	Amount	
Host Country Gross	2015	523,567	2015	518,816	https://research.stlouisfed.or

Domestic Product (GDP) ($M USD)					g/fred2/series/ TWNNGDPD USD
Foreign Direct Investment		Host Country Statistical source*	USG or international statistical source	USG or international Source of data: BEA; IMF; Eurostat; UNCTAD, Other	
U.S. FDI in partner country ($M USD, stock positions)	2015	23,631	2014	17,073	BEA
Host country's FDI in the United States ($M USD, stock positions)	2015	14,209	2014	5,676	BEA
Total inbound stock of FDI as % host GDP	2015	26.2	2014	13.0	UNCTAD

* Local GDP data source: Directorate General of Budget, Accounting, and Statistics (DGBAS). * Local FDI data source: Ministry of Economic Affairs (MOEA). Taiwan FDI data reflect approved investments and do not take into account disinvestment.

STARTING BUSINESS IN TAIWAN - BASIC INFORMATION

MARKET OVERVIEW

With a population of 23 million, Taiwan is a thriving democracy, vibrant market economy, and a highly attractive export market, especially for U.S. firms. Taiwan is our ninth largest trading partner, putting it ahead of Brazil, India, and Italy. It is also our sixth largest agricultural market, and our fifth largest source of foreign students in U.S. higher education. Taiwan is the fourth largest holder in the world of foreign exchange reserves, with over US$ 382 billion in 2010. The Taiwan economy has rebounded sharply from the global financial crisis and enjoyed 10.47% GDP growth last year, low unemployment, and an appreciating currency that makes U.S. goods and services more attractive than ever to Taiwan buyers.

Taiwan's real GDP increased by 10.47% in 2010, mainly driven by strong export growth and private investment expansion. In 2011, local exports to the emerging markets, especially East Asia, will continue to pick up while the growth of exports to the advanced economies is expected to slow down. The innovation of high-tech products should boost export shipments of locally-made ICT items. In addition, the tariff reductions and exemptions on the early harvest program of the Economic Cooperation Framework Agreement (ECFA), effective on January 1, 2011, will also help Taiwan's exports to China. However, Taiwan's export growth may be significantly impacted by the New Taiwan dollar appreciation against the

U.S. dollar. Local private consumption is expected to continuously expand as a result of the recent economic recovery and low unemployment. Improving ties with China is expected to ease the current cross-Strait and investment restrictions and encourage more foreign investments in Taiwan. With these changing factors, local officials forecast the economic growth for 2011 will be moderate and at an annual rate of about 5.03%.

Total exports increased by 34.8% to $274.64 billion in 2010 and imports rose 44.2% to $251.4 billion. China (including Hong Kong) is Taiwan's largest trading partner, accounting for 29.0% of total trade and 14.95% of Taiwan's imports in 2010. Japan follows, with 13.3% of total trade, including 20.66% of Taiwan's imports. The U.S. is now Taiwan's third-largest trading partner, importing 10.8% of Taiwan's exports and exporting 10.1% of Taiwan's imports.

MARKET CHALLENGES

Taiwan is a sophisticated consumer market, plugged into consumer trends in Japan and Korea, awash in products from China and other lower-cost producers in Asia, and well aware of market developments in America and around the globe. Taiwan is generally a target market for high-quality, differentiated products rather than commodity items.

At the same time, it is generally a very price-sensitive market, and imported products must conform to certain standards and labeling regulations required for importing products into this market. Generally, a local agent will assist with this regulatory aspect.

A special concern by American firms over the past few decades has been the protection of intellectual property rights (IPR). Right holders continue to express some concern regarding infringement of copyrighted material on the Internet; illegal textbook copying on and around university campus; inadequate protection for the packaging, configuration, and outward appearance of products (trade dress); and the availability of counterfeit pharmaceuticals in Taiwan.

MARKET OPPORTUNITIES

Taiwan's accession to the World Trade Organization (WTO) in 2009 and the WTO Government Procurement Agreement in 2009 led to further dismantling of non-tariff barriers and a general lowering of the remaining tariffs. These actions further enhance U.S. opportunities in this market, including high-value-added components and other inputs for high-tech manufacturing (e.g., petrochemical products and electronic production and test equipment), food and other agricultural products, and "American lifestyle" goods and services sought by Taiwan's affluent population, running the gamut from luxury consumer goods to healthcare products.

Taiwan's imports are dominated by raw materials and capital goods, which account for more than 90% of the total. Taiwan imports a wide variety of electronic, optical and precision instruments, information and communications products, transportation equipment, machinery, and electrical products. With few natural resources, Taiwan also imports coal, oil and gas to meet most of its energy needs. Taiwan's high-tech sector relies heavily on technology licenses and imports of specialty components from the United States.

MARKET ENTRY STRATEGY

Most new-to-market exporters entering Taiwan begin by finding a local partner to serve as an agent, distributor, and/or representative. Agents are the most common partnerships used by foreign firms to gain their initial foothold here. The vast majority of Taiwan firms are small and medium sized enterprises (SMEs). They are quite active in trading and manufacturing, and offer a large pool of prospective trade partners that can capably represent U.S. companies in Taiwan.

Taiwan's banking and international remittance systems are well developed, and there are no foreign exchange regulations that would significantly hamper a U.S. exporter from getting paid. Irrevocable letters of credit are widely used and

"L/Cs" from leading Taiwan financial institutions can generally be confirmed by

SELLING U.S. PRODUCTS AND SERVICES

USING AN AGENT OR DISTRIBUTOR

Most foreign firms gain their initial foothold in the Taiwan market by using a local agent. Many Taiwan firms prefer the partnering aspect of an agent relationship. Although some companies are willing to act only as distributors, there is concern that foreign firms that are merely seeking distributors may not be serious about the market and will not support their distributors. Some U.S. exporters that sell equipment or machinery may find it necessary to locate a partner willing and able to do some assembly, manufacture in Taiwan, or provide after service. Although not necessarily formal joint ventures, these efforts require a higher degree of commitment to the market than simply selling through an agent. If the size of the market warrants, companies may consider setting up a branch office or subsidiary in Taiwan. Taiwan welcomes foreign investment, and although procedures are sometimes bureaucratic, establishing an office in Taiwan is relatively easy.

The U.S. Commercial Service in Taiwan provides a number of services to help U.S. firms, large and small, export their goods and services to Taiwan. Through our office in Taipei (covering northern and central Taiwan) and a branch office in Kaohsiung (covering southern Taiwan), we offer a variety of resources and services (including business matchmaking services, product launches, market research, agent distributor searches, advocacy, trade missions, trade shows, and due diligence) to assist U.S. companies entering the Taiwan market. CS Taiwan contact details are: Tel: 886-22720-1550, Fax: 886-2-2757-7162, Email taipei.office.box@trade.gov Information is also available at: http://www.buyusa.gov/taiwan/en

The first step in using these services is contacting an Export Assistance Center in the United States. A comprehensive list of U.S. Export Assistance Centers (USEAC) can be found at https://emenu.ita.doc.gov/emenu.nsf/ . These offices can help U.S. exporters determine which services are most suited for their export needs as well as which international markets are suitable for their products and services.

Establishing an Office

Establishing a subsidiary, branch, or representative office in Taiwan is generally not particularly burdensome. However, there are a number of structures and issues to consider, and an array of forms and procedures to complete. In addition, a Chinese company name is required. Consultations with reputable local attorneys and accountants are strongly recommended in order to identify the key issues relevant to each business and to complete all the necessary steps for establishing a new entity.

The Ministry of Economic Affairs (MOEA) website has information on investing and setting up a company in Taiwan. Please visit http://www.moea.gov.tw and http://www.moeaic.gov.tw

The U.S. Commercial Service in Taiwan maintains an online listing of local professional service providers, including local attorneys, accountants, consultants, and other professionals. The listing can be found at http://www.buyusa.gov/taiwan/en/businessserviceproviders.htm

Franchising

Franchise operations in Taiwan have been very popular for fast food restaurants, casual restaurants, convenience stores, health and drug stores, spa services, organic products stores, language schools, hair salons, real estate brokerage services, apparel stores, shoe stores and sporting goods. In recent years, Taiwan's investors have become more conservative in adopting new foreign franchises. This is due to the high capital investment required by foreign franchise operators and the increasing competition from local franchises. In order to succeed in the Taiwan market, well-known U.S. franchises should provide considerable support to their local partners, including management best practices, systems integration, personnel and customer service training, and consistency in product quality.

A variety of franchise arrangements exist in Taiwan, ranging from shared joint venture partnerships to a model in which stores are managed and operated by a master franchisee or a regionally based conglomerate. Currently, there is no specific body of laws that regulate franchising in Taiwan. Franchise agreements are generally subject to the Civil Code with some regulated by the Fair Trade Law. The laws, regulations and practices concerning the intellectual property aspects of international franchising are the same as those of Taiwan domestic franchising regardless of whether the transaction involves a foreign entity or is a purely domestic arrangement.

Successful franchisors in Taiwan usually use a reliable professional service provider, such as an attorney and/or accountant, for advice on the structure and implementation of a franchising agreement.

DIRECT MARKETING

Online shopping and TV shopping have become very popular retail sales channels in Taiwan in recent years. Online shopping is expanding robustly, growing by 21.5% from 2009 to $12 billion in 2010, according to the Market Intelligence & Consulting Institute (MIC) under the semi-official Institute for Information Industry (III). B2C accounted for the largest proportion (57.3%) of the direct marketing sales value. Young people aged 20-39 are the main buyers using online shopping. TV shopping in Taiwan reached about US$1.7 billion in revenue sales in 2010.

In addition, multi-level marketing has become a popular second job in Taiwan, which is ranked the ninth in the world in terms of multi-level marketing sales volume. Recent figures indicate that there are approximately 5.6 million people, out of a total Taiwan population of about 23 million, working for multi-level sales businesses in Taiwan, which specialize primarily in healthcare, skin care products, and household items.

JOINT VENTURES/LICENSING

Foreign investors who wish to establish new enterprises in Taiwan through joint venture activities or by furnishing technical know-how, trademarks, patent rights, or other management services to a locally incorporated business enterprise must file an application for approval by the Investment Commission (IC) of the Ministry of Economic Affairs (MOEA). The IC generally issues a decision within two months of receiving a completed application. Capital should not be remitted for joint-venture investment until approvals are first obtained. Information regarding regulations for approval and consideration of foreign investment or technical cooperation is available at IC's website: http://www.moeaic.gov.tw

SELLING TO THE GOVERNMENT

Taiwan acceded to the World Trade Organization's (WTO) Government Procurement Agreement (GPA) in July 2009. According to Taiwan's GPA Agreement, U.S. firms will now compete on equal terms with domestic firms when government tenders for covered entities under the Agreement that meet or exceed the following threshold values:

Federal government contracts valued at over US$194,000 for goods and services and approximately US$7.45 million for construction services.

State-level government contracts valued at over US$296,000 for goods and services and approximately US$22.2 million for construction services during the first year after the Agreement goes into effect. The construction services threshold will drop to US$7.45 million after the third year the Agreement is in effect and will remain at this level.

Government-controlled entities such as utilities and universities/colleges with contracts for goods and services valued at US$593,000 and construction services valued at US$22.2 million for the first year. The construction services threshold will drop to US$7.45 million after the third year the Agreement is in effect and will remain at this level.

The following are statistics on Taiwan's government procurement cases in 2009, which were submitted in a report to WTO. In total,

Taiwan's GPA-covered entities put out to bid 1,016 contracts with a total worth US$5.3 billion.

U.S. firms won 92 contracts worth US$99 million. 46 of the contracts were with federal government entities, 45 with government-controlled entities, and one with state-level government level contract.

U.S. firms' performance was comparable to EU firms who won 81 contracts worth US$136.9 million, and exceeded Japanese firms who won 27 contracts worth US$32.4 million.

Federal Government Entities

The 46 contracts U.S. firms won at the Federal government level were worth US$25.9 million.

Federal government ministries that purchased from U.S. firms included the Office of the President (19 contracts); Ministry of Transport and Communications (7); National Science Council (6); Atomic Energy Council (5); and Department of Health (3).

The types of goods and services that Central Government entities were purchasing from U.S. firms included: aircraft components; refrigeration and air conditioning equipment; electrical components; lab equipment; chemicals; research and development services.

Government-Controlled Entities

The 45 contracts U.S. firms won at Government-controlled entities, such as utilities and universities/colleges, were worth US$72.8 million.

State-Level Entities

The 1 contract a U.S. firm won for the Taipei City Government was worth US$0.3 million.

Among the 45 total contracts won by U.S. firms, 24 included contracts with Taiwan's government-controlled hospitals (Nat'l Taiwan University Hospital; National Cheng Kung University Hospital; Veterans General Hospital-Taipei; Veterans General Hospital-Kaohsiung); eight contracts with the Taiwan Power Company; seven contracts with Chinese Petroleum Corporation, Taiwan; and six contracts with four separate universities covered under the GPA.

In response to foreign companies' concerns about maintaining fairness in contractual obligations, Taiwan's Public Construction Commission has prepared a model contract template as a reference for government procuring entities. The conditions in this model contract are the same to all bidders - domestic or foreign.

U.S. exporters are encouraged to visit the Commercial Service Taiwan's GPA website http://www.buyusa.gov/taiwan/en/taiwan_gpa.html to find guidance and information on participating in Taiwan's GPA opportunities.

DISTRIBUTION AND SALES CHANNELS

The most common distribution route in Taiwan moves products from suppliers to distributors, from distributors to retailers, and then from retailers to consumers. Some suppliers shorten distribution channels by distributing products directly through retailers. Multi-level marketing is accepted in Taiwan, and some direct-selling organizations are well established here. Foreign firms, especially small- and medium-sized companies, generally rely on agents to sell their merchandise to distributors. For certain products such as apparel, however, the distribution channels tend to be more complex.

Taiwan has four major ports: Kaohsiung, Keelung, Taichung, and Hualien. They also serve as the island's major distribution centers.

SELLING FACTORS/TECHNIQUES

The most important consideration for the majority of Taiwan buyers is price, which is also the most common complaint regarding U.S. goods. American businesses are frequently frustrated that Taiwan firms do not necessarily factor in life-cycle costs when negotiating a purchase. Although attitudes are changing, most Taiwan firms will only pay a higher price for a product if they see a near-term payoff. The second and third most important considerations for Taiwan buyers are quality and after-sales service.

Labeling and instructions and/or sales literature in the Chinese language are required when selling products in the Taiwan market. Detailed information about labeling is available in Chapter 7 of this report.

ELECTRONIC COMMERCE

Taiwan's Internet infrastructure is very well developed and fully capable of supporting the development of electronic commerce, although relevant policies are still evolving. Over 90 percent of Taiwan's companies have corporate networks and a network infrastructure, and 5.8 million (or 76.1% of) households have access to the Internet. According to the Taiwan Institute for Information Industry, Internet sales are expected to increase by 20% from $11.2 billion in 2010 to $13.5 billion in 2011.

In November 2001, the Electronic Signature Law was promulgated, which adopts the principles of the U.N. Commission on International Trade Law's Model Law on Electronic Commerce and recognizes the legal validity of electronic contracts, records, and signatures. To address the issue of identity theft, Taiwan passed the Computer-Processed Personal Data Protection Act in 2011.

Taiwan has not joined the United States in APEC to advocate for a permanent moratorium on taxation of Internet transactions, and the Ministry of Finance imposes business taxes on Internet vendors who sell products for profit and have monthly sales over NT$60,000 (approximately US$1,850).

TRADE PROMOTION AND ADVERTISING

Taiwan businesses are active in the global marketplace. They read trade journals from the U.S., Europe, and Japan, participate in major international trade events, and are well aware of current trends in their industries. There are local trade shows for most major industries and the Taiwan External Trade Development Council (TAITRA) is either the organizer or co-organizer for many of these shows (usually in conjunction with the relevant industry associations).

A local partner can give the best advice on where and how to advertise, but participation in major trade shows and advertisements in relevant Taiwan trade journals and industry newspapers are also important.

Information on trade shows in Taiwan can be obtained from TAITRA's website at http://www.taiwantrade.com.tw. TAITRA also offers several lists, including a frequently updated calendar for international conferences and trade exhibitions held at the Taipei World Trade Center. TAITRA-sponsored trade shows can be found at http://www.taipeitradeshows.com.tw . Most trade exhibitions in Taiwan are export-oriented. Some have a significant number of non-Taiwan exhibitors.

U.S. companies that do not have representatives or agents in Taiwan should target professional journals and magazines. The following are some of Taiwan's major industry/commercial newspapers and business publications with their respective websites:

Commercial Times: http://news.chinatimes.com
Economic Daily News: http://www.udngroup.com/UDNENGLISH/edn.htm
Business Weekly: http://businessweekly.com.tw
Commonwealth: http://www.cw.com.tw
Management Magazine: http://www.managementmagazine.com.tw
Director of Taiwan: http://www.taiwannews.com.tw

Taiwan's advertising sector is comparable to that of other developed economies and covers a wide range of media. The Cable, Radio and Television Act governs TV advertising. All commercials must be pre-approved by the relevant official department. Reference to associated laws and other official department is also necessary to understand the full picture with regard to Do's and Don'ts in the Taiwan market, particularly with regard to the protection of children and women. The duration of advertisements shall not exceed one-sixth of the total transmission time of each program. There are some restrictions to advertising, especially for alcohol and tobacco commercials on television and radio.

The Commercial Service in Taiwan also offers the Featured U.S. Exporters (FUSE), Business Service Provider (BSP), and Single Company Promotion (SCP) services to help U.S. companies promote their products and services in Taiwan. CS Taiwan will be organizing U.S. Pavilions in a variety of industry shows in Taiwan and promoting several conferences in Taiwan recruiting U.S. companies' participation. If a U.S. company would rather exhibit in the U.S. but still meet Taiwan buyers, CS Taiwan regularly recruits and leads Taiwan buyer trade missions to major U.S. trade shows under the auspices of the

U.S. Department of Commerce's International Buyer Program. For further details, please see the CS Taiwan website: http://www.buyusa.gov/taiwan/en

PRICING

Branding is an important factor in developing a pricing strategy, especially in the consumer goods sector. Generally speaking, price margins at the distributor level for international brands are lower than for local or regional brands. Distributor price margins range on average between 15 percent and 40 percent, depending on whether the distributor controls the marketing. Price breaks and discounts for large-volume purchases are commonly offered.

A five percent value-added tax (VAT) of the sales amount is imposed on all products and services sold in Taiwan. Imports are subject to VAT calculated on the landed price, including duties and commodity taxes on certain products. Products including rubber tires, cement, non-alcoholic beverages, oil and gas, certain electrical appliances, flat glass, and motor vehicles are subject to commodity taxes that range from eight percent to 50 percent ad valorem or other specific basis. In addition to customs duties, all imports are assessed a commercial harbor service charge, which is based on cargo weight and net ship tonnage.

SALES SERVICE/CUSTOMER SUPPORT

Taiwan's buyers, especially purchasing commercial and industrial products, consider many factors when making purchase decisions. These factors include technical support, after-sales service, product performance, durability, software availability, and overall commitment. U.S. firms should, however, be aware of the fact that price is often paramount.

PROTECTING YOUR INTELLECTUAL PROPERTY

Taiwan has continued efforts to improve its IPR legal regime and enforcement. The Taiwan Intellectual Property Office (TIPO) under the Ministry of Economic Affairs as well as other relevant agencies have adopted programs to crack down on Internet and physical piracy. In January 2007, the Legislative Yuan passed the Intellectual Property Litigation Law, which stipulates that civil, criminal, and administrative litigation involving intellectual property rights will be tried in a special IPR court. In March 2007, the Legislative Yuan passed the IP Court Organization Law that established a specialized IP court in July 2008.

For more information, please refer to Chapter 6 of this report and the IPR toolkit on the AIT website at http://www.ait.org.tw/en/ipr-Toolkit.html

PROTECTING YOUR INTELLECTUAL PROPERTY IN TAIWAN:

Several general principles are important for the effective management of intellectual property ("IP") rights in Taiwan. First, it is important to have an overall strategy to protect your IP. Second, IP is protected differently in Taiwan than in the U.S. Third, rights must be registered and enforced in Taiwan, under local laws. It is vital that companies understand that intellectual property is primarily a private right and that the US government generally cannot enforce rights for private individuals in Taiwan.

Your U.S. trademark and patent registrations will not protect you in Taiwan. Registration of patents and trademarks is on a first-in-time, first-in-right basis, so you should consider applying for trademark and patent protection even before selling your products or services in the Taiwan market.

Additionally, there is no such thing as an "international copyright" that will automatically protect an author's writings throughout the entire world. Protection against unauthorized use in a particular country depends, basically, on the national laws of that country. However, most countries do offer copyright protection to foreign works under certain conditions, and these conditions have been greatly simplified by international copyright treaties and conventions.

It is the responsibility of the rights' holders to register, protect, and enforce their rights where relevant, retaining their own counsel and advisors. Companies may wish to seek advice from local attorneys or IP consultants who are experts in Taiwan law. The U.S. Commercial Service in Taiwan has an online listing of local lawyers at: http://www.buyusa.gov/taiwan/en/businessserviceproviders.htm

While the U.S. Government (USG) stands ready to assist, there is little the government can do if the rights holders have not taken these fundamental steps necessary to securing and enforcing their IP in a timely fashion. Moreover, in many countries, rights holders who delay enforcing their rights on a mistaken belief that the USG can provide a political resolution to a legal problem may find that their rights have been eroded or abrogated due to legal doctrines such as statutes of limitations, laches, estoppel, or unreasonable delay in prosecuting a law suit. In no instance should U.S. Government advice be seen as a substitute for the obligation of a rights holder to promptly pursue its case.

It is always advisable to conduct due diligence on potential partners. Negotiate from the position of your partner and give your partner clear incentives to honor the contract. A good partner is an important ally in protecting IP rights. Consider carefully, however, whether to permit your partner to register your IP rights on your behalf. Doing so may create a risk that your partner will list itself as the IP owner and fail to transfer the rights should the partnership end. Keep an eye on your cost structure and reduce the margins (and the incentive) of would-be bad actors. Projects and sales require constant attention. Work with legal counsel familiar with Taiwan laws to create a solid contract that includes non-compete clauses, and confidentiality/non-disclosure provisions.

It is also recommended that small and medium-size companies understand the importance of working together with U.S. trade associations and organizations to support efforts to protect IP and stop counterfeiting. There are a number of these organizations, both Taiwan or U.S.-based. These include:

The U.S. Chamber and local American Chambers of Commerce
National Association of Manufacturers (NAM)
International Intellectual Property Alliance (IIPA)
International Trademark Association (INTA)
The Coalition Against Counterfeiting and Piracy
International Anti-Counterfeiting Coalition (IACC)
Pharmaceutical Research and Manufacturers of America (PhRMA)
Biotechnology Industry Organization (BIO)

IP RESOURCES

A wealth of information on protecting IP is freely available to U.S. rights holders. Some excellent resources for companies regarding intellectual property include the following:

For information about patent, trademark, or copyright issues -- including enforcement issues in the U.S. and other countries -- call the STOP! Hotline:

1-866-999-HALT or register at www.StopFakes.gov

For more information about registering trademarks and patents (both in the U.S. as well as in foreign countries), contact the U.S. Patent and Trademark Office (USPTO) at: 1-800-786-9199.

For more information about registering for copyright protection in the U.S., contact the U.S. Copyright Office at: 1-202-707-5959.

For more information about how to evaluate, protect, and enforce intellectual property rights and how these rights may be important for businesses, a free online training program is available at www.StopFakes.gov

For information on obtaining and enforcing intellectual property rights and market-specific IP Toolkits visit:

www.StopFakes.gov This site is linked to the USPTO website for registering trademarks and patents, both in the U.S. as well as in foreign countries. www.StopFakes.gov is also linked to the U.S. Customs & Border Protection website to record registered trademarks and copyrighted works to assist customs in blocking imports of IP-infringing products and allows you to register for Webinars on protecting IP.

DUE DILIGENCE

Prior to entering into a relationship with an unknown Taiwan company, a U.S. firm would be wise to confirm the reputation of the company. However, Taiwan's privacy laws often make it difficult to collect background information on individuals.

Local attorneys and accountants can be excellent sources of information, as can trade/industry associations.

The Commercial Service offers an International Company Profile (ICP) service to help

U.S. firms with due diligence in Taiwan. For further details, please visit http://www.buyusa.gov/taiwan/en/findbuyers.html#_section2

LOCAL PROFESSIONAL SERVICES

Taiwan has a comprehensive, modern legal system, as well as a respectable number of well-regarded local and international law firms and legal consultants. Many Taiwan attorneys active in international business have studied law in the United States, speak English, and understand the concerns of U.S. businesses. Consultations with a competent local attorney prior to engaging in business in the Taiwan market are highly recommended.

Likewise, the major U.S. and global accounting firms and insurance companies have active offices in Taiwan. Any U.S. firms interested in entering the Taiwan market should make a point of meeting with these professional advisors. Not only can they provide advice on their specific areas of expertise, but also on a range of business and cultural matters.

Up-to-date lists of professional firms may be obtained from the American Chamber of Commerce in Taiwan by e-mail: amcham@amcham.com.tw or from their website http://www.amcham.com.tw

The U.S. Commercial Service in Taiwan maintains an online listing of local professional service providers, including local attorneys, accountants, consultants, and other professionals. The listing can be found at http://www.buyusa.gov/taiwan/en/businessserviceproviders.htm

Web Resources Ministry of Economic Affairs (MOEA): http://www.moea.gov.tw Board of Foreign Trade, MOEA: http://www.trade.gov.tw Investment Commission, MOEA: http://www.moeaic.gov.tw National Information & Communications Initiative, Executive

Yuan: http://www.nici.nat.gov.tw National Tax Administration, MOF: http://www.ntat.gov.tw The Fair Trade Commission, Executive Yuan: http://www.ftc.gov.tw Taiwan Intellectual Property Office, MOEA: http://www.tipo.gov.tw

LIST OF ATTORNEYS

AMERICAN INSTITUTE IN TAIWAN
美國在台協會

American Institute in Taiwan
No. 7, Lane 134, Xin Yi Road, Sec. 3, Taipei, Taiwan
台北市信義路三段 134 巷 7 號
Tel: 886-2-2162-2000 Fax: 886-2-2162-2239
E-mail: Amcit-ait-t@state.gov

The attorneys listed below have expressed an interest in representing American citizens in Taiwan. The American Institute in Taiwan assumes no responsibility or liability for the professional ability reputation of, or the quality of services provided by, the following persons or firms. Inclusion on this list is in no way an endorsement by the Department of State or AIT. Firms practicing in the Taipei area are listed first, followed by a list of firms practicing in Northern Taiwan and Central Taiwan. Names are listed alphabetically, and the order in which they appear has no other significance. The information in the list on professional credentials, areas of expertise and language ability are provided directly by the lawyers. You may receive additional information about the individuals by contacting the local bar association or the local licensing authorities.

No. 7, Lane 134, Xin Yi Road, Sec. 3, Taipei, Taiwan 台北市信義路三段134巷7號
Tel: 886-2-2162-2000 Fax: 886-2-2162-2239
E-mail: Amcit-ait-t@state.gov

Attorneys listed as Resident Foreign Attorneys are not licensed to practice before courts in Taiwan. However, in many cases such attorneys are either associated with a Taiwan law firm or have lawyers in their offices who can appear before the court.

The Republic of China Bar Association can be reached by telephone at (02) 2331-2865, by fax at (02) 2375-5594, or by email at bartw@ms27.hinet.net . However, please note that English is not spoken. The address of the Association is 5F, No. 130, Chungking South Road, Section 1, Taipei.

To call Taipei from the United States, dial 011-886-2 plus the eight-digit number. To call Hsinchu and Taoyuan from the United States, dial 011-886-3 plus the seven-digit number. To call or Taichung from the United States, dial 011-886-4 plus the eight-digit number.

Registered mail may be sent through the Taiwan postal system and return receipts obtained. International reply coupons should be used when a prepaid reply is desired.

AIT's Kaohsiung branch office maintains a separate list of attorneys practicing in southern Taiwan. A copy of that list may be obtained by contacting AIT-Kaohsiung through AIT's website, by telephone at 07-238-7744, or by fax at 07-238-5237. To call Kaohsiung from the United States, dial 011-886-7 plus the seven-digit number.

ATTORNEYS IN THE TAIPEI AREA

Ace Tax, Patent & Law Office/ Yale & Yale Law Office

Address: 7F, No. 132, Section 3, Xinyi Road, Taipei, Taiwan
Tel: (886-2) 2705-8077; 2705-6999 Fax: (886-2) 2705-8099
Email: acelaw72@gmail.com ; yaleandyale@hotmail.com
Website: www.yaleyale.com
Areas of practice: Anti-dumping, countervailing, safeguard, WTO, arbitration, aviation, banking and financial law, BOT, child custody (divorce), construction, contracts, corporations, criminal, customs, estates, foreign investment, governmental relations, high tech, immigration, information technology, insurance, international, labor relations, licensing, litigation (civil, criminal, and administrative), maritime, marketing, patent/trademark/copying law, real estate, security, taxes, telecommunications.

Asia Law International Attorneys

Address: 17F, Suite B, No. 167, Dunhua North Road, Taipei, Taiwan
Tel: (886-2) 2717-1999
Email: info@asialaw.biz
Website: www.asialaw.biz
Areas of practice: Diverse legal matters for companies doing business in Asia, particularly commercial and corporate transactions and disputes, with an emphasis on technology and intellectual property rights.

Baker & McKenzie, Taipei

Address: 15F, Hung Tai Center, No. 168, Dunhua North Road, Taipei, Taiwan
Tel: (886-2) 2712-6151 Fax: (886-2) 2712-8292
Email: taipei@bakerandmckenzie.com
Website: http://www.bakermckenzie.com/Taiwan/Taipei/
Areas of practice: Banking and financial law, collections, contracts, corporations, marketing agreements, foreign investment, labor relations, insurance, real estate, patent/trademark/copyright law, maritime, aviation, taxes, and government relations.

CHEN CHANG & ASSOCIATES

Address: 3F-7, Taipei Entrepreneur Building, No. 2, Fuxing North Road, Taipei, Taiwan
Tel: (886-2) 2741-5091 Fax: (886-2) 2741-5090
Email: chenclaw@ms22.hinet.net
Areas of Practice: Banking and financial law, contracts, corporations, marketing agreements, foreign investment, labor relations, insurance, patent/trademark/copyright law, maritime, aviation, criminal law.

CHIEN YEH LAW OFFICES, TAIPEI

Address: 62F, Taipei 101 Tower, No. 7, Section 5, Xinyi Road, Taipei, Taiwan
Tel: (886-2) 8101-1973 Fax: (886-2) 8101-1972
Email: eleanorchin@chienyeh.com.tw
Website: http://www.chienyeh.com.tw
Contact: Eleanor Chin, Managing Partner
Areas of practice: Mergers and acquisitions, intellectual property, institutional investment, international investment, IPO and OTC listing, corporate governance, commercial investment, corporate reorganization, liquidation, bankruptcy, securities

finance dispute resolution, government procurement and construction bids, public construction arbitration, private investment in infrastructure (BOT, BOO, BT), business, consumer protection, labor, employment and fair trading, insurance, real estate, technology and science, land law and administrative litigation, criminal law, medical and health law.

DEEP & FAR, ATTORNEYS-AT-LAW

Address: 13F, No. 27, Section 3, Zhongshan North Road, Taipei, Taiwan
Tel: (886-2) 2585-6688 Fax: (886-2) 2598-9900
Email: email@deepnfar.com.tw
Website: http://www.deepnfar.com.tw
Areas of practice: Child custody, marriage/divorce, estates, contracts, corporations, marketing agreements, foreign investment, labor relations, insurance, real estate, patent/trademark/copyright law, personal injury, maritime, immigration, criminal law, and government relations.

DING & DING LAW OFFICES

Address: 10F, No. 458, Section 4, Xinyi Road, Taipei, Taiwan
Tel: (886-2) 2762-5659 Fax: (886-2) 2761-7682
Email: ddinglaw@ms12.hinet.net
Areas of practice: Banking and financial law, contracts, corporations, marketing agreements, foreign investment, labor relations, insurance, patent/trademark/copyright law, maritime, aviation, taxes, and government relations.

Eiger Law, Taipei
Address: 12F, Building A, No. 25, Section 4, Ren'ai Road, Taipei, Taiwan
Tel: (886-2) 2771-0086 Fax: (886-2) 2771-0186
Website: www.eigerlaw.com
Contacts: Nathan Kaiser & John Eastwood
Email: nathan.kaiser@eigerlaw.com ; john.eastwood@eigerlaw.com
Areas of practice: Corporate law, fair trade and competition, mergers and acquisitions, foreign investment, commercial contracts, international trade, construction and infrastructure, labor and employment law, real estate, intellectual-property, licensing and technical cooperation, telecommunications, litigation and arbitration.

First International Law & Intellectual Property Offices
Address: 3F, No. 43, Section 1, Minsheng East Road, Taipei, Taiwan
Tel: (886-2) 2521-5900 Fax: (886-2) 2521-5311
Email: office@firstlaw.com.tw
Website: http://www.firstlaw.com.tw
Areas of practice: Trademark, patent, copyright, establishment of company or its branch office, labor relationship, stock's ownership dispute, construction dispute, real estate, etc.

Formosa Transnational, Attorneys-at-Law
Address: 13F, No. 136, Section 3, Ren'ai Road, Taipei, Taiwan
Tel: (886-2) 2755-7366 Fax: (886-2) 2755-6486
Email: ftlaw@taiwanlaw.com
Website: http://www.taiwanlaw.com

Areas of practice: Adoptions, child custody, marriage/divorce, estates, banking and financial law, collections, contracts, corporations, marketing agreements, foreign investment, labor relations, insurance, real estate, patent/trademark/copyright law, personal injury, maritime, aviation, immigration, criminal law, and taxes.

Formosan Brothers, Attorneys-at-Law
Address: 8F, No. 376, Section 4, Ren'ai Road, Taipei, Taiwan
Tel: (886-2) 2705-8086 Fax: (886-2) 2701-4705
Email: fblaw@mail.fblaw.com.tw
Website: http://www.fblaw.com.tw
Areas of practice: Adoptions, child custody, marriage/divorce, estates, banking and financial law, collections, contracts, corporations, marketing agreements, foreign investment, labor relations, insurance, real estate, patent/trademark/copyright law, personal injury, maritime, immigration, criminal law, and taxes.

Jones Day, Taipei
Address: 8F, No. 2, Section 2, Dunhua South Road, Taipei, Taiwan
Tel: (886-2) 7712-3399 Fax: (886-2) 2704-6791
Contact: Jack Huang
Email: jhuang@jonesday.com
Website: http://www.jonesday.com/taipei
Areas of practice: Banking and financial law, collections, contracts, corporations, marketing agreements, foreign investment, patent/trademark/copyright law, personal injury, maritime, criminal law, and taxes.

Kew & Lord, Attorneys-at-Law
Address: 9F, No. 17, Section 3, Ren'ai Road, Taipei, Taiwan
Tel: (886-2) 2771-3393 Fax: (886-2) 2772-5911
Email: kewnlord@ms19.hinet.net
Areas of practice: Criminal law, human rights law, general commercial law.

Lee & Li, Attorneys-at-Law
Address: 7F, No. 201, Dunhua North Road, Taipei, Taiwan
Tel: (886-2) 2715-3300 Fax: (886-2) 2713-3966
Email: attorneys@leeandli.com
Webpage: www.leeandli.com
Areas of practice: Estates, banking and financial law, collections, contracts, corporations, marketing agreements, foreign investment, labor relations, insurance, real estate, patent/trademark/copyright law, maritime, aviation, immigration, taxes, and government relations.

Lin & Partners, Attorneys-at-Law
Address: 27F, No. 99, Section 2, Dunhua South Road, Taipei, Taiwan
Tel: (886-2) 2705-5929 Fax: (886-2) 2731-2896
Email: attorneys@linandpartners.com.tw
Website: www.linandpartners.com.tw
Areas of Specialization: Banking and finance, commercial and personal insolvency, mergers and acquisitions, securities, general corporate law, contracts, construction law, international business transactions, foreign investment, antitrust, China-related matters, electronic commerce, privacy and data protection, intellectual property, computer law, technology law, administrative, taxation, maritime, aviation, labor law, commercial, civil and criminal litigation, and alternative dispute resolution.

Thomas Liu Law Offices
Address: 4F-2, No. 1, Fuzhou Street, Taipei, Taiwan
Tel: (886-2) 2396-8519 Fax: (886-2) 2356-7056
Email: liulawo@yahoo.com.tw
Areas of practice: Adoptions, child custody, marriage/divorce, estates, contracts, corporations, marketing agreements, labor relations, insurance, real estate, patent/trademark/copyright law, personal injury, immigration, and criminal law.

OmniService Law Offices
Address: 8F, No. 27-5, Section 2, Zhongzheng East Road, New Taipei City, Taiwan
Tel: (886-2) 8809-1122 Fax: (886-2) 8809-7890
Email: wchern@omniservice.com.tw
Website: http://www.omniservice.com.tw
Areas of practice: International and domestic business transactions, intellectual property, banking, construction, real estate, labor and general legal matters.

Pamir Law Group
Address: 7F, No. 214, Dunhua North Road, Taipei, Taiwan
Tel: (886-2) 5588-1799 Fax: (886-2) 5588-1790
Email: info@pamirlaw.com
Website: www.pamirlaw.com
Areas of practice: General corporate and commercial matters including contract (outsourcing, distribution, OEM), employment, estate planning, finance, intellectual property, litigation/arbitration, mergers and acquisitions, venture capital/high-tech matters, China-related and cross-border matters, family law, government procurement and criminal law matters.

Taiwan Commercial Law Offices
Address: Suite 501, No. 131, Section 3, Minsheng East Road, Taipei, Taiwan
Tel: (886-2) 2717-6658 Fax: (886-2) 2717-7429
Email: info@tclo.com.tw
Website: http://www.tclo.com.tw/
Areas of practice: Banking and financial law, collections, contracts, corporations, marketing agreements, foreign investment, labor relations, insurance, real estate, patent/trademark/copyright law, aviation, and immigration law.

Saint Island International Patent & Law Offices
Address: 7F, No. 248, Section 3, Nanjing East Road, Taipei, Taiwan
Tel: (886-2) 2775-1823 Fax: (886-2) 2731-6377
Email: siiplo@mail.saint-island.com.tw
Website: http://www.saint-island.com.tw
Areas of practice: Contracts, marketing agreements, patent/trademark/copyright law, aviation.

Tai E International Patent & Law Office
Address: 9F, No. 112, Section 2, Chang'an East Road, Taipei, Taiwan
Tel: (886-2) 2506-1023 Fax: (886-2) 2501-1666
Email: lawoffice@taie.com.tw
Website: http://www.taie.com.tw
Areas of practice: Child custody, marriage/divorce, estates, collections, contracts, corporations, marketing agreements, foreign investment, labor relations, insurance, real estate, patent/trademark/copyright law, personal injury, immigration, and criminal law.

Tsar & Tsai Law Firm, Taipei
Address: 8F, No. 245, Section 1, Dunhua South Road, Taipei, Taiwan
Tel: (886-2) 2781-4111 Fax: (886-2) 2731-5581
Email: law@tsartsai.com.tw
Website: www.tsartsai.com.tw
Areas of practice: Banking and financial law, contracts, corporations, marketing agreements, foreign investment, labor relations, insurance, patent/trademark/copyright law, taxes, and government relations.

Wang & Wang
Address: 4F-2, No. 146, Songjiang Road, Taipei, Taiwan
Tel: (886-2) 2537-2694 Fax: (886-2) 2541-9662
Email: tpo@wangandwang.com
Website: http://www.wangandwang.com
Areas of practice: Estates, contracts, corporations, marketing agreements, foreign investment, labor relations, patent/trademark/copyright law, and government relations.

Winkler Partners
12F, No. 86, Section 1, Chongqing South Road, Taipei, Taiwan Tel: (886-2) 2311-2345
Fax: (886-2) 2311-2688 Email: info@winklerpartners.com
Website: www.winklerpartners.com
Areas of practice: Banking and financial law, contracts, corporations, marketing agreements, foreign investment, patent/trademark/copyright law, government relations.

Wong & Company Law Offices
Address: 9F, No. 39, Section 1, Zhongxiao West Road, Taipei, Taiwan
Tel: (886-2) 2382-0255 Fax: (886-2) 2382-0244
Email: attorney@wongandcompany.com.tw
Areas of practice: Adoptions, child custody, marriage/divorce, estates, banking and financial law, collections, contracts, marketing agreements, foreign investment, labor relations, insurance, real estate, patent/trademark/copyright law, personal injury, maritime, aviation, immigration, criminal law, taxes, and government relations.

World Law Offices
Address: 9F-1, No. 72, Section 2, Nanjing East Road, Taipei, Taiwan
Tel: (886-2) 2561-0361 Fax: (886-2) 2561-0363
Email: worldlaw@ms6.hinet.net
Areas of practice: Adoptions, child custody, marriage/divorce, estates, collections, contracts, corporations, marketing agreements, foreign investment, labor relations, real estate, patent/trademark/copyright law, personal injury, aviation, criminal law, and government relations.

WTW Taipei Commercial Law Firm
Address: 7F, No. 149, Section 2, Minsheng East Road, Taipei, Taiwan
Tel: (886-2) 2516-9577 Fax: (886-2) 2516-9715
Contacts: David Enterline & Dennis Tsai
Email: david@wtwct.com.tw ; dennis@wtwct.com.tw
Website: www.wtwct.com.tw
Areas of practice: Telecommunication and information technology, investment, e-commence, child custody, marriage/divorce, estate, banking and financial law, collections, contracts, corporations, mergers and acquisitions, capital markets and securities, commercial agreements, foreign investment, insurance, real estate,

intellectual property-patent/trademark/copyright law, personal injury, labor relations, aviation, immigration, criminal law, taxes, dispute resolution mediation, arbitration and litigation, administrative law, fair trade and consumer rights, government relations and procurement..

Yangming Partners
Address: 10F, No. 89, Songren Road, Taipei, Taiwan
Tel: (886-2) 8725-6677 Fax: (886-2) 2729-5577
Email: yangming@yangminglaw.com
Website: www.yangminglaw.com
Areas of practice: Banking and financial law, contracts, corporations, marketing agreements, foreign investment, patent/trademark/copyright law, government relations.

ATTORNEYS PRACTICING IN NORTHERN AND CENTRAL TAIWAN

TAOYUAN

Rong-Teh Tsai, Attorney-at-Law
Address: No. 93, Datong Road, Taoyuan City, Taiwan
Tel: (886-3) 334-6223 Fax: (886-3) 333-4671
Email: h0367@ms17.hinet.net
Areas of practice: Adoptions, marriage/divorce, labor relations, insurance, personal injury, criminal law, taxes, and government relations.

HSINCHU

Lee & Li, Attorneys-at-Law
Address: 5F, No. 1, Science Park Life Hub, Industry East Second Road, Hsinchu Science Park, Hsinchu, Taiwan
Tel: (886-3) 579-9911 Fax: (886-3) 579-7880
Email: attorneys@leeandli.com
Website: www.leeandli.com
Areas of practice: Estates, banking and financial law, collections, contracts, corporations, marketing agreements, foreign investment, labor relations, insurance, real estate, patent/trademark/copyright law, maritime, aviation, immigration, taxes, and government relations.

Tsar & Tsai Law Firm, Hsinchu
Address: A6, 3F, No. 1, Lixin First Road, Hsinchu Science Park, Hsinchu, Taiwan
Tel: (886-3) 563-3999 Fax: (886-3) 577-9965
Email: law@tsartsai.com.tw
Website: www.tsartsai.com.tw
Area of practice: Patent/trademark/copyright law, foreign investment, commercial agreements, corporations, labor relations, tax, insurance, banking and financial law, and government relations.

TAICHUNG

Clayton P. Yang, Attorney-at-Law
Address: 9F-2, No. 308, Section 2, Wenxin Road, Taichung, Taiwan
Tel: (886-4) 2313-8662 Fax: (886-4) 2314-4779

Email: claylaw@ms26.hinet.net
Areas of practice: General law.

LIST OF ATTORNEYS PRACTICING CRIMINAL LAW

The attorneys listed below practice criminal law and have expressed an interest in representing American citizens in Taiwan. All of the law firms have English-speaking staff, and all are willing to take cases outside Taipei.

The American Institute in Taiwan assumes no responsibility for the professional ability or integrity of the persons or firms whose names appear on the list below. Firms practicing in the Taipei area are listed first, followed by a list of firms practicing in northern Taiwan outside Taipei. The names listed are arranged alphabetically by firm, and the order in which they appear has no other significance.

Attorneys listed as Resident Foreign Attorneys are not licensed to practice before courts in Taiwan. However, in many cases such attorneys are either associated with a Taiwan law firm or have lawyers in their offices who can appear before the court.

The Republic of China Bar Association can be reached by telephone at (02) 2331-2865, by fax at (02) 2375-5594, or by e-mail at bartw@ms27.hinet.net . However, please note that English is not spoken. The address of the Association is 5F, No. 130, Chungking South Road, Section 1, Taipei.

To call Taipei from the United States, dial 011-886-2 plus the eight-digit number. To call Hsinchu and Taoyuan from the United States, dial 011-886-3 plus the seven-digit number. To call or Taichung from the United States, dial 011-886-4 plus the seven-digit number.

Registered mail may be sent through the Taiwan postal system and return receipts obtained. International reply coupons should be used when a prepaid reply is desired.

AIT's Kaohsiung branch office maintains a separate list of attorneys practicing in southern Taiwan. A copy of that list may be obtained by contacting AIT-Kaohsiung through AIT's website, by telephone at 07-224-0154, ext. 15, or by fax at 07-223-8237. To call Kaohsiung from the United States, dial 011-886-7 plus the seven-digit number.

ATTORNEYS IN THE TAIPEI AREA

Ace Tax, Patent & Law Office/ Yale & Yale Law Office
Address: 7F, No. 132, Section 3, Xinyi Road, Taipei, Taiwan
Tel: (886-2) 2705-8077; 2705-6999 Fax: (886-2) 2705-8099
Email: acelaw72@gmail.com ; yaleandyale@hotmail.com
Website: www.yaleyale.com
Chen Chang & Associates
Address: 3F-7, Taipei Entrepreneur Building, No. 2, Fuxing North Road, Taipei, Taiwan
Tel: (886-2) 2741-5091 Fax: (886-2) 2741-5090

Email: chenclaw@ms22.hinet.net
Chien Yeh Law Offices, Taipei
Address: 62F, Taipei 101 Tower, No. 7, Section 5, Xinyi Road, Taipei, Taiwan
Tel: (886-2) 8101-1973 Fax: (886-2) 8101-1972
Email: eleanorchin@chienyeh.com.tw
Website: http://www.chienyeh.com.tw
Deep & Far, Attorneys-at-Law
Address: 13F, No. 27, Section 3, Zhongshan North Road, Taipei, Taiwan
Tel: (886-2) 2585-6688 Fax: (886-2) 2598-9900
Email: email@deepnfar.com.tw
Website: http://www.deepnfar.com.tw
Eiger Law
Address: 12F, Building A, No. 25, Section 4, Ren'ai Road, Taipei, Taiwan
Tel: (886-2) 2771-0086 Fax: (886-2) 2771-0186
Email: nathan.kaiser@eigerlaw.com ; john.eastwood@eigerlaw.com
Website: www.eigerlaw.com
Formosa Transnational, Attorneys-at-Law
Address: 13F, No. 136, Section 3, Ren'ai Road, Taipei, Taiwan
Tel: (886-2) 2755-7366 Fax: (886-2) 2755-6486
Email: ftlaw@taiwanlaw.com
Website: http://www.taiwanlaw.com
Formosan Brothers, Attorneys-at-Law
Address: 8F, No. 376, Section 4, Ren'ai Road, Taipei, Taiwan
Tel: (886-2) 2705-8086 Fax: (886-2) 2701-4705
Email: fblaw@mail.fblaw.com.tw
Website: http://www.fblaw.com.tw
Jones Day, Taipei
Address: 8F, No. 2, Section 2, Dunhua South Road, Taipei, Taiwan
Tel: (886-2) 7712-3399 Fax: (886-2) 2704-6791
Email: jhuang@jonesday.com
Website: http://www.jonesday.com/taipei
Kew & Lord, Attorneys-at-Law
Address: 9F, No. 17, Section 3, Ren'ai Road, Taipei, Taiwan
Tel: (886-2) 2771-3393 Fax: (886-2) 2772-5911
Email: kewnlord@ms19.hinet.net
Thomas Liu Law Offices
Address: 4F-2, No. 1, Fuzhou Street, Taipei, Taiwan
Tel: (886-2) 2396-8519 Fax: (886-2) 2356-7056
Email: liulawo@yahoo.com.tw
Tai E International Patent & Law Office
Address: 9F, No. 112, Section 2, Chang'an East Road, Taipei, Taiwan
Tel: (886-2) 2506-1023 Fax: (886-2) 2501-1666
Email: lawoffice@taie.com.tw
Website: http://www.taie.com.tw
Wong & Company Law Offices
Address: 9F, No. 39, Section 1, Zhongxiao West Road, Taipei, Taiwan
Tel: (886-2) 2382-0255 Fax: (886-2) 2382-0244

Email: attorney@wongandcompany.com.tw
World Law Offices
Address: 9F-1, No. 72, Section 2, Nanjing East Road, Taipei, Taiwan
Tel: (886-2) 2561-0361 Fax: (886-2) 2561-0363
Email: worldlaw@ms6.hinet.net
WTW Taipei Commercial Law Firm
Address: 7F, No. 149, Section 2, Minsheng East Road, Taipei, Taiwan
Tel: (886-2) 2516-9577 Fax: (886-2) 2516-9715
Email: david@wtwct.com.tw ; dennis@wtwct.com.tw
Website: www.wtwct.com.tw

ATTORNEYS PRACTICING IN NORTHERN TAIWAN OUTSIDE TAIPEI

TAICHUNG

Chien Yeh Law Offices, Taichung
21F-1, No.201, Section 2, Wenxin Road, Taichung, Taiwan
Tel: (886-4) 2251-1973 Fax: (886-4) 2252-1974
Email: alanli@chienyeh.com.tw
Website: http://www.chienyeh.com.tw/
Clayton P. Yang, Attorney-at-Law
Address: 9F-2, No. 308, Section 2, Wenxin Road, Taichung, Taiwan
Tel: (886-4) 2313-8662 Fax: (886-4) 2314-4779
Email: claylaw@ms26.hinet.net

TAOYUAN

Rong-Teh Tsai, Attorney-at-Law
Address: No. 93, Datong Road, Taoyuan City, Taiwan
Tel: (886-3) 334-6223 Fax: (886-3) 333-4671
Email: h0367@ms17.hinet.net

TRADE AND PROJECT FINANCING

How Do I Get Paid (Methods of Payment)

METHODS OF PAYMENT

There are four common methods of international payment: cash in advance, letters of credit (L/C), documentary collections, such as documents against payment (D/P) and documents against acceptance (D/A), and open account (O/A). Cash in advance terms are generally used in new relationships where transactions are small and the buyer has no choice but to pre-pay. Bank-to-bank letters of credit (L/C) are the most common form of international payment because they provide a high degree of protection for both the seller and the buyer. D/P and D/A terms are commonly used in ongoing relationships and provide a measure of protection for both the seller and the buyer. Open account (O/A) is used only when the seller has significant trust and faith in the buyer's ability and willingness to pay once the goods have been shipped. O/A terms give maximum security to the buyer and greatest risk to the seller.

The Commercial Section of the American Institute in Taiwan (AIT) recommends that

U.S. exporters minimize financial risk by requiring their Taiwan trading partners to finance their imports through L/Cs. A large majority of Taiwan's importers utilize L/Cs with validity of up to 180 days. On the whole, U.S. companies find Taiwan's trade finance system to be efficient and report no widespread pattern of deferred payment.

Banks authorized to handle foreign exchange may issue L/Cs. This includes all 37 local banks (and their branch offices), six U.S. banks and their branches, and 23 third-country banks. All banks in Taiwan that are authorized to handle foreign exchange have correspondent relations with one or more U.S. banks. This relationship includes test-key exchanges.

HOW DOES THE BANKING SYSTEM OPERATE

As of 2010, Taiwan has a Central Bank, 37 domestic banks (with 3,326 branch offices), and 29 foreign banks (with 98 branch offices). In addition, there are 26 credit cooperatives, 276 farmers' credit unions, and 25 fishermen's credit unions. These banks, cooperatives, and credit unions have traditionally played a dominant role in finance on the island.

The Central Bank performs all of the functions normally associated with central banks in other countries. It issues currency, manages foreign-exchange reserves, handles treasury receipts and disbursements, sets interest-rate policy, oversees the operations of local financial institutions, and serves as a lender of last resort.

Taiwan's domestic banks offer a wide range of services – receiving deposits, making loans, handling trade financing and providing guarantees, and discounting bills and notes. Most are also involved in the securities business, in underwriting and trading securities and managing bond and debenture issues, as well as in providing savings-account facilities. The Mega International Commercial Bank assists with long-term financing for industries and projects, while the Export-Import Bank of the Republic of China and the Farmers Bank focus on trade financing and agricultural development, respectively.

Foreign banking institutions have played an important role on the financial scene. Foreign banks are essentially treated like domestic commercial banks; they are permitted to engage in trade financing, foreign-exchange dealings, private and corporate lending, and various kinds of trust businesses. In order to build a greater overall market presence, many foreign banking institutions also concentrate on the development of consumer loan and credit card services.

FOREIGN-EXCHANGE CONTROLS

There are no foreign exchange (FX) limitations for trade, insurance, and authorized investment transactions. Similarly, there are no FX limitations on repatriating capital and profits related to direct and portfolio investment, provided that such investment has been permitted or approved by Taiwan authorities. There are no limitations on inward and outward remittances not involving any exchange between the NT dollar and the foreign currency. All other inward or outward remittances for business firms are subject to a US$50 million annual ceiling per account if such remittances involve exchange between the NT dollar and the foreign currency. Individuals are allowed to remit a maximum of US$5 million yearly to or from overseas if such remittance involves exchange between the NT dollar and the foreign currency.

U.S.BANKS AND LOCAL CORRESPONDENT BANKS

U.S.Commercial Banks Operating in Taiwan

Citibank N.A. Taipei, Taiwan Branch Manager: Audrey Chen Tel: 886-2-2725-9800 15F, No. 1, Song Zhi Road Fax: 886-2-2725-2988 Taipei, Taiwan http://www.jpmorganchase.com Tel: 886-2-8726-9821 Fax: 886-2-8786-7980 State Street Bank & Trust Company http://www.citibank.com.tw VP & General Manager: Jane Huang

19F, No. 207 DunHua S. Rd., Sec. 2, JPMorgan Chase Bank, N.A. Taipei, Taiwan Senior Country Officer: Carl K. Chien Tel: 886-2-2735-1200 8F, No. 108 XinYi Rd., Sec. 5 Fax: 886-2-2735-1012 http://www.statestreet.com

Wells Fargo Bank, N.A.
General Manager: Michael Lin
17F, No. 44 Chung Shan N. Rd., Sec. 2
Taipei, Taiwan
Tel: 886-2-8175-8688
Fax: 886-2-2567-8516
http://www.wellsfargo.com

Bank of America
CEO: Eric Liu
43 and 48F, No. 7 Xin Yi Rd., Sec. 5
Taipei, Taiwan
Tel: 886-2-8101-1288
Fax: 886-2-8101-1130
http://www.bankofamerica.com

The Bank of New York Mellon General Manager: James Liu 4F, No. 245 Dun Hwa S. Rd., Sec. 1 Taipei, Taiwan Tel: 886-2-2771-6612 Fax: 886-2-2771-2640 http://www.bankofny.com

Major Local Correspondent Banks

Bank of Taiwan Chang Hwa Commercial Bank The First Commercial Bank Hua Nan Commercial Bank, Ltd. Mega Int'l Commercial Bank Co., Ltd. Citibank Taiwan Limited

China Trust Commercial Bank Land Bank of Taiwan Taishin International Bank Taiwan Cooperative Bank Shanghai Commercial & Savings Bank Cathay United Bank

PROJECT FINANCING

Taiwan does not rely on money from multilateral institutions to facilitate investment projects. In the public sector, the Taiwan authorities rely heavily on bond issuance to cover the huge outlays connected with construction of major public works. Beginning in 1997, some major public projects were opened to private investment on a build-operatetransfer (BOT) basis. Private investment projects can easily be financed through banks on the island. Moreover, many Taiwan investors, especially large-sized companies, employ financial instruments (including corporate bonds) to raise funds in capital markets, both at home and abroad.

Web Resources Export-Import Bank of the United States: http://www.exim.gov Country Limitation Schedule: http://www.exim.gov/tools/country/country_limits.html OPIC: http://www.opic.gov Trade and Development Agency: http://www.tda.gov/ SBA's Office of International Trade: http://www.sba.gov/oit/ USDA Commodity Credit Corporation: http://www.fsa.usda.gov/ccc/default.htm

U.S. Agency for International Development: http://www.usaid.gov Central Bank (Taiwan): http://www.cbc.gov.tw/mp1.html

Financial Supervisory Commission, Executive Yuan: http://www.fscey.gov.tw

IMPORTANT CONTACTS

AMERICAN INSTITUTE IN TAIWAN (AIT)

Commercial Section Chief: Helen Hwang Suite 3207, No. 333 Keelung Rd., Sec. 1, Taipei, Taiwan Tel: 886-2-2720-1550 ext. 382 Fax: 886-2-2757-7162 Website: http://www.buyusa.gov/taiwan

Agriculture Trade Office Director: Valerie Brown-Jones Suite 704, No. 136 Jen Ai Rd., Sec. 3, Taipei, Taiwan Tel: 886-2-2705-6536 ext. 287 Fax: 886-2-2706-4885 Website: http://www.ait.org.tw

Agriculture Section Chief: Jeffrey Hesse No. 7, Lane 134, Hsin Yi Rd., Sec. 3, Taipei, Taiwan Tel: 886-2-2162-2000 ext. 2317 Fax: 886-2-2162-2238 Website: http://www.ait.org.tw

Economic Section Chief: Alan R. Tousignant No. 7, Lane 134, Hsin Yi Rd., Sec. 3, Taipei, Taiwan Tel: 886-2-2162-2000 ext. 2374 Fax: 886-2-2162-2240 Website: http://www.ait.org.tw

WASHINGTON, D.C.-BASED COUNTRY CONTACTS

U.S. Department of Commerce Trade Information Center 1401 Constitution Ave., NW, Washington, D.C. 20230 Tel: 1-800-USA-TRADE

Fax: 202-482-4473 Website: http://www.export.gov

AIT/Washington Trade and Commercial Programs Director: Rick Ruzicka Suite 1700, 1700 N. Moore Street Arlington, VA 22209 Tel: 703-525-8474; Fax: 703-841-1385 Website: http://www.ait.org.tw/en/ait washington.html

U.S.Department of Commerce US & Foreign Commercial Service, East/Asia Pacific Regional Director: Patrick Santillo Room 3122, 14th and Constitution Ave. NW, Washington, D.C. 20230 Tel: 202-482-0423; Fax: 202-501-6165 Website: http://www.export.gov

U.S.Department of Agriculture Foreign Agricultural Service (FAS) Office of Trade Program South Building, 1400 Independence Ave. SW, Washington, D.C. 20250 Tel: 202-690-3576 Website: http://www.usda.gov

TRADE OR INDUSTRY ASSOCIATIONS

American Chamber of Commerce in Taipei President: Andrea Wu Suite 706, No. 129 Minsheng E. Road, Sec. 3, Taipei, Taiwan Tel: 886-2-2718-8226 Fax: 886-2-2718-8182 Website: http://www.amcham.com.tw

Importers and Exporters Association of Taipei Chairman: Kuo Chao Liu No. 350 Sungchiang Rd.,Taipei, Taiwan Tel: 886-2-2581-3521 Fax: 886-2-2523-8782 Website: http://www.ieatpe.org.tw

Chinese National Association of Industry & Commerce Chairman: Kenneth C.M. Lo 13F, No. 390 FuXing S. Rd., Sec. 1, Taipei, Taiwan Tel: 886-2-2707-0111 Fax: 886-2-2707-0977 Website: http://www.cnaic.org

US-Taiwan Business Council President: Paul D. Wolfowitz Suite 1703, 1700 North Moore Street Arlington, Virginia 22209 Tel: 703-465-2930; Fax: 703-465-2937 Website: http://www.us-taiwan.org

Taiwan External Trade Development Council (TAITRA) President and CEO: Yuen-Chuan Chao 5-7F, No. 333 Keelung Rd., Sec. 1, Taipei, Taiwan Tel: 886-2-2725-5200 Fax: 886-2-2757-6652 Website: http://www.taitra.org.tw

Chinese National Federation of Industries Chairman: Preston W. Chen 12F, No. 390 FuXing S. Rd., Sec. 1, Taipei, Taiwan Tel: 886-2-2703-3500 Fax: 886-2-2705-8317 Website: http://www.cnfi.org.tw

TAIWAN AGENCIES

Ministry of Economic Affairs (MOEA) Minister: Shih, Yen-shiang No. 15 FuZhou St., Taipei, Taiwan Tel: 886-2-2321-2200 Fax: 886-2-2391-9398 Website: http://www.moea.gov.tw

Ministry of Finance (MOF) Minister: Lee, Sush-Der No. 2 AiGuo W. Rd., Taipei, Taiwan Tel: 886-2-2322-8000 Fax: 886-2-2356-8774 Website: http://www.mof.gov.tw

Board of Foreign Trade (BOFT), MOEA Director General: Chih-Peng Huang No. 1 HuKou St., Taipei, Taiwan Tel: 886-2-2321-0271 Fax: 886-2-2351-7080 Website: http://www.trade.gov.tw

Financial Supervisory Commission (FSC) Chairman: Sean C. Chen 18F, No. 7 SianMin Blvd., Sec. 2, Banciao City, Taipei County, Taiwan Tel: 886-2-8968-0899 Fax: 886-2-8968-1215 Website: http://www.fscey.gov.tw

Ministry of Transportation and Communications (MOTC) Minister: Mao, Chi-Kuo No. 50, Ren-Ai Rd., Sec. 1, Taipei, Taiwan Tel: 886-2-2349-2900 Fax: 886-2-2349-2491 Website: http://www.motc.gov.tw

Council of Agriculture (COA) Minister: Chen, Wu-Hsiung No. 37 NanHai Rd., Taipei, Taiwan Tel: 886-2-2381-2991 Fax: 886-2-2331-0341 Website: http://www.coa.gov.tw

Department of Health (DOH) Minister: Chih-Liang Yaung No. 36 Tacheng St., Taipei, Taiwan Tel: 886-2-8590-6666 Fax: 886-2-8590-6051 Website: http://www.doh.gov.tw

Environmental Protection Administration (EPA) Minister: Shen, Shih-Hung No. 83 ZhongHua Rd., Sec. 1, Taipei, Taiwan Tel: 886-2-2311-7722 Fax: 886-2-2311-6071 Website: http://www.epa.gov.tw

Bureau of Standards, Metrology and Inspection (BSMI), MOEA Director General: Chen Jay-San No. 4 Jinan Rd., Sec. 1, Taipei, Taiwan Tel: 886-2-2343-1700 Fax: 886-2-2356-0998 Website: http://www.bsmi.gov.tw Small & Medium Enterprise Administration, MOEA Director General: Dr. Robert Sun-Quae Lai 3F, No 95 Roosevelt Rd., Sec. 2, Taipei Taiwan Tel: 886-2-2366-2200 Fax: 886-2-2367-3896 Website: http://www.moeasmea.gov.tw

OTHER U.S. GOVERNMENT CONTACTS

U.S. Department of State Bureau of Economic and Business Affairs Office of Commercial and Business Affairs 2201 C Street NW Washington, D.C. 20520 Tel: 202-647-4000 Fax: 202-647-3953 Website: http://www.state.gov

Export-Import Bank of the United States 811 Vermont Avenue, N.W. Washington, D.C. 20571 Tel: 202-565-3910 Fax: 202-565-3930 Website: www.exim.gov

Overseas Private Investment Corporation 1100 New York Avenue, NW Washington, D.C. 20527 Tel: 202-336-8400 Fax: 202-336-7949 Website: http://www.opic.gov

BUSINESS TRAVELING

US STATE DEPARTMENT: SUGGESTIONS FOR TRELERS

COUNTRY DESCRIPTION: Taiwan is a stable democracy and has a strong and well-developed economy. Tourist facilities are widely available.

ENTRY REQUIREMENTS: Passport required. Taiwan previously required that U.S. visitors to Taiwan hold passports valid for at least six months. This is no longer the case: Taiwan now considers U.S. passports valid for return to the United States for six months beyond the expiration date of the passport. For specific information about entry requirements, travelers may contact the Taipei Economic and Cultural Representative Office (TECRO), 4201 Wisconsin Avenue, N.W., Washington, D.C. 20056-2137, via either its main telephone number,(202) 895-1800, or its visa section telephone number,(202) 895-1814. The main fax number at TECRO is (202) 363-0999, and the visa section fax number is (202) 895-0017. There is also an Internet address: http://www.taipei.org/teco.htm. The Taipei Economic and Cultural Office (TECO) also has offices in Atlanta, Boston, Chicago, Guam, Honolulu, Houston, Kansas City, Los Angeles, Miami, New York, San Francisco and Seattle.

INFORMATION ON CRIME AND SAFETY: Although there has been an increase in the crime rate over the last year, due in part to local enforcement reporting methods, the overall crime rate in Taiwan remains relatively low. Nonetheless, there has been intense public concern in Taipei resulting from several violent crime cases in 1996-97. Residential burglaries and thefts are the predominant crimes affecting foreigners in Taiwan, but other more serious crimes do occasionally occur. Generally, U.S. citizen visitors to Taiwan should follow the basic security precautions that would apply in any large city. Women should exercise caution when traveling alone in taxis, especially at night, as there have been incidents reported involving violence directed towards unaccompanied female taxi passengers; calling for a radio-dispatched taxi is an option. Local police departments have foreign affairs sections which are normally staffed by English-speaking officers. Police contact numbers for the major cities in Taiwan are as follows: Taipei (02)2556-6007, Kaohsiung (07) 215-4342, Tainan (06) 222-9704, Taichung (04) 327-3875, Taitung (089) 334-756, Pingtung (08) 733-6283. The loss or theft abroad of a U.S. passport should be reported immediately to the local police, and to the American Institute in Taiwan, at Taipei or Kaohsiung. Useful information on guarding valuables and protecting personal security while traveling abroad is provided in the Department of State pamphlet, *A Safe Trip Abroad*. It is available by mail from the Superintendent of Documents, U.S. Government Printing Office, Washington, D.C. 20402, via the Internet at http://www.access.gpo.gov/su_docs, or via the Bureau of Consular Affairs home page at http://travel.state.gov.

CRIMINAL PENALTIES: When outside the U.S., a U.S. citizen is subject to local laws and regulations, which sometimes differ significantly from those in the United States and do not afford the protections available to the individual under U.S. law. Penalties for breaking the law can be more severe than in the United States for similar offenses. Persons violating the law, even unknowingly, may be expelled, arrested or imprisoned. Criminal penalties for possession, use, or trafficking of illegal drugs are strict, and convicted offenders can expect severe jail sentences and fines. Taiwan law provides for the death penalty for some narcotics offenses.

COMPULSORY MILITARY SERVICE: Taiwan law provides for compulsory military service. Men between the ages of 18 and 45 who were born in Taiwan or who have ever held a Taiwan passport should be aware that they may be subject to compulsory military service in Taiwan, even if they are also U.S. citizens, and even if they have entered Taiwan on U.S. passports. Affected individuals are urged to consult with the nearest office of the Taipei Economic and Cultural Office (TECO) in the United States before visiting Taiwan to determine whether they are subject to the military service requirement.

MEDICAL FACILITIES: Health facilities in Taiwan are fully adequate for routine medical treatment. Doctors and hospitals may expect immediate cash payment for health services, and U.S. medical insurance is not always valid outside the United States. The Medicare/Medicaid program does not provide for payment of medical services outside the United States.

MEDICAL INSURANCE: Serious medical problems requiring hospitalization and/or medical evacuation to the United States can cost from $10,000 to $100,000. Supplemental overseas medical insurance, including coverage for medical evacuation, may prove useful. Check with your own insurance company to confirm whether your policy applies overseas, and whether it includes a provision for medical evacuation. Ascertain whether payment will be made to the overseas hospital or doctor, or whether you will be reimbursed later for expenses you incur. Some insurance policies also include coverage for psychiatric treatment and for disposition of remains in the event of death. Useful information on medical emergencies abroad, including overseas insurance programs, is provided in the Department of State, Bureau of Consular Affairs' brochure *Medical Information for Americans Traveling Abroad*, available via the Bureau's home page and autofax service.

For additional health information, travelers may call the toll-free numbers of the Centers for Disease Control and Prevention's international travelers hotline 1-877-FYI-TRIP (1-877-394-8747), may use the CDC autofax service, 1-888-CDC-FAXX (1-888-232-3299), or may access the CDC home page on the Internet: http://www.cdc.gov.

AVIATION SAFETY OVERSIGHT: The U.S. Federal Aviation Administration (FAA) has assessed the Civil Aviation Authority of Taiwan as Category 1 -- in compliance with international aviation safety standards for oversight of Taiwan's air carrier operations. For further information, travelers may contact the Department of Transportation within the U.S. at 1-800-322-7873, or visit the FAA Internet home page at http://www.faa.gov/avr/iasa/index.htm. The U.S. Department of Defense (DOD) separately assesses some foreign air carriers for suitability as official providers of air services. For information regarding the DOD policy on specific carriers, travelers may contact DOD at 618-256-4801.

TRAFFIC SAFETY AND ROAD CONDITIONS: Roads in Taiwan's major cities are generally congested, and driving conditions are made worse by large numbers of scooters and motorcycles that weave in and out of traffic. Special caution should be taken when driving on mountain roads, which are typically narrow, winding, and poorly banked, and which may be made impassable by mudslides after heavy rains.

REGISTRATION AND PASSPORTS: U.S. citizens are encouraged to register at the American Institute in Taiwan, and to obtain updated information on travel and security. The American Institute in Taiwan does not issue U.S. passports but accepts passport applications and forwards them to the Passport Agency in Honolulu for processing. Processing time takes three to four weeks. In an emergency, the American Institute in Taiwan can issue a travel letter to permit a U.S. citizen who has lost a passport to return to the United States.

CHILDREN'S ISSUES: For information on international adoption of children, international parental child abduction, and international child support enforcement issues, please refer to our Internet site at http://travel.state.gov/children's_issues.html or telephone (202) 736-7000.

AMERICAN INSTITUTE IN TAIWAN: Unofficial relations with the people of Taiwan are conducted through the American Institute in Taiwan, whose offices are authorized by law to perform American citizen services. For assistance, U.S. citizen travelers may contact the American Institute in Taiwan at No. 7 Lane 134, Hsin Yi Road Section 3, Taipei, Taiwan; telephone (886-2) 2709-2000; fax: (886-2) 2709-0908; or the American Institute in Taiwan branch office at No. 2 Chung Cheng 3rd Road, 5th Floor, Kaohsiung, Taiwan, telephone: (886-7) 224-0154; fax: (886-7) 223-8237. In case of emergencies after working hours, the duty officer at the American Institute in Taiwan at Taipei may be contacted at (886-2) 2709-2013.

GETTING THERE

Air

The national airline is *China Airlines (CI)*. *EVA Air* offers flights to destinations throughout Asia, Europe, North America, Australia and New Zealand. Other airlines serving Taiwan include *British Asia Airways*, *Continental Airlines*, *Singapore Airlines* and *Thai Airways*.

Approximate flight time: From Taipei to Los Angeles is 14 hours.

International airports

Chiang Kai-shek–Taipei (TPE) is 40km (25 miles) southwest of the city (travel time – 30 minutes). Airport facilities include an outgoing duty-free shop (0800-2100), post office, car hire, bank/bureau de change (0900-1700), bar/restaurant (0900-2100) and tourist information. Buses depart every 15 minutes for both *Sung Shan* (domestic) airport and the main railway station. Taxis and buses are available to the city centre.

Kaohsiung International (KHH) is 9km (4 miles) from the town centre. Airport facilities include an outgoing duty-free shop (0800-1900), car hire (0900-1900), bank/bureau de change (0900-1900) and bar/restaurant (0900-1900). A regular bus service is available (travel time – 30 minutes). There is a taxi service to the town.

Sea

There are sea links with Macau, Hong Kong and Japan.

GETTING AROUND

Air

China Airlines, *Eva Air*, *Far Eastern Air Transport*, *Formosa Airlines* and five other domestic airlines run services to local destinations from *Sung Shan* airport, Taipei.

Sea

There are reasonable connections from local ports. For details contact port authorities.

Train

Services are provided to destinations all over the island by the *Taiwan Railway Administration*. The main tourist routes are Taipei–Taichung–Chiayi–Tainan–Kaohsiung (a top-class service), Taipei–Taichung–Sun Moon Lake (with the last leg of the journey by bus), Chiayi–Alishan (with spectacular mountain scenery) and Taipei–New Hualian–Taitung (scenic coastal route). Air-conditioned electric trains run at least hourly from Taipei to Kaohsiung; some trains have restaurant cars. Children under three travel free; children aged 3-13 pay half fare. Train tickets can be purchased at many major hotels in Taipei, as well as at the main railway station.

Road

Traffic drives on the right. There is an adequate road system joining all major cities. A highway links Taipei and Kaohsiung. Some main streets have English signs.

Bus
There are both local and long-distance bus and coach services.
Taxi
These are plentiful and inexpensive (metered). The destination must be written in Chinese for the driver.
Car rental
This is available in major towns.

Documentation: An International Driving Permit is required.

Urban

A number of private bus companies provide extensive services in Taipei. Two lines of a Mass Rapid Transit (MRT) system, a monorail train system serving Taipei and its suburbs, opened in 1996. Metered taxis are available in Taipei; tipping is not expected, but it is starting to come into practice.

Travel Times

The following chart gives approximate journey times (in hours and minutes) from Taipei to other major cities/towns.

	Air	Road	Train
Kaohsiung	0.40	5.30	4.40
Tainan	0.40	4.30	4.10
Taichung	0.30	2.30	2.30
Hualien	0.30	7.00	3.00
Taitung	0.50	10.00	5.30
Sun Moon L.	-	4.30	-
Alishan	-	6.00	-
Kenting	-	6.30	-
Makung	0.40	-	-

ACCOMMODATION

Hotels

There are over 398 tourist hotels in the country offering a broad range of accommodation and services. Prices range from US$30-50 a day for smaller hotels with US$90-150 a day being average. For details, contact the Press Division of the Taipei Representative Office in the UK or the Taiwan Visitors Bureau. Many hotels belong to the International Tourist Hotel Association of Taipei, 8th Floor-1, 369 Fu Shing N Road. Tel: (2) 27 17 21 55. Fax: (2) 27 17 24 53.

Grading: Hotels are rated on a scale of 1 to 5 'Plum Blossoms' using a system equivalent to the more familiar 5-star system, with three Plum Blossoms being about average:

4 to 5 Plum Blossoms: 50 hotels (half of which are in Taipei) are in these categories. The hotels are luxury class with a range of services and facilities, eg tennis courts, swimming pools and beauty salons.

2 and 3 Plum Blossoms: The 80 hotels in these categories are clean, comfortable and functional.

Camping

Campsites are available.

Youth Dorms

Dormitory and non-dormitory rooms are available in major cities and in scenic areas.

MONEY

Currency

New Taiwan Dollar (NT$) = 100 cents. Notes are in denominations of NT$1000, 500, 100 and 50. Coins are in denominations of NT$50, 10, 5 and 1, and 50 cents.

Currency exchange

All travelers are required to make a currency declaration in writing together with the baggage declaration. Unused currency can be reconverted on departure, on production of exchange receipts.

Credit cards

Accepted in most hotels, restaurants and shops.

Travelers' checks

Accepted in most hotels, restaurants and shops. To avoid additional exchange rate charges, travelers are advised to take travelers' checks in US Dollars.

Exchange rate indicators against the US Dollar

The following figures are included as a guide to the movements of the New Taiwan Dollar against Sterling and the US Dollar:

Date	Aug'99	Nov'99	May'00	Aug'00
$1.00=	32.17	31.73	30.74	31.10

Currency restrictions

The import and export of local currency is limited to NT$40,000. Free import of foreign currency is allowed, subject to declaration. The export of foreign currency is limited to the equivalent of US$5000 or up to the amount imported and declared. All exchange receipts must be retained.

Banking hours: 9AM-3.30PM Monday to Friday; 9AM-12PM Saturday.

SUPPLEMENTS

FREQUENCY SEGMENTS AND FREQUENCY BANDWIDTH FOR PREVIOUSLY RELEASED OPERATING CONCESSION LICENSES SHALL BE AS FOLLOWS:

Year	Frequency segments	Frequency bandwidth
2013	700 MHz	A1: Uplink 703MHz～713MHz; Downlink 758MHz～768MHz (10MHz each)
		A2: Uplink 713MHz～723MHz; Downlink 768MHz～778MHz (10MHz each)
		A3: Uplink 723MHz～733MHz; Downlink 778MHz～788MHz (10MHz each)
		A4: Uplink 733MHz～748MHz; Downlink 788MHz～803MHz (15MHz each)
	900MHz	B1: Uplink 885MHz～895MHz; Downlink 930MHz～940MHz (10MHz each)
		B2: Uplink 895MHz～905MHz; Downlink 940MHz～950MHz (10MHz each)
		B3: Uplink 905MHz～915MHz; Downlink 950MHz～960MHz (10MHz each)
	1800 MHz	C1: Uplink 1710MHz～1725MHz; Downlink 1805MHz～1820MHz (15MHz each)
		C2: Uplink 1725MHz～1735MHz; Downlink 1820MHz～1830MHz (10MHz each)
		C3: Uplink 1735MHz～1745MHz; Downlink 1830MHz～1840MHz (10MHz each)
		C4: Uplink 1745MHz～1755MHz; Downlink 1840MHz～1850MHz (10MHz each)
		C5: Uplink 1755MHz～1770MHz; Downlink 1850MHz～1865MHz (15MHz each)
2015	2500MHz & 2600MHz (paired frequency segment)	D1: 2500MHz～2520MHz; 2620MHz～2640MHz (paired, 20MHz each)
		D2: 2520MHz～2540MHz; 2640MHz～2660MHz (paired, 20MHz each)
		D3: 2540MHz～2560MHz; 2660MHz～2680MHz (paired, 20MHz each)
		D4: 2560MHz～2570MHz; 2680MHz～2690MHz (paired, 10MHz each)
	2500MHz & 2600MHz (unpaired frequency	D5: 2570MHz～2595MHz, including guard band:2570MHz～2575MHz (25MHz unpaired frequency segment, with 5MHz guard band)

	frequency segment)	D6：2595MHz~2620MHz, including guard band:2615MHz~2620MHz （25MHz unpaired frequency segment, with 5MHz guard band）

COUNTRIES BY NUMBER OF BROADBAND INTERNET SUBSCRIPTIONS

	Fixed-broadband subscriptions				Mobile-cellular subscriptions			
Country or area	Number	Rank	%	Rank	Number	Rank	%	Rank
China	174,285,380	1	13.0	66	231,614,860	2	17.2	75
United States	87,974,583	2	28.0	24	234,412,672	1	74.7	9
Japan	35,556,075	3	27.9	25	144,077,507	3	113.1	2
Germany	27,674,074	4	34.0	13	33,336,214	11	41.0	40
France	24,780,180	5	37.8	8	34,233,625	10	52.2	27
United Kingdom	21,455,580	6	34.0	14	45,419,806	9	72.0	14
Russia	20,630,858	7	14.5	61	75,344,817	6	52.9	25
South Korea	18,354,447	8	37.6	9	51,810,697	8	106.0	4
Brazil	18,275,780	9	9.2	85	73,021,400	7	36.6	44
India[8]	16,600,000	10	1.2	137	104,280,000	4	7.6	98
Italy	13,548,539	11	22.1	45	31,710,663	12	51.8	28
Mexico	12,588,657	12	10.9	76	11,180,208	23	9.7	94
Spain	11,410,276	13	24.3	37	25,044,744	13	53.2	24
Canada	11,282,326	14	32.9	16	17,163,076	19	50.0	32
Turkey	8,411,176	15	10.5	80	13,017,505	21	16.3	79
Netherlands	6,598,394	16	39.4	6	10,202,005	26	61.0	20
Poland	6,388,846	17	16.6	54	18,921,448	16	49.3	33
Taiwan	5,548,270	18	23.9	38	10,715,720	25	46.1	34
Australia	5,516,663	19	25.1	34	21,184,928	15	96.2	6
Argentina	4,592,231	20	10.9	77	5,233,135	35	12.4	85
Vietnam	4,535,696	21	5.0	104	17,378,598	17	19.0	73

Country or area	Number	Rank	%	Rank	Number	Rank	%	Rank
Thailand	4,182,458	22	6.2	97	95,940	119	0.1	145
Colombia	3,781,987	23	8.4	89	2,237,977	63	4.9	110
Ukraine	3,636,319	24	8.1	93	2,465,179	59	5.5	106
Belgium	3,560,000	25	34.1	12	3,520,543	47	33.7	48
Romania	3,473,257	26	15.9	57	5,179,188	48	23.7	63
Switzerland	3,317,304	27	41.9	3	3,281,402	50	41.4	39
Iran	3,208,379	28	4.1	110	—	—	—	—
Pakistan	2,969,090	29	1.7	150	31,779,549	12	18.8	75
Sweden	2,929,963	30	32.2	18	9,219,679	26	101.3	5
Belarus	2,561,813	31	26.6	28	3,167,236	51	32.8	51
Greece	2,532,270	32	23.5	40	4,789,637	38	45.5	35
Malaysia	2,447,906	33	8.4	88	3,945,130	45	13.5	84
Portugal	2,409,117	34	22.3	43	3,500,632	48	32.5	52
Philippines	2,308,994	35	2.2	125	3,969,394	44	3.8	116
Hungary	2,283,075	36	22.9	41	2,299,506	61	23.1	64
Hong Kong	2,257,221	38	31.6	20	5,256,334	34	73.5	10
Chile	2,122,498	39	12.4	70	4,771,695	39	29.0	57
Denmark	2,118,541	40	38.2	7	4,851,519	37	88.5	7
Indonesia	3,030,983	29	1.2	136	79,225,759	5	31.9	54
Austria	2,074,252	41	25.2	33	4,564,834	41	55.5	23
Venezuela	1,889,309	42	6.7	95	1,332,277	68	4.8	112
Saudi Arabia	1,817,083	43	6.8	94	11,351,726	23	42.8	37
Norway	1,736,182	44	36.9	10	3,983,527	42	84.6	8
Egypt	2,279,666	37	2.7	121	22,471,109	14	27.9	60
Kazakhstan	1,702,964	45	9.7	84	7,356,441	29	42.0	38
Czech Republic	1,689,534	46	16.6	56	4,473,330	42	44.0	36
Israel	1,687,881	47	22.2	44	4,974,376	36	66.5	17
Finland	1,602,457	48	30.4	23	5,606,178	33	106.5	3
Peru	1,413,353	49	4.8	107	820,295	77	2.8	121
Singapore	1,396,352	50	26.1	29	6,600,483	30	123.3	1

Country or area	Number	Rank	%	Rank	Number	Rank	%	Rank
Azerbaijan	1,310,022	51	13.8	63	3,160,514	53	33.3	50
Bulgaria	1,241,914	52	17.6	53	2,835,021	55	40.3	41
New Zealand	1,202,952	53	27.8	26	2,823,031	56	65.2	18
Algeria	1,137,832	54	3.0	116	—	—	—	—
Ireland	1,071,995	55	22.7	42	3,033,242	54	64.2	19
South Africa	1,065,044	56	2.2	126	12,698,521	22	26.0	62
Croatia	909,090	58	20.3	48	2,341,270	60	52.3	26
Ecuador	825,732	59	5.4	102	3,380,114	48	23.2	67
Slovakia	798,776	60	14.6	59	1,916,230	63	34.9	46
Serbia	740,467	61	10.2	81	2,922,357	54	40.2	42
Lithuania	688,475	62	19.5	49	301,488	106	8.6	97
Morocco	675,586	63	2.1	127	3,244,494	50	10.0	93
United Arab Emirates	624,007	64	11.7	72	2,704,509	57	50.9	30
Uruguay	550,643	65	16.6	55	1,060,462	69	32.0	53
Bangladesh	546,074	66	0.3	153	325,389	105	0.2	142
Tunisia	513,569	67	4.8	106	558,647	89	5.2	108
Slovenia	491,467	68	24.6	36	740,605	80	37.1	43
Lebanon	482,344	69	11.7	74	13,042	139	0.3	141
Latvia	471,847	70	21.5	47	1,122,768	68	51.2	29
Costa Rica	465,536	71	10.0	82	673,615	84	14.5	82
Dominican Republic	446,420	72	4.4	108	1,557,377	65	15.4	80
Moldova	433,482	73	11.9	71	185,439	111	5.1	109
Sri Lanka	428,338	74	2.0	128	953,986	73	4.4	114
Bosnia and Herzegovina	418,692	75	10.8	78	421,641	95	10.9	88
Georgia	416,366	76	9.1	86	1,023,112	71	22.4	66
Syria	403,300	77	1.8	129	415,918	96	1.8	126
Estonia	327,243	78	25.7	31	924,699	74	72.5	12
Macedonia	304,547	79	14.6	58	449,646	93	21.6	68

Country or area	Number	Rank	%	Rank	Number	Rank	%	Rank
Panama	288,280	80	8.2	91	526,893	91	15.0	81
El Salvador	235,403	81	3.9	111	335,716	104	5.5	105
Cyprus	218,783	82	19.2	51	384,270	98	33.8	47
Uzbekistan	205,006	83	0.7	146	5,869,645	30	20.7	71
Armenia	197,181	84	6.6	96	820,272	78	27.6	58
Jordan	195,136	85	3.0	117	697,167	82	10.7	90
Trinidad and Tobago	166,948	86	13.6	65	18,028	132	1.5	131
Luxembourg	165,994	87	32.6	17	369,430	100	72.6	11
Yemen	162,008	88	0.7	147	46,571	126	0.2	143
Qatar	160,050	89	8.2	92	1,407,253	66	72.1	13
Bahrain	159,015	90	12.7	67	838,004	76	67.1	16
Albania	148,882	91	5.0	103	552,676	90	18.4	74
Macau	147,130	92	25.5	32	—	—	—	—
Kyrgyzstan	144,179	93	2.6	122	—	—	—	—
Mauritius	138,820	94	10.6	79	282,302	107	21.5	69
Malta	129,848	95	31.7	19	236,229	109	57.6	21
Jamaica	125,188	96	4.3	109	45,505	127	1.6	128
Nepal	119,563	97	0.4	151	—	—	—	—
Mongolia	115,561	98	3.6	114	848,391	75	26.7	61
Bolivia	111,029	99	1.1	139	690,768	83	6.7	102
Iceland	107,895	100	34.5	11	224,568	110	71.7	15
Laos	96,291	101	1.5	134	50,648	124	0.8	134
Nicaragua	95,023	102	1.7	131	58,365	123	1.0	133
Senegal	94,548	103	0.7	145	486,490	92	3.8	117
Oman	75,770	104	2.5	123	1,751,590	64	56.7	22
Paraguay	72,612	105	1.1	138	358,545	101	5.5	107
Zimbabwe	69,282	106	0.5	148	3,743,226	45	29.7	55
Barbados	68,547	107	23.8	39	104,810	116	36.4	45
Honduras	64,216	108	0.8	144	347,217	103	4.2	115
Ghana	62,124	109	0.3	156	8,209,743	27	33.3	49

Country or area	Number	Rank	%	Rank	Number	Rank	%	Rank
Namibia	60,188	110	2.8	119	624,257	86	28.8	56
Libya	58,379	111	1.0	140	775,545	79	13.8	83
Montenegro	54,439	112	8.3	90	177,437	112	27.0	59
Ivory Coast	52,685	113	0.2	157	—	—	—	—
New Caledonia	48,165	114	18.5	52	6,033	141	2.3	123
Kenya	43,013	115	0.1	167	954,896	72	2.2	124
Kuwait	43,003	116	1.6	132	—	—	—	—
Ethiopia	40,126	117	0.0	176	402,173	97	0.4	138
French Polynesia	39,878	118	14.5	60	15,971	135	5.8	104
Uganda	36,332	119	0.1	165	2,542,911	58	7.6	100
Suriname	32,192	120	5.7	98	—	—	—	—
Cambodia	30,653	121	0.2	158	1,032,781	70	6.9	101
Liechtenstein	29,504	122	80.4	1	—	—	—	—
Guyana	28,593	123	3.9	112	—	—	—	—
Angola	27,987	124	0.2	162	278,966	108	1.5	129
Andorra	26,346	125	31.0	22	—	—	—	—
Saint Lucia	22,415	126	13.8	62	—	—	—	—
Maldives	21,718	127	5.5	101	84,700	122	21.5	70
Cape Verde	19,791	128	3.8	113	117,986	114	22.5	65
Mozambique	19,753	129	0.1	168	431,988	94	1.8	127
Brunei	19,650	130	4.8	105	31,080	130	7.6	99
Sudan	18,472	131	0.1	172	5,607,848	31	16.4	78
Chad	18,000	132	0.2	161	—	—	—	—
Cayman Islands	17,750	133	33.8	15	—	—	—	—
Botswana	16,407	134	0.8	143	348,124	102	16.6	76
Bhutan	16,015	135	2.2	124	17,851	133	2.5	122
Nigeria	15,311	136	0.0	185	17,339,012	18	10.2	91
Grenada	14,945	137	13.7	64	—	—	—	—
Zambia	14,785	138	0.1	166	90,643	121	0.7	137

Country or area	Number	Rank	%	Rank	Number	Rank	%	Rank
Burkina Faso	14,166	139	0.1	169	—	—	—	—
Monaco	13,889	140	45.5	2	15,494	138	50.8	31
Saint Kitts and Nevis	13,792	141	27.2	27	—	—	—	—
Fiji	13,734	142	1.5	133	96,277	118	10.8	89
Djibouti	13,343	143	1.7	130	—	—	—	—
Saint Vincent and the Grenadines	12,890	144	12.5	69	—	—	—	—
Gibraltar	11,879	145	40.9	4	2,954	143	10.2	92
Greenland	11,177	146	19.4	50	2,803	144	4.9	111
Seychelles	10,546	147	11.7	73	7,809	140	8.7	96
Belize	10,077	148	3.1	115	419	147	0.1	146
San Marino	9,962	149	31.0	21	3,521	142	11.0	87
Madagascar	9,242	150	0.0	177	—	—	—	—
Dominica	9,186	151	12.6	68	—	—	—	—
The Bahamas	8,730	152	2.8	120	—	—	—	—
Papua New Guinea	8,077	153	0.1	164	—	—	—	—
British Virgin Islands	7,785	154	25.0	35	—	—	—	—
Mauritania	6,013	155	0.2	160	108,434	115	3.2	120
Burma	6,004	156	0.0	184	15,830	136	0.0	147
Tajikistan	5,904	157	0.1	171	—	—	—	—
Togo	5,569	158	0.1	170	47,892	125	0.7	135
Benin	5,183	159	0.1	172	33,596	129	0.4	139
Gabon	5,147	160	0.3	154	—	—	—	—
Antigua and Barbuda	5,016	161	5.6	99	17,703	134	19.9	72
Cuba	4,984	162	0.0	175	—	—	—	—
Anguilla	3,974	163	25.8	30	—	—	—	—
Tanzania	3,753	164	0.0	187	698,531	81	1.5	130

Country or area	Number	Rank	%	Rank	Number	Rank	%	Rank
Swaziland	3,717	165	0.3	155	166,485	113	12.0	86
Niger	3,596	166	0.0	182	—	—	—	—
Rwanda	2,806	167	0.0	181	379,331	99	3.2	119
Vanuatu	2,646	168	1.0	141	—	—	—	—
Lesotho	2,529	169	0.1	163	—	—	—	—
Solomon Islands	2,198	170	0.4	152	36,969	128	6.3	103
Mali	2,014	171	0.0	183	101,954	117	0.7	136
Saint Helena	1,683	172	21.8	46	—	—	—	—
Tonga	1,518	173	1.4	135	—	—	—	—
Equatorial Guinea	1,372	174	0.2	159	—	—	—	—
Turkmenistan	1,365	175	0.0	178	—	—	—	—
Wallis and Futuna	1,363	176	8.8	87	—	—	—	—
Malawi	1,306	177	0.0	187	565,267	88	3.5	118
Cook Islands	1,212	178	11.2	75	—	—	—	—
Falkland Islands[9]	1,187	179	40.5	5	—	—	—	—
Cameroon	1,006	180	0.0	190	—	—	—	—
Kiribati	993	181	1.0	142	—	—	—	—
São Tomé and Príncipe	960	182	0.5	149	—	—	—	—
Guinea	762	183	0.0	189	—	—	—	—
Palau	621	184	3.0	118	—	—	—	—
Tuvalu	592	185	5.6	100	—	—	—	—
East Timor	583	186	0.1	174	—	—	—	—
Montserrat	512	187	9.9	83	854	146	16.5	77
The Gambia	497	188	0.0	178	22,435	131	1.2	132
Burundi	422	189	0.0	191	—	—	—	—
Republic of the Congo	393	190	0.0	185	90,906	120	2.1	125
Comoros	192	191	0.0	180	—	—	—	—

Country or area	Number	Rank	%	Rank	Number	Rank	%	Rank
Eritrea	122	192	0.0	192	—	—	—	—
Liberia	78	193	0.0	192	—	—	—	—
Guatemala	—	—	—	—	632,624	85	4.5	113
Haiti	—	—	—	—	15,781	137	0.2	144
Nauru	—	—	—	—	904	145	9.6	95

NATIONAL COMMUNICATIONS COMMISSION CONTACTS

Office	Tel No.	Fax No.	Address
Counter-1	0800-177-177	(02)2343-3994	No.50, Sec. 1, RenAi Rd., Taipei City 10052, Taiwan (R.O.C.)
Counter-2	0800-177-177	(02)2343-3994	No.16, Sec. 2, JiNan Rd., Taipei City 10054, Taiwan (R.O.C.)
Dept. of Planning	(02)3343-8156	(02)2343-3938	No.50, Sec. 1, RenAi Rd., Taipei City 10052, Taiwan (R.O.C.)
Dept. of Network Infrastructure	(02)3343-8276	(02)2343-3636	No.16, Sec. 2, JiNan Rd., Taipei City 10054, Taiwan (R.O.C.)
Dept. of Platforms and Businesses	(02)3343-8382 (02)3343-8379	(02)2343-3600 (02)2343-3651	No.50, Sec. 1, RenAi Rd., Taipei City 10052, Taiwan (R.O.C.)
Dept. of Frequency and Resources	(02)3343-8409	(02)2343-3699	No.16, Sec. 2, JiNan Rd., Taipei City 10054, Taiwan (R.O.C.)
Dept. of Broadcasting and Content	(02)3343-8580	(02)3343-2642	No.50, Sec. 1, RenAi Rd., Taipei City 10052, Taiwan (R.O.C.)
Dept. of Legal Affairs	(02)3343-8616	(02)2343-3874	No.50, Sec. 1, RenAi Rd., Taipei City 10052, Taiwan (R.O.C.)
Secretariat	(02)3343-8798	(02)2343-3809	No.50, Sec. 1, RenAi Rd., Taipei City 10052, Taiwan (R.O.C.)

Personnel Office	(02)3343-8815	(02)2343-3686	No.16, Sec. 2, JiNan Rd., Taipei City 10054, Taiwan (R.O.C.)
Civil Service Ethics Office	(02)3343-8851	(02)2343-3695	No.16, Sec. 2, JiNan Rd., Taipei City 10054, Taiwan (R.O.C.)
Budget, Accounting and Statistics Office	(02)3343-8878	(02)2343-3675	No.16, Sec. 2, JiNan Rd., Taipei City 10054, Taiwan (R.O.C.)
Dept. of Northern Region Affairs	(02)3343-8973	(02)2343-3991	No.143, YanPing S. Rd., Taipei City 10066, Taiwan (R.O.C.)
Dept. of Central Region Affairs	(04)2254-0844	(04)2259-5861	660, Sec. 2, Liming Rd., Taichung City 40873, Taiwan (R.O.C.)
Dept. of Southern Region Affairs	(07)239-1111	(07)239-1107	No.142, JinTian Rd., Kaohsiung City 80051, Taiwan (R.O.C.)
Telecommunications Investigation Corp	(02)2343-3983	(02)2343-3989	No.18, Ln. 111, Sec. 3, Xinyi Rd., Taipei City 10658, Taiwan (R.O.C.)
Telecommunications Investigation Corp 1st Squadron	(02)2343-3980	(02)2700-2615	No.18, Ln. 111, Sec. 3, Xinyi Rd., Taipei City 10658, Taiwan (R.O.C.)
Telecommunications Investigation Corp 2st Squadron	(04)2253-0539	(04)2253-0685	660, Sec. 2, Liming Rd., Taichung City 40873, Taiwan (R.O.C.)
Telecommunications Investigation Corp 3st Squadron	(07)239-1161	(07)239-1143	No.142, JinTian Rd., Kaohsiung City 80051, Taiwan (R.O.C.)

STRATEGIC GOVERNMENT AND BUSINESS CONTACTS

REPRESENTATIVE OFFICES

UNITED STATES REPRESENTATIVE OFFICES

American Institute in Taiwan, Washington Headquarters
Suite 1700, 1700 North Moore Street, Arlington, VA 22209
Tel: 703-525-8474; fax 703-841-1385.

American Institute in Taiwan, Taipei Office
No. 7, Lane 134, Hsin Yi Road, Section 3, Taipei, Taiwan
Tel: 011-886-2-2709-2000; fax 011-886-2-2702-7675

American Institute in Taiwan, Kaohsiung Office
5F, No. 2, Chung Cheng 3rd Road; Kaohsiung, Taiwan 800
Tel: 011-886-7-224-0154; fax 011-886-7-223-8237

Taiwan Representative Office

Taipei Economic and Cultural Representative Office (TECRO)
4201 Wisconsin Ave. NW, Washington, DC 20056-2137
Tel: 202-895-1800; fax 202-363-0999.

1. U.S. TRADE RELATED CONTACTS

American Institute in Taiwan (AIT)
Commercial Section
Chief: William Brekke
Deputy Chief: Rosemary Gallant
Suite 3207, 333 Keelung Rd., Sec. 1, Taipei, Taiwan
Tel: 886-2-2720-1550, Fax: 886-2-2757-7162

Agriculture Section
Chief: Debra Henke
Trade Officer: Daniel Martinez
7, Lane 134, Hsin Yi Rd., Sec. 3, Taipei, Taiwan
Tel: 886-2-2709-2000, 886-2-2332-7981
Fax: 886-2-2709-2054, 886-2-2305-2120

Economic Section
Chief: Marc Wall
Deputy Chief: Matthew Matthews
7, Lane 134, Hsin Yi Rd., Sec. 3, Taipei, Taiwan
Tel: 886-2-2709-2000, Fax: 886-2-2706-3023

WASHINGTON-BASED COUNTRY CONTACTS

AIT/Washington
Trade and Commercial Programs
Director: Ray Sander
Suite 1700, 1700 N. Moore Stret
Arlington, VA 22209
Tel: 703-525-8474, Fax: 703-841-1385

U.S. Department of Commerce
Taiwan Desk Officers
Laurette Newsom
Room 2327, 14th and Constitution Ave. NW
Washington, D.C. 20230
Tel: 202-482-4681, Fax: 202-482-4098

U.S. Department of Commerce
US&FCS East Asia Pacific
Director: Alice Davenport
Room 1229, 14th and Constitution Ave. NW

Washington, D.C. 20230
Tel: 202-482-2429, Fax: 202-482-5179

U.S. Department of Commerce
Trade Information Center
Room 7424, 14th and Constitution Ave. NW
Washington, D.C. 20230
Tel: 1-800-USA-TRADE

U.S. Department of Agriculture
Foreign Agricultural Service
Trade Assistance and Promotion Office
South Building, 14th and Independent Ave. SW
Washington, D.C. 20250
Tel: 202-720-7420

2. AMCHAM AND/OR BILATERAL BUSINESS COUNCILS

American Chamber of Commerce
President: Jeffrey Williams
Rm. 1012, 96 Chungshan N. Rd., Sec. 2, Taipei, Taiwan
Tel: 886-2-2581-7089, Fax: 886-2-2542-3376

China External Trade Development Council
Secretary-General: Ricky Y.S. Kao
3-8F, 333 Keelung Rd., Sec. 1, Taipei, Taiwan
Tel: 886-2-2725-5200, Fax: 886-2-2757-6653

3. TRADE OR INDUSTRY ASSOCIATIONS

Chinese National Asociation of Industry & Commerce
Chairman: Jeffrey Koo
13F, 390 Fuhsing S. Rd., Sec. 1, Taipei, Taiwan
Tel: 886-2-2707-0111, Fax: 886-2-2701-7601

Chinese National Federation of Industries
Chairman: Kao Chin-yen
12F, 390 Fuhsing S. Rd., Sec. 1, Taipei, Taiwan
Tel: 886-2-2703-3500, Fax: 886-2-2703-3982

4. PUBLIC AGENCIES

Ministry of Economic Affairs (MOEA)
Minister: Wang Chih-Kang
15 Foochow St., Taipei, Taiwan
Tel: 886-2-2321-8124, Fax: 886-2-2391-9398

Ministry of Finance (MOF)
Minister: Paul C. H. Chiu
2 Aikuo W. Rd., Taipei, Taiwan
Tel: 886-2-2322-8006, Fax: 886-2-2321-1205

Board of Foreign Trade (BOFT), MOEA
Director General: Chen Ruey-long
1 Hukou St., Taipei, Taiwan
Tel: 886-2-2321-0717, Fax: 886-2-2351-3603

Ministry of Transportation and Communications (MOTC)
Minister: Fong-Cheng Lin
2 Changsha St., Sec. 1, Taipei, Taiwan
Tel: 886-2-2349-2000, Fax: 886-2-2389-6009

Directorate General of Telecommunications, MOTC
Director General: Chien Jen-Ter
16 Chi-Nan Rd., Taipei, Taiwan
Tel: 886-2-2343-3953, Fax: 886-2-2343-3772

Council of Agriculture (COA), Executive Yuan
Chairman: Peng Tso-Kwei
37 Nanhai Rd., Taipei, Taiwan
Tel: 886-2-2311-9175, Fax: 886-2-2361-4397

Council for Economic Planning and Development (CEPD)
Chairman: Chiang Pin-kung
3, Paoching Rd., Taipei, Taiwan
Tel: 886-2-2316-5306, Fax: 886-2-2370-0403

Department of Health (DOH), Executive Yuan
Director-General: Chan Chi-Shean M.D.
100 Aikuo E. Rd., Taipei, Taiwan
Tel: 886-2-2396-7166, Fax: 886-2-2341-8994

Environmental Protection Administration (EPA), Executive Yuan
Administrator: Hsung-hsiung Tsai
41 Chunghwa Rd., Sec. 1, Taipei, Taiwan
Tel: 886-2-2321-7888, Fax: 886-2-2371-9759

5. MARKET RESEARCH FIRMS (PARTIAL LISTING)

Dun & Bradstreet International Ltd., Taiwan Branch
General Manager: James B. Barnett
12F, 188 Nanking E. Rd., Sec. 5, Taipei, Taiwan
Tel: 886-2-2756-2922, Fax: 886-2-2749-1936

AC Nielsen
Managing Director: Titan Wang
12F, 188 Nanking E. Rd., Sec. 5, Taipei, Taiwan
Tel: 886-2-2756-8668, Fax: 886-2-2754-8883

Investec-Coopers Lybrand Consulting Ltd.
Managing Director: Michael McNabb
3/F, 367 Fu Hsing N. Rd., Taipei, Taiwan
Tel: 886-2-2715-2822, Fax: 886-2-2545-1185

6. COMMERCIAL BANKS (PARTIAL LISTING)

American Express Bank, Ltd.
Senior Director & Gen. Mgr: Howard Law
3rd & 4th Fl, 214 Tunhwa N. Rd., Taipei, Taiwan
Tel: 886-2-2715-1581, Fax: 886-2-2713-0263

Citibank, N.A.
Corporate Officer: Peper Baumann
52 Minsheng E. Rd., Sec. 4, Taipei, Taiwan
Tel: 886-2-2715-5931, Fax: 886-2-2712-7388

Bank Boston, N.A. Taipei Branch
VP Corporate Banking: Francis Wu
5F, 137 Nanking E. Rd., Sec. 2, Taipei, Taiwan
Tel: 886-2-2506-3443, Fax: 886-2-2517-1653

Bank of Taiwan
Chairman: James C.T. Lo
120, Chungking S. Rd., Sec. 1, Taipei, Taiwan
Tel: 886-2-2349-3456, Fax: 886-2-2331-5840

International Commercial Bank of China
Chairman: James T.T. Yuan
100 Chilin Rd., Taipei, Taiwan
Tel: 886-2-2563-3156, Fax: 886-2-2561-1216

The Multilateral Development Bank
Office Director: Janet Thomas
14th and Constitution, NW
Washington, D.C. 20007
Tel: 202-482-3399, Fax: 202-482-5179

TITLE
Taiwan Aviation and Aerospace Industry Handbook
Taiwan Aviation and Aerospace Industry Handbook
Taiwan Business and Investment Opportunities Yearbook
Taiwan Business and Investment Opportunities Yearbook
Taiwan Business and Investment Opportunities Yearbook Volume 1 Strategic Information and Opportunities
Taiwan Business and Investment Opportunities Yearbook Volume 2 Leading Export-Import, Business, Investment Opportunities and Projects
Taiwan Business Intelligence Report - Practical Information, Opportunities, Contacts
Taiwan Business Intelligence Report - Practical Information, Opportunities, Contacts
Taiwan Business Law Handbook - Strategic Information and Basic Laws
Taiwan Business Law Handbook - Strategic Information and Basic Laws
Taiwan Business Law Handbook - Strategic Information and Basic Laws
Taiwan Business Law Handbook - Strategic Information and Basic Laws
Taiwan Business Success Guide - Basic Practical Information and Contacts
Taiwan Clothing & Textile Industry Handbook
Taiwan Clothing & Textile Industry Handbook
Taiwan Company Laws and Regulations Handbook
Taiwan Company Laws and Regulations Handbook - Strategic Information and Basic Laws
Taiwan Constitution and Citizenship Laws Handbook - Strategic Information and Basic Laws
Taiwan Country Study Guide - Strategic Information and Developments
Taiwan Country Study Guide - Strategic Information and Developments Volume 1 Strategic Information and Developments
Taiwan Country Study Guide Volume 1 Strategic Information and Developments
Taiwan Criminal Laws, Regulations and Procedures Handbook - Strategic Information, Regulations, Procedures
Taiwan Customs, Trade Regulations and Procedures Handbook
Taiwan Customs, Trade Regulations and Procedures Handbook
Taiwan Diplomatic Handbook - Strategic Information and Developments
Taiwan Diplomatic Handbook - Strategic Information and Developments
Taiwan Ecology & Nature Protection Handbook
Taiwan Ecology & Nature Protection Handbook
Taiwan Ecology & Nature Protection Laws and Regulation Handbook
Taiwan Economic & Development Strategy Handbook
Taiwan Economic & Development Strategy Handbook
Taiwan Education System and Policy Handbook
Taiwan Electoral, Political Parties Laws and Regulations Handbook - Strategic Information, Regulations, Procedures
Taiwan Energy Policy, Laws and Regulation Handbook
Taiwan Export-Import Trade and Business Directory
Taiwan Export-Import Trade and Business Directory
Taiwan Foreign Policy and Government Guide
Taiwan Foreign Policy and Government Guide

TITLE
Taiwan Government and Business Contacts Handbook
Taiwan Government and Business Contacts Handbook
Taiwan Healthcare Sector Organization, Management and Payment Systems Handbook - Strategic Information, Programs and Regulations
Taiwan Immigration Laws and Regulations Handbook - Strategic Information and Basic Laws
Taiwan Industrial and Business Directory
Taiwan Insolvency (Bankruptcy) Laws and Regulations Handbook - Strategic Information and Basic Laws
Taiwan Intelligence & Security Activities & Operations Handbook
Taiwan Intelligence & Security Activities & Operations Handbook
Taiwan Internet and E-Commerce Investment and Business Guide - Strategic and Practical Information: Regulations and Opportunities
Taiwan Internet and E-Commerce Investment and Business Guide - Strategic and Practical Information: Regulations and Opportunities
Taiwan Investment and Business Guide - Strategic and Practical Information
Taiwan Investment and Business Guide - Strategic and Practical Information
Taiwan Investment and Business Guide - Strategic and Practical Information
Taiwan Investment and Business Guide - Strategic and Practical Information
Taiwan Investment and Business Guide Volume 2 Business, Investment Opportunities and Incentives
Taiwan Investment and Business Profile - Basic Information and Contacts for Succesful investment and Business Activity
Taiwan Investment and Trade Laws and Regulations Handbook
Taiwan Justice System and National Police Handbook
Taiwan Justice System and National Police Handbook
Taiwan Labor Laws and Regulations Handbook - Strategic Information and Basic Laws
Taiwan Land Ownership and Agriculture Laws Handbook
Taiwan Medical & Pharmaceutical Industry Handbook
Taiwan Medical & Pharmaceutical Industry Handbook
Taiwan Military Policy and Defense Strategy Handbook
Taiwan Military Policy and Defense Strategy Handbook
Taiwan Military Service Guide
Taiwan Mineral & Mining Sector Investment and Business Guide - Strategic and Practical Information
Taiwan Mineral & Mining Sector Investment and Business Guide - Strategic and Practical Information
Taiwan Mining Laws and Regulations Handbook
Taiwan National Defense and Security Report
Taiwan National Defense Report
Taiwan National Police Handbook
Taiwan National Police Handbook
Taiwan National Security and Defense Law and Regulations Handbook
Taiwan National Security and Defense Law and Regulations Handbook
Taiwan President Handbook

TITLE
Taiwan President Handbook
Taiwan Province of China Investment, Trade Strategy and Agreements Handbook - Strategic Information and Basic Agreements
Taiwan Recent Economic and Political Developments Yearbook
Taiwan Research & Development Policy Handbook
Taiwan Space Agency and Programs Handbook
Taiwan Space Agency and Programs Handbook
Taiwan Starting Business (Incorporating) in Taiwan Guide
Taiwan Starting Business (Incorporating) in....Guide
Taiwan Tax Guide
Taiwan Tax Guide
Taiwan Tax Guide Volume 1 Strategic Information and Basic Regulations
Taiwan Taxation Laws and Regulations Handbook
Taiwan Telecom Laws and Regulations Handbook
Taiwan Telecommunication Industry Business Opportunities Handbook
Taiwan Telecommunication Industry Business Opportunities Handbook
Taiwan Transportation Policy and Regulations Handbook
Taiwan: Business in Taiwan for Everyone: Practical Information and Contacts for Success
Taiwan: Doing Business and Investing in Taiwan Guide
Taiwan: Doing Business and Investing in Taiwan Guide
Taiwan: How to Invest, Start and Run Profitable Business in Taiwan Guide - Practical Information, Opportunities, Contacts
Taiwan: Investing in Taiwan Guide
Taiwan: Investing in Taiwan Guide: Strategic and Practical Information
Taiwan: Starting Business (Incorporating) in Taiwan Guide

INFORMATION STRATEGY, INTERNET AND E-COMMERCE DEVELOPMENT HANDBOOKS LIBRARY

Price: $99.95 Each

World Business Information Catalog: http://www.ibpus.com

TITLE
Albania Information Strategy, Internet and E-Commerce Development Handbook - Strategic Information, Programs, Regulations
Algeria Information Strategy, Internet and E-Commerce Development Handbook - Strategic Information, Programs, Regulations
Angola Information Strategy, Internet and E-Commerce Development Handbook - Strategic Information, Programs, Regulations
Argentina Information Strategy, Internet and E-Commerce Development Handbook - Strategic Information, Programs, Regulations
Armenia Information Strategy, Internet and E-Commerce Development Handbook - Strategic Information, Programs, Regulations
Australia Information Strategy, Internet and E-Commerce Development Handbook - Strategic Information, Programs, Regulations
Austria Information Strategy, Internet and E-Commerce Development Handbook - Strategic Information, Programs, Regulations
Azerbaijan Information Strategy, Internet and E-Commerce Development Handbook - Strategic Information, Programs, Regulations
Bangladesh Information Strategy, Internet and E-Commerce Development Handbook - Strategic Information, Programs, Regulations
Belarus Information Strategy, Internet and E-Commerce Development Handbook - Strategic Information, Programs, Regulations
Belgium Information Strategy, Internet and E-Commerce Development Handbook - Strategic Information, Programs, Regulations
Bermuda Information Strategy, Internet and E-Commerce Development Handbook - Strategic Information, Programs, Regulations
Bolivia Information Strategy, Internet and E-Commerce Development Handbook - Strategic Information, Programs, Regulations
Bosnia and Herzegovina Information Strategy, Internet and E-Commerce Development Handbook - Strategic Information, Programs, Regulations
Botswana Information Strategy, Internet and E-Commerce Development Handbook - Strategic Information, Programs, Regulations
Brazil Information Strategy, Internet and E-Commerce Development Handbook - Strategic Information, Programs, Regulations
Bulgaria Information Strategy, Internet and E-Commerce Development Handbook - Strategic Information, Programs, Regulations
Cambodia Information Strategy, Internet and E-Commerce Development Handbook - Strategic Information, Programs, Regulations
Cameroon Information Strategy, Internet and E-Commerce Development Handbook - Strategic Information, Programs, Regulations
Canada Information Strategy, Internet and E-Commerce Development Handbook - Strategic Information, Programs, Regulations
Chile Information Strategy, Internet and E-Commerce Development Handbook - Strategic Information, Programs,

TITLE
Regulations
China Information Strategy, Internet and E-Commerce Development Handbook - Strategic Information, Programs, Regulations
Colombia Information Strategy, Internet and E-Commerce Development Handbook - Strategic Information, Programs, Regulations
Cook Islands Information Strategy, Internet and E-Commerce Development Handbook - Strategic Information, Programs, Regulations
Costa Rica Information Strategy, Internet and E-Commerce Development Handbook - Strategic Information, Programs, Regulations
Croatia Information Strategy, Internet and E-Commerce Development Handbook - Strategic Information, Programs, Regulations
Cuba Information Strategy, Internet and E-Commerce Development Handbook - Strategic Information, Programs, Regulations
Cyprus Information Strategy, Internet and E-Commerce Development Handbook - Strategic Information, Programs, Regulations
Czech Republic Information Strategy, Internet and E-Commerce Development Handbook - Strategic Information, Programs, Regulations
Denmark Information Strategy, Internet and E-Commerce Development Handbook - Strategic Information, Programs, Regulations
Dominican Republic Information Strategy, Internet and E-Commerce Development Handbook - Strategic Information, Programs, Regulations
Dubai Information Strategy, Internet and E-Commerce Development Handbook - Strategic Information, Programs, Regulations
Ecuador Information Strategy, Internet and E-Commerce Development Handbook - Strategic Information, Programs, Regulations
Egypt Information Strategy, Internet and E-Commerce Development Handbook - Strategic Information, Programs, Regulations
El Salvador Information Strategy, Internet and E-Commerce Development Handbook - Strategic Information, Programs, Regulations
Equatorial Guinea Information Strategy, Internet and E-Commerce Development Handbook - Strategic Information, Programs, Regulations
Estonia Information Strategy, Internet and E-Commerce Development Handbook - Strategic Information, Programs, Regulations
Fiji Information Strategy, Internet and E-Commerce Development Handbook - Strategic Information, Programs, Regulations
Finland Information Strategy, Internet and E-Commerce Development Handbook - Strategic Information, Programs, Regulations
France Information Strategy, Internet and E-Commerce Development Handbook - Strategic Information, Programs, Regulations
Georgia Republic Information Strategy, Internet and E-Commerce Development Handbook - Strategic Information, Programs, Regulations
Germany Information Strategy, Internet and E-Commerce Development Handbook - Strategic Information, Programs, Regulations
Greece Information Strategy, Internet and E-Commerce Development Handbook - Strategic Information, Programs, Regulations
Guatemala Information Strategy, Internet and E-Commerce Development Handbook - Strategic Information, Programs, Regulations
Guernsey Information Strategy, Internet and E-Commerce Development Handbook - Strategic Information, Programs, Regulations
Guyana Information Strategy, Internet and E-Commerce Development Handbook - Strategic Information, Programs, Regulations
Haiti Information Strategy, Internet and E-Commerce Development Handbook - Strategic Information, Programs, Regulations
Honduras Information Strategy, Internet and E-Commerce Development Handbook - Strategic Information, Programs, Regulations
Hungary Information Strategy, Internet and E-Commerce Development Handbook - Strategic Information, Programs, Regulations
Iceland Information Strategy, Internet and E-Commerce Development Handbook - Strategic Information, Programs, Regulations
India Information Strategy, Internet and E-Commerce Development Handbook - Strategic Information, Programs, Regulations

TITLE
Indonesia Information Strategy, Internet and E-Commerce Development Handbook - Strategic Information, Programs, Regulations
Iran Information Strategy, Internet and E-Commerce Development Handbook - Strategic Information, Programs, Regulations
Iraq Information Strategy, Internet and E-Commerce Development Handbook - Strategic Information, Programs, Regulations
Ireland Information Strategy, Internet and E-Commerce Development Handbook - Strategic Information, Programs, Regulations
Israel Information Strategy, Internet and E-Commerce Development Handbook - Strategic Information, Programs, Regulations
Italy Information Strategy, Internet and E-Commerce Development Handbook - Strategic Information, Programs, Regulations
Jamaica Information Strategy, Internet and E-Commerce Development Handbook - Strategic Information, Programs, Regulations
Japan Information Strategy, Internet and E-Commerce Development Handbook - Strategic Information, Programs, Regulations
Jordan Information Strategy, Internet and E-Commerce Development Handbook - Strategic Information, Programs, Regulations
Kazakhstan Information Strategy, Internet and E-Commerce Development Handbook - Strategic Information, Programs, Regulations
Kenya Information Strategy, Internet and E-Commerce Development Handbook - Strategic Information, Programs, Regulations
Korea, North Information Strategy, Internet and E-Commerce Development Handbook - Strategic Information, Programs, Regulations
Korea, South Information Strategy, Internet and E-Commerce Development Handbook - Strategic Information, Programs, Regulations
Kuwait Information Strategy, Internet and E-Commerce Development Handbook - Strategic Information, Programs, Regulations
Kyrgyzstan Information Strategy, Internet and E-Commerce Development Handbook - Strategic Information, Programs, Regulations
Laos Information Strategy, Internet and E-Commerce Development Handbook - Strategic Information, Programs, Regulations
Latvia Information Strategy, Internet and E-Commerce Development Handbook - Strategic Information, Programs, Regulations
Lebanon Information Strategy, Internet and E-Commerce Development Handbook - Strategic Information, Programs, Regulations
Libya Information Strategy, Internet and E-Commerce Development Handbook - Strategic Information, Programs, Regulations
Lithuania Information Strategy, Internet and E-Commerce Development Handbook - Strategic Information, Programs, Regulations
Macao Information Strategy, Internet and E-Commerce Development Handbook - Strategic Information, Programs, Regulations
Macedonia, Republic Information Strategy, Internet and E-Commerce Development Handbook - Strategic Information, Programs, Regulations
Madagascar Information Strategy, Internet and E-Commerce Development Handbook - Strategic Information, Programs, Regulations
Malaysia Information Strategy, Internet and E-Commerce Development Handbook - Strategic Information, Programs, Regulations
Malta Information Strategy, Internet and E-Commerce Development Handbook - Strategic Information, Programs, Regulations
Mauritius Information Strategy, Internet and E-Commerce Development Handbook - Strategic Information, Programs, Regulations
Mauritius Information Strategy, Internet and E-Commerce Development Handbook - Strategic Information, Programs, Regulations
Mexico Information Strategy, Internet and E-Commerce Development Handbook - Strategic Information, Programs, Regulations
Micronesia Information Strategy, Internet and E-Commerce Development Handbook - Strategic Information, Programs, Regulations
Moldova Information Strategy, Internet and E-Commerce Development Handbook - Strategic Information, Programs, Regulations
Monaco Information Strategy, Internet and E-Commerce Development Handbook - Strategic Information,

TITLE
Programs, Regulations
Mongolia Information Strategy, Internet and E-Commerce Development Handbook - Strategic Information, Programs, Regulations
Morocco Information Strategy, Internet and E-Commerce Development Handbook - Strategic Information, Programs, Regulations
Myanmar Information Strategy, Internet and E-Commerce Development Handbook - Strategic Information, Programs, Regulations
Namibia Information Strategy, Internet and E-Commerce Development Handbook - Strategic Information, Programs, Regulations
Netherlands Information Strategy, Internet and E-Commerce Development Handbook - Strategic Information, Programs, Regulations
New Zealand Information Strategy, Internet and E-Commerce Development Handbook - Strategic Information, Programs, Regulations
Nicaragua Information Strategy, Internet and E-Commerce Development Handbook - Strategic Information, Programs, Regulations
Nigeria Information Strategy, Internet and E-Commerce Development Handbook - Strategic Information, Programs, Regulations
Norway Information Strategy, Internet and E-Commerce Development Handbook - Strategic Information, Programs, Regulations
Opportunities
Pakistan Information Strategy, Internet and E-Commerce Development Handbook - Strategic Information, Programs, Regulations
Panama Information Strategy, Internet and E-Commerce Development Handbook - Strategic Information, Programs, Regulations
Peru Information Strategy, Internet and E-Commerce Development Handbook - Strategic Information, Programs, Regulations
Philippines Information Strategy, Internet and E-Commerce Development Handbook - Strategic Information, Programs, Regulations
Poland Information Strategy, Internet and E-Commerce Development Handbook - Strategic Information, Programs, Regulations
Portugal Information Strategy, Internet and E-Commerce Development Handbook - Strategic Information, Programs, Regulations
Romania Information Strategy, Internet and E-Commerce Development Handbook - Strategic Information, Programs, Regulations
Russia Information Strategy, Internet and E-Commerce Development Handbook - Strategic Information, Programs, Regulations
Saudi Arabia Information Strategy, Internet and E-Commerce Development Handbook - Strategic Information, Programs, Regulations
Scotland Information Strategy, Internet and E-Commerce Development Handbook - Strategic Information, Programs, Regulations
Serbia Information Strategy, Internet and E-Commerce Development Handbook - Strategic Information, Programs, Regulations
Singapore Information Strategy, Internet and E-Commerce Development Handbook - Strategic Information, Programs, Regulations
Slovakia Information Strategy, Internet and E-Commerce Development Handbook - Strategic Information, Programs, Regulations
Slovenia Information Strategy, Internet and E-Commerce Development Handbook - Strategic Information, Programs, Regulations
South Africa Information Strategy, Internet and E-Commerce Development Handbook - Strategic Information, Programs, Regulations
Spain Information Strategy, Internet and E-Commerce Development Handbook - Strategic Information, Programs, Regulations
Sri Lanka Information Strategy, Internet and E-Commerce Development Handbook - Strategic Information, Programs, Regulations
Sudan Information Strategy, Internet and E-Commerce Development Handbook - Strategic Information, Programs, Regulations
Suriname Information Strategy, Internet and E-Commerce Development Handbook - Strategic Information, Programs, Regulations
Sweden Information Strategy, Internet and E-Commerce Development Handbook - Strategic Information, Programs, Regulations
Switzerland Information Strategy, Internet and E-Commerce Development Handbook - Strategic Information,

TITLE
Programs, Regulations
Syria Export Import &Business Directory
Taiwan Information Strategy, Internet and E-Commerce Development Handbook - Strategic Information, Programs, Regulations
Tajikistan Information Strategy, Internet and E-Commerce Development Handbook - Strategic Information, Programs, Regulations
Thailand Information Strategy, Internet and E-Commerce Development Handbook - Strategic Information, Programs, Regulations
Tunisia Information Strategy, Internet and E-Commerce Development Handbook - Strategic Information, Programs, Regulations
Turkey Information Strategy, Internet and E-Commerce Development Handbook - Strategic Information, Programs, Regulations
Turkmenistan Information Strategy, Internet and E-Commerce Development Handbook - Strategic Information, Programs, Regulations
Uganda Information Strategy, Internet and E-Commerce Development Handbook - Strategic Information, Programs, Regulations
Ukraine Information Strategy, Internet and E-Commerce Development Handbook - Strategic Information, Programs, Regulations
United Arab Emirates Information Strategy, Internet and E-Commerce Development Handbook - Strategic Information, Programs, Regulations
United Kingdom Information Strategy, Internet and E-Commerce Development Handbook - Strategic Information, Programs, Regulations
United States Information Strategy, Internet and E-Commerce Development Handbook - Strategic Information, Programs, Regulations
Uruguay Information Strategy, Internet and E-Commerce Development Handbook - Strategic Information, Programs, Regulations
US Information Strategy, Internet and E-Commerce Development Handbook - Strategic Information, Programs, Regulations
Uzbekistan Information Strategy, Internet and E-Commerce Development Handbook - Strategic Information, Programs, Regulations
Venezuela Information Strategy, Internet and E-Commerce Development Handbook - Strategic Information, Programs, Regulations
Vietnam Information Strategy, Internet and E-Commerce Development Handbook - Strategic Information, Programs, Regulations

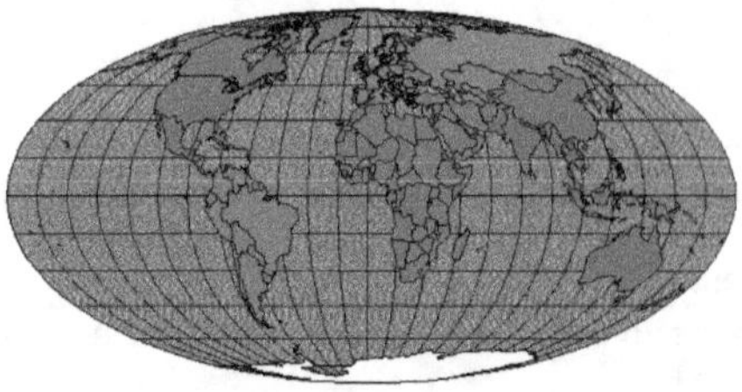

WORLD RESEARCH AND DEVELOPMENT POLICY LIBRARY

Price: $99.95 Each

Australia Research & Development Policy Handbook
Austria Research & Development Policy Handbook
Bangladesh Research & Development Policy Handbook
Belgium Research & Development Policy Handbook
Canada Research & Development Policy Handbook
China Research & Development Policy Handbook
Costa Rica Research & Development Policy Handbook
Cuba Research & Development Policy Handbook
Czech Republic Research & Development Policy Handbook
Egypt Research & Development Policy Handbook
Estonia Research & Development Policy Handbook
Finland Research & Development Policy Handbook
France Research & Development Policy Handbook
Germany Research & Development Policy Handbook
Greece Research & Development Policy Handbook
Hungary Research & Development Policy Handbook
India Research & Development Policy Handbook
Indonesia Research & Development Policy Handbook
Israel Research & Development Policy Handbook
Italy Research & Development Policy Handbook
Japan Research & Development Policy Handbook
Korea, South Research & Development Policy Handbook
Kuwait Research & Development Policy Handbook
Laos Research & Development Policy Handbook
Latvia Research & Development Policy Handbook
Lithuania Research & Development Policy Handbook
Malaysia Research & Development Policy Handbook
Mexico Research & Development Policy Handbook
Myanmar Research & Development Policy Handbook

**For additional analytical, business and investment opportunities information,
Please contact Global Investment & Business Center, USA
at (202) 546-2103. Fax: (202) 546-3275. E-mail: rusric@erols.com**

Pakistan Research & Development Policy Handbook
Palau Research & Development Policy Handbook
Palestine Research & Development Policy Handbook
Philippines Research & Development Policy Handbook
Russia Research & Development Policy Handbook
Singapore Research & Development Policy Handbook
South Africa Research & Development Policy Handbook
Sri Lanka Research & Development Policy Handbook
Sweden Research & Development Policy Handbook
Taiwan Research & Development Policy Handbook
Thailand Research & Development Policy Handbook
Turkey Research & Development Policy Handbook
Ukraine Research & Development Policy Handbook
United Kingdom Research & Development Policy Handbook
United States Research & Development Policy Handbook

NEW! WORLD OFFSHORE TAX GUIDES

Price: $149.95 each

1. Andorra Offshore Tax Guide
2. Anguilla Offshore Tax Guide
3. Bahamas Offshore Tax Guide
4. Barbados Offshore Tax Guide
5. Belize Offshore Tax Guide
6. Bermuda Offshore Tax Guide
7. British Virgin Islands Offshore Tax Guide
8. Cayman Islands Offshore Tax Guide
9. Cook Islands Offshore Tax Guide
10. Costa Rica Offshore Tax Guide
11. Cyprus Offshore Tax Guide
12. Dubai Offshore Tax Guide
13. Gibraltar Offshore Tax Guide
14. Grenada Offshore Tax Guide
15. Guernsey Offshore Tax Guide
16. Hong Kong Offshore Tax Guide
17. Ireland Offshore Tax Guide
18. Isle of Man Offshore Tax Guide
19. Jersey Offshore Tax Guide
20. Labuan Offshore Tax Guide
21. Liechtenstein Offshore Tax Guide
22. Luxembourg Offshore Tax Guide
23. Madeira Offshore Tax Guide
24. Malta Offshore Tax Guide
25. Mauritius Offshore Business and Investment Opportunities Handbook
26. Mauritius Offshore Tax Guide
27. Monaco Offshore Tax Guide
28. Nauru Offshore Tax Guide
29. Netherlands Antilles Offshore Tax Guide
30. Panama Offshore Tax Guide
31. Seychelles Offshore Tax Guide
32. Switzerland Offshore Tax Guide
33. Turks & Caicos Islands Offshore Tax Guide
34. Vanuatu Offshore Tax Guide

WORLD BUSINESS INTELLIGENCE REPORTS LIBRARY

World Business Information Catalog, USA: http://www.ibpus.com
Email: ibpusa3@gmail.com

Price: $99.95 Each

TITLE
Abkhazia (Republic of Abkhazia) Business Intelligence Report-- Strategic, Practical Information, Contacts
Afghanistan Business Intelligence Report-- Strategic, Practical Information, Contacts
Aland Business Intelligence Report-- Strategic, Practical Information, Contacts
Albania Business Intelligence Report-- Strategic, Practical Information, Contacts
Algeria Business Intelligence Report-- Strategic, Practical Information, Contacts
Andorra Business Intelligence Report-- Strategic, Practical Information, Contacts
Angola Business Intelligence Report-- Strategic, Practical Information, Contacts
Anguilla Business Intelligence Report-- Strategic, Practical Information, Contacts
Antigua and Barbuda Business Intelligence Report-- Strategic, Practical Information, Contacts
Antilles (Netherlands) Business Intelligence Report-- Strategic, Practical Information, Contacts
Argentina Business Intelligence Report-- Strategic, Practical Information, Contacts
Armenia Business Intelligence Report-- Strategic, Practical Information, Contacts
Aruba Business Intelligence Report-- Strategic, Practical Information, Contacts
Australia Business Intelligence Report-- Strategic, Practical Information, Contacts
Austria Business Intelligence Report-- Strategic, Practical Information, Contacts
Azerbaijan Business Intelligence Report-- Strategic, Practical Information, Contacts
Bahamas Business Intelligence Report-- Strategic, Practical Information, Contacts
Bahrain Business Intelligence Report-- Strategic, Practical Information, Contacts
Bangladesh Business Intelligence Report-- Strategic, Practical Information, Contacts
Barbados Business Intelligence Report-- Strategic, Practical Information, Contacts
Belarus Business Intelligence Report-- Strategic, Practical Information, Contacts
Belgium Business Intelligence Report-- Strategic, Practical Information, Contacts
Belize Business Intelligence Report-- Strategic, Practical Information, Contacts
Benin Business Intelligence Report-- Strategic, Practical Information, Contacts
Bermuda Business Intelligence Report-- Strategic, Practical Information, Contacts
Bhutan Business Intelligence Report-- Strategic, Practical Information, Contacts
Bolivia Business Intelligence Report-- Strategic, Practical Information, Contacts
Bosnia and Herzegovina Business Intelligence Report-- Strategic, Practical Information, Contacts
Botswana Business Intelligence Report-- Strategic, Practical Information, Contacts
Brazil Business Intelligence Report-- Strategic, Practical Information, Contacts
Brunei Business Intelligence Report-- Strategic, Practical Information, Contacts
Bulgaria Business Intelligence Report-- Strategic, Practical Information, Contacts
Burkina Faso Business Intelligence Report-- Strategic, Practical Information, Contacts
Burundi Business Intelligence Report-- Strategic, Practical Information, Contacts
Cambodia Business Intelligence Report-- Strategic, Practical Information, Contacts
Cameroon Business Intelligence Report-- Strategic, Practical Information, Contacts
Canada Business Intelligence Report-- Strategic, Practical Information, Contacts

For additional analytical, business and investment opportunities information,
Please contact Global Investment & Business Center, USA
at (202) 546-2103. Fax: (202) 546-3275. E-mail: ibpusa3@gmail.com

TITLE
Cape Verde Business Intelligence Report-- Strategic, Practical Information, Contacts
Cayman Islands Business Intelligence Report-- Strategic, Practical Information, Contacts
Central African Republic Business Intelligence Report-- Strategic, Practical Information, Contacts
Chad Business Intelligence Report-- Strategic, Practical Information, Contacts
Chile Business Intelligence Report-- Strategic, Practical Information, Contacts
China Business Intelligence Report-- Strategic, Practical Information, Contacts
Colombia Business Intelligence Report-- Strategic, Practical Information, Contacts
Comoros Business Intelligence Report-- Strategic, Practical Information, Contacts
Congo Business Intelligence Report-- Strategic, Practical Information, Contacts
Congo, Democratic Republic Business Intelligence Report-- Strategic, Practical Information, Contacts
Cook Islands Business Intelligence Report-- Strategic, Practical Information, Contacts
Costa Rica Business Intelligence Report-- Strategic, Practical Information, Contacts
Cote d'Ivoire Business Intelligence Report-- Strategic, Practical Information, Contacts
Croatia Business Intelligence Report-- Strategic, Practical Information, Contacts
Cuba Business Intelligence Report-- Strategic, Practical Information, Contacts
Cyprus Business Intelligence Report-- Strategic, Practical Information, Contacts
Czech Republic Business Intelligence Report-- Strategic, Practical Information, Contacts
Denmark Business Intelligence Report-- Strategic, Practical Information, Contacts
Djibouti Business Intelligence Report-- Strategic, Practical Information, Contacts
Dominica Business Intelligence Report-- Strategic, Practical Information, Contacts
Dominican Republic Business Intelligence Report-- Strategic, Practical Information, Contacts
Ecuador Business Intelligence Report-- Strategic, Practical Information, Contacts
Egypt Business Intelligence Report-- Strategic, Practical Information, Contacts
El Salvador Business Intelligence Report-- Strategic, Practical Information, Contacts
Equatorial Guinea Business Intelligence Report-- Strategic, Practical Information, Contacts
Eritrea Business Intelligence Report-- Strategic, Practical Information, Contacts
Estonia Business Intelligence Report-- Strategic, Practical Information, Contacts
Ethiopia Business Intelligence Report-- Strategic, Practical Information, Contacts
Falkland Islands Business Intelligence Report-- Strategic, Practical Information, Contacts
Faroes Islands Business Intelligence Report-- Strategic, Practical Information, Contacts
Fiji Business Intelligence Report-- Strategic, Practical Information, Contacts
Finland Business Intelligence Report-- Strategic, Practical Information, Contacts
France Business Intelligence Report-- Strategic, Practical Information, Contacts
Gabon Business Intelligence Report-- Strategic, Practical Information, Contacts
Gambia Business Intelligence Report-- Strategic, Practical Information, Contacts
Georgia Business Intelligence Report-- Strategic, Practical Information, Contacts
Germany Business Intelligence Report-- Strategic, Practical Information, Contacts
Ghana Business Intelligence Report-- Strategic, Practical Information, Contacts
Gibraltar Business Intelligence Report-- Strategic, Practical Information, Contacts
Greece Business Intelligence Report-- Strategic, Practical Information, Contacts
Greenland Business Intelligence Report-- Strategic, Practical Information, Contacts
Grenada Business Intelligence Report-- Strategic, Practical Information, Contacts
Guam Business Intelligence Report-- Strategic, Practical Information, Contacts
Guatemala Business Intelligence Report-- Strategic, Practical Information, Contacts
Guernsey Business Intelligence Report-- Strategic, Practical Information, Contacts
Guinea Business Intelligence Report-- Strategic, Practical Information, Contacts

TITLE
Guinea-Bissau Business Intelligence Report-- Strategic, Practical Information, Contacts
Guyana Business Intelligence Report-- Strategic, Practical Information, Contacts
Haiti Business Intelligence Report-- Strategic, Practical Information, Contacts
Honduras Business Intelligence Report-- Strategic, Practical Information, Contacts
Hungary Business Intelligence Report-- Strategic, Practical Information, Contacts
Iceland Business Intelligence Report-- Strategic, Practical Information, Contacts
India Business Intelligence Report-- Strategic, Practical Information, Contacts
Indonesia Business Intelligence Report-- Strategic, Practical Information, Contacts
Iran Business Intelligence Report-- Strategic, Practical Information, Contacts
Iraq Business Intelligence Report-- Strategic, Practical Information, Contacts
Ireland Business Intelligence Report-- Strategic, Practical Information, Contacts
Israel Business Intelligence Report-- Strategic, Practical Information, Contacts
Italy Business Intelligence Report-- Strategic, Practical Information, Contacts
Jamaica Business Intelligence Report-- Strategic, Practical Information, Contacts
Japan Business Intelligence Report-- Strategic, Practical Information, Contacts
Jersey Business Intelligence Report-- Strategic, Practical Information, Contacts
Jordan Business Intelligence Report-- Strategic, Practical Information, Contacts
Kazakhstan Business Intelligence Report-- Strategic, Practical Information, Contacts
Kenya Business Intelligence Report-- Strategic, Practical Information, Contacts
Kiribati Business Intelligence Report-- Strategic, Practical Information, Contacts
Korea, North Business Intelligence Report-- Strategic, Practical Information, Contacts
Korea, South Business Intelligence Report-- Strategic, Practical Information, Contacts
Kosovo Business Intelligence Report-- Strategic, Practical Information, Contacts
Kurdistan Business Intelligence Report-- Strategic, Practical Information, Contacts
Kuwait Business Intelligence Report-- Strategic, Practical Information, Contacts
Kyrgyzstan Business Intelligence Report-- Strategic, Practical Information, Contacts
Laos Business Intelligence Report-- Strategic, Practical Information, Contacts
Latvia Business Intelligence Report-- Strategic, Practical Information, Contacts
Lebanon Business Intelligence Report-- Strategic, Practical Information, Contacts
Lesotho Business Intelligence Report-- Strategic, Practical Information, Contacts
Liberia Business Intelligence Report-- Strategic, Practical Information, Contacts
Libya Business Intelligence Report-- Strategic, Practical Information, Contacts
Liechtenstein Business Intelligence Report-- Strategic, Practical Information, Contacts
Lithuania Business Intelligence Report-- Strategic, Practical Information, Contacts
Luxembourg Business Intelligence Report-- Strategic, Practical Information, Contacts
Macao Business Intelligence Report-- Strategic, Practical Information, Contacts
Macedonia Business Intelligence Report-- Strategic, Practical Information, Contacts
Madagascar Business Intelligence Report-- Strategic, Practical Information, Contacts
Madeira Business Intelligence Report-- Strategic, Practical Information, Contacts
Malawi Business Intelligence Report-- Strategic, Practical Information, Contacts
Malaysia Business Intelligence Report-- Strategic, Practical Information, Contacts
Maldives Business Intelligence Report-- Strategic, Practical Information, Contacts
Mali Business Intelligence Report-- Strategic, Practical Information, Contacts
Malta Business Intelligence Report-- Strategic, Practical Information, Contacts
Man Business Intelligence Report-- Strategic, Practical Information, Contacts
Marshall Islands Business Intelligence Report-- Strategic, Practical Information, Contacts

TITLE
Mauritania Business Intelligence Report-- Strategic, Practical Information, Contacts
Mauritius Business Intelligence Report-- Strategic, Practical Information, Contacts
Mayotte Business Intelligence Report-- Strategic, Practical Information, Contacts
Mexico Business Intelligence Report-- Strategic, Practical Information, Contacts
Micronesia Business Intelligence Report-- Strategic, Practical Information, Contacts
Moldova Business Intelligence Report-- Strategic, Practical Information, Contacts
Monaco Business Intelligence Report-- Strategic, Practical Information, Contacts
Mongolia Business Intelligence Report-- Strategic, Practical Information, Contacts
Montserrat Business Intelligence Report-- Strategic, Practical Information, Contacts
Montenegro Business Intelligence Report-- Strategic, Practical Information, Contacts
Morocco Business Intelligence Report-- Strategic, Practical Information, Contacts
Mozambique Business Intelligence Report-- Strategic, Practical Information, Contacts
Myanmar Business Intelligence Report-- Strategic, Practical Information, Contacts
Nagorno-Karabakh Republic Business Intelligence Report-- Strategic, Practical Information, Contacts
Namibia Business Intelligence Report-- Strategic, Practical Information, Contacts
Nauru Business Intelligence Report-- Strategic, Practical Information, Contacts
Nepal Business Intelligence Report-- Strategic, Practical Information, Contacts
Netherlands Business Intelligence Report-- Strategic, Practical Information, Contacts
New Caledonia Business Intelligence Report-- Strategic, Practical Information, Contacts
New Zealand Business Intelligence Report-- Strategic, Practical Information, Contacts
Nicaragua Business Intelligence Report-- Strategic, Practical Information, Contacts
Niger Business Intelligence Report-- Strategic, Practical Information, Contacts
Nigeria Business Intelligence Report-- Strategic, Practical Information, Contacts
Niue Business Intelligence Report-- Strategic, Practical Information, Contacts
Northern Cyprus (Turkish Republic of Northern Cyprus) Business Intelligence Report-- Strategic, Practical Information, Contacts
Northern Mariana Islands Business Intelligence Report-- Strategic, Practical Information, Contacts
Norway Business Intelligence Report-- Strategic, Practical Information, Contacts
Oman Business Intelligence Report-- Strategic, Practical Information, Contacts
Pakistan Business Intelligence Report-- Strategic, Practical Information, Contacts
Palau Business Intelligence Report-- Strategic, Practical Information, Contacts
Palestine (West Bank & Gaza) Business Intelligence Report-- Strategic, Practical Information, Contacts
Panama Business Intelligence Report-- Strategic, Practical Information, Contacts
Papua New Guinea Business Intelligence Report-- Strategic, Practical Information, Contacts
Paraguay Business Intelligence Report-- Strategic, Practical Information, Contacts
Peru Business Intelligence Report-- Strategic, Practical Information, Contacts
Philippines Business Intelligence Report-- Strategic, Practical Information, Contacts
Pitcairn Islands Business Intelligence Report-- Strategic, Practical Information, Contacts
Poland Business Intelligence Report-- Strategic, Practical Information, Contacts
Polynesia French Business Intelligence Report-- Strategic, Practical Information, Contacts
Portugal Business Intelligence Report-- Strategic, Practical Information, Contacts
Qatar Business Intelligence Report-- Strategic, Practical Information, Contacts
Romania Business Intelligence Report-- Strategic, Practical Information, Contacts
Russia Business Intelligence Report-- Strategic, Practical Information, Contacts
Rwanda Business Intelligence Report-- Strategic, Practical Information, Contacts
Sahrawi Arab Democratic Republic Volume 1 Strategic Information and Developments

TITLE
Saint Kitts and Nevis Business Intelligence Report-- Strategic, Practical Information, Contacts
Saint Lucia Business Intelligence Report-- Strategic, Practical Information, Contacts
Saint Vincent and The Grenadines Business Intelligence Report-- Strategic, Practical Information, Contacts
Samoa (American) A Business Intelligence Report-- Strategic, Practical Information, Contacts
Samoa (Western) Business Intelligence Report-- Strategic, Practical Information, Contacts
San Marino Business Intelligence Report-- Strategic, Practical Information, Contacts
Sao Tome and Principe Business Intelligence Report-- Strategic, Practical Information, Contacts
Saudi Arabia Business Intelligence Report-- Strategic, Practical Information, Contacts
Scotland Business Intelligence Report-- Strategic, Practical Information, Contacts
Senegal Business Intelligence Report-- Strategic, Practical Information, Contacts
Serbia Business Intelligence Report-- Strategic, Practical Information, Contacts
Seychelles Business Intelligence Report-- Strategic, Practical Information, Contacts
Sierra Leone Business Intelligence Report-- Strategic, Practical Information, Contacts
Singapore Business Intelligence Report-- Strategic, Practical Information, Contacts
Slovakia Business Intelligence Report-- Strategic, Practical Information, Contacts
Slovenia Business Intelligence Report-- Strategic, Practical Information, Contacts
Solomon Islands Business Intelligence Report-- Strategic, Practical Information, Contacts
Somalia Business Intelligence Report-- Strategic, Practical Information, Contacts
South Africa Business Intelligence Report-- Strategic, Practical Information, Contacts
Spain Business Intelligence Report-- Strategic, Practical Information, Contacts
Sri Lanka Business Intelligence Report-- Strategic, Practical Information, Contacts
St. Helena Business Intelligence Report-- Strategic, Practical Information, Contacts
St. Pierre & Miquelon Business Intelligence Report-- Strategic, Practical Information, Contacts
Sudan (Republic of the Sudan) Business Intelligence Report-- Strategic, Practical Information, Contacts
Sudan South Business Intelligence Report-- Strategic, Practical Information, Contacts
Suriname Business Intelligence Report-- Strategic, Practical Information, Contacts
Swaziland Business Intelligence Report-- Strategic, Practical Information, Contacts
Sweden Business Intelligence Report-- Strategic, Practical Information, Contacts
Switzerland Business Intelligence Report-- Strategic, Practical Information, Contacts
Syria Business Intelligence Report-- Strategic, Practical Information, Contacts
Taiwan Business Intelligence Report-- Strategic, Practical Information, Contacts
Tajikistan Business Intelligence Report-- Strategic, Practical Information, Contacts
Tanzania Business Intelligence Report-- Strategic, Practical Information, Contacts
Thailand Business Intelligence Report-- Strategic, Practical Information, Contacts
Timor Leste (Democratic Republic of Timor-Leste) Business Intelligence Report-- Strategic, Practical Information, Contacts
Togo Business Intelligence Report-- Strategic, Practical Information, Contacts
Tonga Business Intelligence Report-- Strategic, Practical Information, Contacts
Trinidad and Tobago Business Intelligence Report-- Strategic, Practical Information, Contacts
Tunisia Business Intelligence Report-- Strategic, Practical Information, Contacts
Turkey Business Intelligence Report-- Strategic, Practical Information, Contacts
Turkmenistan Business Intelligence Report-- Strategic, Practical Information, Contacts
Turks & Caicos Business Intelligence Report-- Strategic, Practical Information, Contacts
Tuvalu Business Intelligence Report-- Strategic, Practical Information, Contacts
Uganda Business Intelligence Report-- Strategic, Practical Information, Contacts
Ukraine Business Intelligence Report-- Strategic, Practical Information, Contacts

TITLE
United Arab Emirates Business Intelligence Report-- Strategic, Practical Information, Contacts
United Kingdom Business Intelligence Report-- Strategic, Practical Information, Contacts
United States Business Intelligence Report-- Strategic, Practical Information, Contacts
Uruguay Business Intelligence Report-- Strategic, Practical Information, Contacts
Uzbekistan Business Intelligence Report-- Strategic, Practical Information, Contacts
Vanuatu Business Intelligence Report-- Strategic, Practical Information, Contacts
Vatican City (Holy See) Business Intelligence Report-- Strategic, Practical Information, Contacts
Venezuela Business Intelligence Report-- Strategic, Practical Information, Contacts
Vietnam Business Intelligence Report-- Strategic, Practical Information, Contacts
Virgin Islands, British Business Intelligence Report-- Strategic, Practical Information, Contacts
Wake Atoll Business Intelligence Report-- Strategic, Practical Information, Contacts
Wallis & Futuna Business Intelligence Report-- Strategic, Practical Information, Contacts
Western Sahara Business Intelligence Report-- Strategic, Practical Information, Contacts
Yemen Business Intelligence Report-- Strategic, Practical Information, Contacts
Zambia Business Intelligence Report-- Strategic, Practical Information, Contacts
Zimbabwe Business Intelligence Report-- Strategic, Practical Information, Contacts

www.ingramcontent.com/pod-product-compliance
Lightning Source LLC
LaVergne TN
LVHW080035210926
848481LV00011B/3201